COMMEMORATIVE PLAQUES

LONDON PLAQUES

5 FASCINATING WALKS
VIEWING THE HOMES OF THE GREAT AND THE GOOD

MAYFAIR, MARYLEBONE AND ST JAMES'S

DOUGLAS J EATON

ELGAR ESTATES PUBLISHING

www.commemorativeplaques.co.uk

First published in 2015 by
Elgar Estates Publishing
Meadow House
Ashington
West Sussex
RH20 3AZ

Design and Origination
MIKE SHORT

All rights reserved.
© Copyright 2015
No part of this publication may be reproduced, stored in a retrieval system, or transmitted, in any form, or by any means, electronic, mechanical, photocopying, recording or otherwise, without the prior permission of Elgar Estates Publishing

A catalogue record for this book is available from the British Library

ISBN 978-1-902269-01-6

Printed and bound by
THOMSON PRESS (INDIA) LTD

CONTENTS

PAGE 5
Foreword by Rt Hon Mark Field MP

PAGES 6-8
Introduction

PAGES 9-52
Walk 1- Mayfair South

PAGES 53-90
Walk 2 - Mayfair North

PAGES 91 -130
Walk 3 - Marylebone West

PAGES 131-174
Walk 4 - Marylebone East

PAGES 175-208
Walk 5 - St James's

PAGE 209
A Message From The Author

PAGES 211 - 213
Index

PAGES 214-215
Where The People Were Born

PAGE 216
Glossary

ACKNOWLEDGEMENTS

Special thanks to Mike Short for his collaboration, research, energy and good humour.
Without his encouragement this book would not have happened.

Thanks also to Heather Hawker, whose enthusiasm showed me that the project had legs.
She agreed to proof-read the book – but don't blame her for any factual errors
– they are all down to me.

Devon Busby was a student at Northbrook College in Worthing when she created our beautiful,
and very original, maps for each of the walks.

The photographs of the buildings and plaques were taken by,
and remain the property of Douglas J Eaton.

This book includes some materials that are not the copyright of Elgar Estates Publishing.
Every reasonable effort has been made to contact copyright holders of material
produced in this book. If any have inadvertently been overlooked, the publishers
would be glad to hear from them and make good in future editions
any errors or omissions brought to their attention.

Comments on the guide's content, and any feedback are more than welcome.
Don't hesitate to contact us at info@commemorativeplaques.co.uk

FOREWORD
Rt Hon Mark Field MP

My selection in the final month of the last millennium for the Cities of London and Westminster seat commenced a love affair with the political, cultural and financial heart of the world's most exciting city. It also sparked in me a passion for urban walking.

As recently as 1800 London was still a collection of villages and its built-up area measured five miles by three. By the end of that century the arrival of the railway had helped London become a vast metropolis recognisable today. Shaped by waves of migration from the English countryside, then from Western Europe and, by the latter half of the twentieth century, from every corner of the globe, London's success has made it a magnet for those seeking their fortunes.

Perhaps this is one of the reasons why one cannot go far in my constituency without happening upon a commemorative plaque revealing a famous writer, politician, poet, scientist, actor or revolutionary who lived here in decades past. Amidst the urban swirl, these timeless reminders of the people and communities that went before reveal so much about British life, its remarkable residents and the range of our nation's achievements.

I have enjoyed countless hours in my walking boots wandering through the capital's central districts and suburbs. I never fail to be fascinated by the inexhaustible variety of London's districts, streets and buildings. Travel on the tube, whizz along in a taxi or stick to the main drag and you will not be taken into London's confidence. You will perhaps instead be struck by a brash and unforgiving place with apparently hostile and impatient inhabitants. But take time to gaze at its historic buildings, stumble upon its ancient villages, take note of its commemorative plaques and London will unfold its hidden secrets to you. In plumbing this rich variety, each and every one of us can find a home.

Rt Hon Mark Field has been the Member of Parliament for the Cities of London and Westminster since 2001.

The constituency contains some of our country's most iconic landmarks, revered institutions and famous streets, such as Buckingham Palace, the Houses of Parliament, Trafalgar Square and St. Paul's Cathedral.

To me London is a living organism. It grows, has personal crises and fosters very individual relationships with each of its inhabitants. Our capital also has a great capacity to unite its people both past and present. While London is ever changing, common threads run through the ages that lend a welcome sense of perspective in troubled times. To walk through London is to be in communion with a place that has been witness to the nation's political and financial crises and the troubled plight or personal joy of people from all walks of life. This fantastic book is the perfect way for Londoners and visitors alike to start or develop their own relationships with this most exciting of cities.

INTRODUCTION

The idea for a 'walking guide' around buildings with commemorative plaques started when I saw a plaque for the poet Shelley in Worthing in West Sussex, and then walked round the corner and encountered another plaque – this time for Oscar Wilde. The plaque informed me that The Importance of Being Earnest had been written in a building on that spot. When I got home I picked out my copy of the play, and had a look through it, and of course, Jack Worthing was the main character in the play......

The next week I was in Hastings in East Sussex, and was looking up at a plaque on a wall in the Old Town.

I was approached by a stranger, who asked – "What are you looking at? "That plaque" says I. "Crickey! I've lived here for twenty years and never noticed it before. Thank you!"

Many of the former homes of the great and the good are identified with commemorative plaques. There are over 1000 plaques in London, and I realised that there could be interest in bringing them to people's attention – tourists and locals – whilst taking a healthy walk. Commemorative plaques can be found on buildings of all shapes and sizes, of all types and dates. They are a highly visible and effective way of celebrating the history of the city: they enable everyone to learn about the history and architecture of London. Our Walks Guide links the buildings to the people who lived there, with a brief biography of the occupants.

London is a great city for walking. The London Mayor's vision is to make it one of the world's most walking-freely cities by 2015. Walking is an enjoyable, free, and accessible activity. Walking is a means of really understanding and appreciating a city up-close. London is unique and blessed with imposing squares, magnificent landmarks, hidden architectural gems, world-class buildings and a real cultural heritage.

It is a city full of places of interest, but is notoriously hard to find your way around when you're walking. Unlike somewhere like New York, the West End is made-up of an unplanned maze of streets. The interconnecting streets of London have evolved organically over the centuries, which adds to its charm and character, but makes it tricky for the pedestrian to navigate.

The idea of erecting "memorial tablets" in London was first proposed by William Ewart MP in 1863. The idea immediately caught the public's imagination, and from 1866 the Royal Society of Arts (nee Society of Arts) erected 35 plaques. In 1901 the scheme was taken over by the London County Council (LCC), and over the next 64 years erected 250 plaques, when the familiar blue colour was adopted.

The LCC was abolished in 1965, and the scheme passed to the new Greater London Council (GLC), who widened the range of people commemorated and erected 262 plaques.

In 1986 English Heritage (EH) took over the scheme and has erected 300 plaques in London. The scheme is driven by proposals from the public, and from the many applications made, an EH panel draws-up a short-list and selects on average 12 new plaques a year.

The round, blue design of the EH plaques has remained constant since the 1930's, although before this they had also been designed as squares or rectangles, and varied in colour between blue, chocolate, sage and terracotta.

Plaques will often tell the passer-by something they didn't already know, and are there to celebrate people and place. They increase engagement by visitors and locals alike in the history and culture of the city.

In order to be eligible for EH to nominate a person for a plaque, they must have been dead for 20 years, or passed the centenary of their birth. They must be considered to have made an important positive contribution to human welfare or happiness, be recognisable to the well-informed passer-by or deserve national recognition, and have resided in London for a significant period. Unless a case is deemed exceptional, such as Palmerston, Disraeli and Gladstone, each figure can only be commemorated with one plaque.

The majority of plaques in the Guide have emanated from the English Heritage stable, but we have included plaques in our Walks from all sources. A number of individuals and groups have erected plaques, where the strict EH rules don't allow inclusion in their scheme. A number of London Boroughs have erected their own plaques, notably in this Guide the City of Westminster's Green Plaques Scheme, the majority of which have been sponsored.

There are now over 100 that have been erected by the Heritage Foundation (HF), which evolved from Comic Heritage, and even earlier the Dead Comic's Society. They pay tribute to the wealth of talent of entertainers and sports men and women, who lived or worked in London. Its Presidents have included Robin Gibbs of the Bee Gees, Ernie Wise, Rick Wakeman, Phil Collins and Sir Norman Wisdom.

There are a number of different types of commemorative plaques, which include not only the various roundel colour varieties, but also slate, stone and bronze tablets, wall tiles, squares, ovals and rectangular shapes.

Over one hundred plaques have been lost over the years, as houses have been demolished. The listing of a building as Grade I or Grade II celebrates its significance through its special architectural and historic interest, and although the majority of houses that display a plaque are not formally listed, a number of buildings have been listed after the installation of a plaque.

Across London there are always buildings being maintained, cleaned, or up-graded, which results in their being covered in scaffolding. Some of the plaques that have been erected, and in some cases whole buildings, are consequently hidden. We have taken the view that the overall 'ambience' of the location is relevant, and where practical and relevant, we have included the 'People' who occupied the building in the Guide. In some cases we have been able to show a picture of what the building used to look like.

In some instances, we have not been able to obtain a picture of the Person detailed. If any readers know where we can access images of these 'faceless' ones – either photographs or paintings – please let us know, so that we can include them in the next edition of the Guide.

Many of the plaques commemorate names that everybody will know, including the likes of Nelson and Churchill.

We have tried to provide a flavour of all of the people in the Guide, by giving each of them a full page of biography, along with a picture of the plaque and the building. Some of the subjects of the plaques will be names that you possibly don't recognise, but they all commemorate significant people and their contribution to society.

The biographies of some of the lesser-known occupants of the houses may encourage you to learn more about them, as they all have a story to tell. There are many people who were experts in their field – how many of us know who was the original pioneer of computers, or who coined the phrase – "The customer is always right"? They are all here!

If we have not highlighted the country of birth, you should assume that they were born in England. There is a glossary of all the subjects in alphabetical order, along with a reference as to in which of the five walks they appear.

We have created five walks, which will each take in the order of two hours to complete, depending on how quickly you walk, how long you spend at each building, and whether you take time out for shopping or some refreshment. You don't have to start a walk at No. 1 as shown on the maps, but we have numbered all of the houses on the maps to help you find your way around. Start where you like! We have also shown some of the key features that you will pass on the walk, including hotels, gardens, statues and churches.

Doug Eaton

MAYFAIR SOUTH W1
CITY OF WESTMINSTER

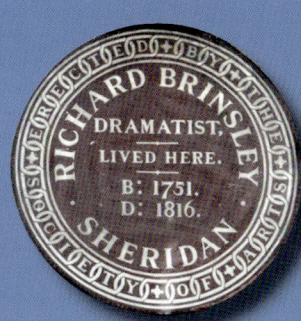

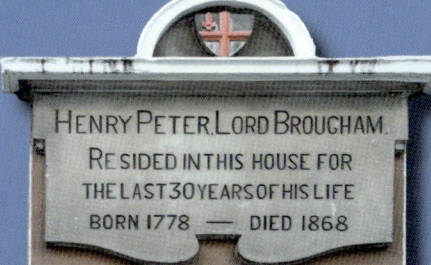

MAYFAIR SOUTH W1
CITY OF WESTMINSTER

This is London's most exclusive and wealthiest district, home of the aristocracy and includes the most important retail activity in the UK. It is also, of course, the most expensive property on the Monopoly board! In fiction it has often been depicted as the home of the upper-class twit.

Hyde Park to the west, Oxford Street to the north, Regent Street to the east and Piccadilly to the south are the rough borders of Mayfair. This walk takes in the southern part of Mayfair, an area dominated by elegant Georgian terraces, originally developed in the 18th century, although a number of the houses have been reconstructed over a variety of periods.

Before the 18th century Mayfair was fields and farmland. The name emanates from an annual fair that took place in what is now Shepherd Market. This two-week event, which started in 1686, was banned in 1708 as a result of the fair's revellers' boisterousness and disorder!

The site of the oldest cottage in Mayfair is celebrated in Stanhope Row, off Curzon Street, where MP Rt. Hon Peter Brook unveiled a plaque, which marks the 50th anniversary of the ending of World War II. It had lasted over four hundred years from 1618 until a German bomb crushed it in 1940.

Royal Academy

Edward Shepherd, a local architect and developer, was commissioned to develop the area, and the square and piazza were developed between 1735 and 1746. Initially, it included a duck pond, a 2-storey market, topped with a theatre. Today, Shepherd Market is known for its chic boutiques, intimate restaurants, out-door cafes and impressive Victorian pubs. It has long held the reputation that the oldest profession flourished here, although this is may now not be the case.

Next to Shepherd Market is Half Moon Street, where MI5 used to have offices, and is where some believe the fictional Wooster and Jeeves of P.G Wodehouse's novels lived. Others believe that they lived at 15 Berkeley Street, where Wodehouse lived in 1922.

He wrote almost 100 books, and very rarely made up any of his locations. Bertie Wooster's fearsome Aunt Dahlia lived around the corner at 47 Charles Street, with Jeeves' club, The Junior Ganymede, now The Only Running Footman pub, opposite. Head towards New Bond Street and at 18 Clifford Street is Bertie's club, The Drone, which was – and still is – the exclusive Buck's Club, where Bucks Fizz was invented.

Heading north from Shepherd Market, the first side of Berkeley Square was built in 1738,

The Winston Churchill and Franklin D Roosevelt Bench in New Bond Street

named after John Berkeley, first Lord Berkeley of Stratton, who took possession of the land to the north of his newly acquired house in Piccadilly. Several original character houses remain on the west side of the square, and the gardens contain just one statue, but an interesting one. It was created by the Pre-Raphaelite sculptor, Alexander Munro, and depicts a semi-draped nymph carrying a vase from which water pours to form a fountain.

Mount Street leads off to the west from the northern end of the square, containing a number of exclusive art galleries and buildings constructed with distinctive ornate pink terracotta facades.

Burlington Arcade

Along Piccadilly is Britain's very first shopping arcade, Burlington Arcade, which contains almost forty bijou shops, purveyors of luxury goods. It sits to the side of Burlington House, now the home of the Royal Academy of Arts, which is unique in that it is an independent and privately funded institution led by artists and architects to promote appreciation of the visual arts. It runs a continuous programme of internationally-acclaimed exhibitions throughout the year. The arcade was built in 1819 by Lord Cavendish to stop passers-by throwing rubbish in his garden!

Sothebys

To the east of Mayfair sits Savile Row, the centre of traditional bespoke tailoring for over 200 years, close to the Royal Institution's 'World of Science' in the Faraday Museum at 21 Albemarle Street. The museum is open 9.00am to 9.00pm, Monday to Friday every week, and entrance is free.

MAYFAIR SOUTH WALK GUIDE

Page	Ref	Person	Place
14	1	Bert AMBROSE	May Fair Hotel, Stratton Street
15	2	Fanny BURNEY ("Madame D'Arblay")	11 Bolton Street
16	3	Charles FOX	46 Clarges Street
17	4	Edward MERYON	17 Clarges Street
18	5	Lord PALMERSTON	94 Piccadilly
19	6	Charles IVES	17 Half Moon Street
20	7	Nancy MITFORD	10 Curzon Street
21	8	Wendy RICHARD	Shepherds Tavern, Shepherd Market
22	9	Richard SHERIDAN	10 Hertford Street
22	9	General John BURGOYNE	10 Hertford Street
23	10	Sir George CAYLEY	20 Hertford Street
24	11	Rufus ISAACS (1st Marquess of Reading)	32 Curzon Street
25	12	Benjamin DISRAELI	19 Curzon Street
26	13	Fitzroy SOMERSET (1st Baron Raglan)	5 Stanhope Gate
27	14	Pasquale PAOLI	80 South Audley Street
28	15	Sir Richard WESTMACOTT	14 South Audley Street
29	16	King CHARLES X of France	72 South Audley Street
30	17	Constance SPRY	65 South Audley Street
31	18	Duke of CLARENCE	22 Charles Street
32	19	Beau BRUMMELL	4 Chesterfield Street
33	19	Anthony EDEN	4 Chesterfield Street
34	20	Somerset MAUGHAM	6 Chesterfield Street
35	21	5th Earl of ROSEBERY	20 Charles Street
36	22	Lady Dorothy NEVILL	45 Charles Street
37	23	Harry SELFRIDGE	9 Fitzmaurice Place
38	23	William PETTY (2nd Earl of Shelburne)	9 Fitzmaurice Place
39	24	George CANNING	50 Berkeley Square
40	25	CLIVE OF INDIA	45 Berkeley Square
41	26	Bernard SUNLEY	24 Berkeley Square
42	27	Terence DONOVAN	30 Bourdon Street
43	28	Sir Norman HARTNELL	26 Bruton Street
44	29	Lord Henry BROUGHAM	5 Grafton Street
45	30	Sir Henry IRVING	15a Grafton Street
46	31	George BASEVI	17 Savile Row
47	32	Richard SHERIDAN	14 Savile Row
48	33	George GROTE	12 Savile Row
49	34	Richard BRIGHT	11 Savile Row
50	35	Allen LANE	8 Vigo Street
51	36	Ziggy STARDUST	23 Heddon Street
52	37	James YEARSLEY	32 Sackville Street

Distance : 2.4 miles (3.9 Km)
Start Point: Green Park
Finish Point: Piccadilly Circus
Underground Stations

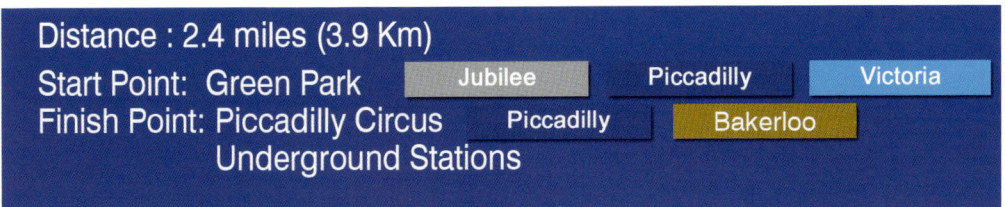

Bert AMBROSE
Musician

Mayfair Hotel, Stratton Street   Map Ref   1

Benjamin Baruch Ambrose was born in the East End of London, the son of a Jewish wool merchant. Nothing is known of his childhood, apart from the fact that he was playing the violin from a very young age. He developed a rare talent as a bandleader in choosing successful songs and arrangements, and selecting the best musicians.

His aunt took him to New York at the age of 15, where the music scene inspired him. He began his professional career soon after arriving, first playing with Emil Coleman at Reisenweber's Restaurant, and then in a big band at the Palais Royal. The bandleader fell ill, and at the age of 20 Ambrose took over, before forming his own 15-piece band to play at the Club de Vingt.

He returned to England in 1922, and as a result of his experience in America, he was invited to play at the Embassy Club in Mayfair, which was bought by his future business partner, restaurateur Luigi. By 1923 Ambrose was making records, and returned briefly to America. He was enticed back by his fan, the Prince of Wales and continued to play at the Embassy, until the Mayfair Hotel opened in 1927, where he played until 1932.

The Mayfair Hotel provided the venue for Ambrose's Saturday night radio programme, and his deal included a flat at the hotel, which he retained even when he returned to the Embassy Club in 1933. After touring Britain with Vera Lynn, he and fellow bandleader Jack Harris bought the Ciro's Club in 1937. He returned once more to the Mayfair Hotel in 1939 for a year, before retiring to his farm in Hertfordshire.

Following the war, he played again at the Ciro's Club until 1947, and then moved on to The Nightingale and to the Café de Paris. With the onset of rock'n'roll, big band music was no longer popular, and in 1958, just as his money ran out, he got the break he needed when he discovered 16 years old Kathy Kirby. He decided to promote her, and she made No.1 in the charts (the Hit Parade in those days!) with "Secret Love", and he continued to manage her until he died in 1971.

Fanny BURNEY ("Madame D'Arblay")
Writer and Royal Servant

11 Bolton Street　　　　　　　　　　　　　　　　　**Map Ref　2**

Frances Burney, the third of six children of Charles and Esther Sleepe Burney was born in Kings Lynn, Lincolnshire. The Burney's were descended from an aristocratic Scottish family, who had "fallen upon difficult times", whilst Frances' mother came from a 'lower social class'. They relocated to London in 1760, and having taken a Doctorate of Music at Oxford University, Charles devoted his life to the arts. Frances' elder sister, Esther, continued the family's musical credentials with aplomb, in a household that was visited by such artistic luminaries as David Garrick, Sir Joshua Reynolds, and George Colman.

Frances, on the other hand, was deemed to be backward, received no formal education, but taught herself to read and write, including French and Italian. Her mother died when she was only ten, and she began to write poems, plays and stories, all of which she destroyed on her fifteenth Birthday. However, her desire to write encouraged her to create a journal, in which she recorded her thoughts and commented about her life. She loved the theatre, and her journals were packed with accounts of plays she had seen.

Her first novel, *Evelina or The History of a Young Woman's Entrance into the World* (1778) was written anonymously, as young women were discouraged from reading, let alone writing fiction. The secret as to her identity eventually seeped-out, and was followed by the publication of *Cecilia* (1782), which resulted in an interest being shown by George III and Queen Charlotte, and lead to her being presented to the royal couple.

In 1789, the Queen offered her the post of '2nd Keeper of the Robes', and although the role was hardly more than that of a 'dresser', you didn't refuse a royal offer! She continued to write her journals, but frustrated with her role, she extricated herself from Court in 1790.

She met French exile General Alexandre D'Arthay in 1792, at the age of 42, married him a year later, and gave birth to their son Alexander in 1794. *Camilla or A Picture of Youth* was published in 1796, and her fourth novel – *The Wanderer or Female Difficulties* in 1813. She lived in France with her husband for 10 years, before returning to England where she wrote *Memoirs of Dr. Burney* (1832) in memory of her father.

"Now I am ashamed of confessing that I have nothing to confess"

Charles FOX
Statesman

46 Clarges Street Map Ref 3

Charles James Fox was born in London, the third of four sons to Henry Fox, 1st Baron Holland and Lady Caroline Lennox, a direct descendent of Charles II. He was an over-indulged child, and allowed to choose the direction of his own education. After attending school in Wandsworth, he went to Eton College and, for a short time, university at Hertford College, Oxford.

His father 'bought' him the Midhurst constituency in West Sussex, to enable him to become an MP, when he was only 19. His early political career was chequered, and even when he had achieved senior office, he spent little time in the roles. He was appointed Junior Lord of the Admiralty in 1770 (under Prime Minister North) and then Lord of the Treasury in 1772.

He was sacked in 1774, and proceeded to oppose the government's policy relating to the American Revolution (1774 – 1782). He served as Foreign Secretary and Leader of the House of Commons for less than four months in 1782 under Prime Minister Rockingham. Fox resigned when Lord Shelburne became Prime Minister, and returned the following year – again briefly – as Foreign Secretary, this time under the Duke of Portland.

Fox was always a strong opponent of George III, whom he regarded as a tyrant. After his fall from ministerial power, he continued to be an active backbench politician and debater in parliament, until his appointment as Foreign Secretary, for seven months in 1806, under Prime Minister Grenville.

Fox had a life-long love of classical literature, and he mixed this with a colourful private life, and was well known for his drinking and gambling. He enjoyed riding and playing cricket, when he wasn't chasing women, until he married the calming influence of Elizabeth Armistead in 1795.

46 Clarges Street is now a private members club called, unsurprisingly, The Fox Club, of which the man himself would undoubtedly have been a member, had he been alive today. The location also boasts a hotel and has a bar and restaurant that is open to the public.

Edward MERYON
Physician

17 Clarges Street Map Ref 4

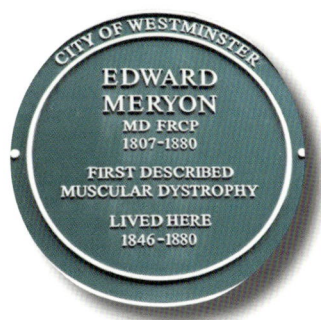

Edward Meryon was born in the East Sussex seaside town of Rye, to John Meryon, who was the harbour commissioner and inn-keeper, and Jane Gotland, a dressmaker. The couple never married. The Meryons were descended from the Huguenots who had moved to England from France in 1682. There is no information available about Meryon's school education.

In 1829, when Meryon was 22, he enrolled at the newly established University College in London to study medicine, where he was an outstanding student. Between 1830 and 1831 he was apprenticed to the apothecary Frederick Bellingham, and was elected a member of the Royal College of Surgeons and the Society of Apothecaries. In 1836 he published The Physical and Intellectual Constitution of Man Considered and two years later established a partnership at 4 Bolton Street in London with the surgeon Thomas Wood. In 1840 he was a founder of the Microscopical Society of London, and in 1842 he was appointed as a lecturer in comparative anatomy at St Thomas Hospital.

Meryon gradually established himself as a respected physician, with a special interest in nervous and muscle diseases. In 1846 he was elected as a Fellow of the Royal Medical and Chirurgical Society, which later became the Royal Society of Medicine. He was the first person to publish his findings after a systematic and detailed study of Muscular Dystrophy, identifying that the basic defect was a breakdown of the muscle fibre membrane. He was particularly impressed by the predilection for males and its familial nature. However, his contributions went unrecognised at the time of their publication, and he was not helped by the research of the French doctor, Guillaume Duchenne was perhaps a better publicist of his findings than Meryon.

He continued to undertake research, particularly in the area of the impact of therapy on the nervous system. In 1869 Meryon was appointed to his most influential role, when he became physician at the newly established London Infirmary for Epilepsy and Paralysis. He married Catherine Bailey-Falkingham in 1833, with whom he had a son and four daughters. His position in Victorian society was confirmed by his membership of the Athenaeum Club in Pall Mall, limited to only those who were pre-eminent in science, literature or the fine arts.

Lord PALMERSTON
Prime Minister

94 Piccadilly   **Map Ref   5**

Born Henry John Temple at Broadlands in Hampshire – later the home of Lord Mountbatten – the son of the Irish Peer, Viscount Palmerston. He attended Harrow School and then St.John's College, Cambridge. His father died when he was 17, and he succeeded to the Irish Peerage.

In 1806 he paid £1500 (£2m in today's money) to become MP for Horsham, West Sussex, the legality of which was challenged, and he was shoehorned in as an MP for the pocket borough of Newtown, Isle of Wight, and – after three attempts - MP for Cambridge University in 1811. He had had swift promotions up the political tree, becoming Lord of the Admiralty (the Duke of Portland was PM) in 1807, he was offered but rejected the job of Chancellor of the Exchequer (under PM Spencer Percival) in 1809, preferring the post of Secretary of War, which he performed for twenty years, under five Prime Ministers.

He switched his political allegiance in 1830 from the Tories to the Whigs, and under PM Lord Grey, he became Secretary of State for Foreign Affairs. One of the most consistent aspects of his foreign policy was his attempt to abolish the slave trade. He upset his Cambridge constituents, becoming MP for Bletchley and then South Hampshire. Between 1832 and 1852 he served both Whig and Tory governments, and became Prime Minister twice – 1855 to 1858, and then at the age of 75, from 1859.

He was known as a womaniser. The Times called him Lord Cupid, and he was cited as a correspondent in a divorce case when he was 79. He courted the displeasure of Queen Victoria, who was not amused by his sexual behaviour: she also tried to have him removed from office because he believed that the government's foreign policy should be to increase Britain's power in the world, against her belief that he should be supporting European royal families.

The property, known originally as Cambridge House, and more recently as the In and Out Club, is being converted into a 48 room, 60,000 sq.ft mansion

Charles IVES
Composer

17 Half Moon Street **Map Ref 6**

Charles Ives was born in Danbury, Connecticut, USA, the son of US Army bandleader, George Ives, and Mary (*nee* Parmalee). His father gave him music lessons, encouraging him to experiment and be innovative with his music. Charles played the drums in his father's band, but his real hope was that his son would become a classical pianist. At the age of 14 he became a church organist and began to write hymns and songs for church services.

At the age of 19 Ives left Danbury, continuing his education at the Hopkins Grammar School, and the following year he entered Yale University to study music. After the sudden death of his father in 1894, he threw himself into the social life that Yale offered, and "Dasher" Ives showed himself to be an excellent sportsman. The influence of his professor at university, Horatio Parker, encouraged Ives to write conventional compositions, but he began to experiment with different styles. He combined the voice of America with the forms of European classical music.

His *First Symphony* was very much in the traditional style of orchestral pieces, but he began to stretch his musical imagination. In 1906 he composed *Central Park in the Dark,* which has been described as the first radical composition of the twentieth century, and in the same year *The Unanswered Question* for the unfamiliar combination of trumpet, flutes and string orchestra. Around 1910, he composed the *Holiday Symphony* and probably his best known piece, *Three Places in New England*.

Acting on some of his father's last words of advice, he decided to forego a musical career, and go into business. At the age of 25 he headed for New York to begin as a clerk with the Mutual Life Insurance Company. 'At night' Ives held organist posts in two prominent churches, played recitals and composed. He became an insurance agent with Charles H Raymond & Co and when the company closed in 1906, he established his own insurance agency with his friend Julian Myrick. His insurance business prospered, creating life-assurance packages for wealthy clients, and laying the foundations for effective estate planning: he published *Life Insurance with Relation to Inheritance Tax* in 1918.

In 1908 he married Harmony Twichell, a nurse he had met at Yale, and lived in New York, combining a successful insurance business with composing music in his spare time. After a series of heart attacks, he began to compose less, although in 1922 he published *114 Songs*, which demonstrated the range of his compositions, and in 1928 his final piece, *Sunrise*. His plaque commemorates the time when he toured Europe with his music.

Nancy MITFORD
Novelist, Biographer

10 Curzon Street   Map Ref   7

Nancy Freeman-Mitford was born in Belgravia in London, and known as one of the "Bright Young Things" on the London social-scene in the inter-war years. She travelled Europe extensively, dressed elegantly, and was famous for her 'Mitford' brand of humour.

She was known for her novels and for the fact that she spied on her sisters, because of their sympathies with Adolf Hitler. Nancy and her sister Jessica were socialists, whereas her parents had strong right-wing political views, supporting the British Union of Fascists, as did three of her five sisters (she also had a brother). One of whom – Diana – secretly married its leader, Sir Oswald Mosley and of her other sisters, Pamela, was a known Jew-hater, and Unity went to Germany, meeting the leaders of the Nazi party.

Her first novel, *Highland Fling* was published in 1931, followed by *Christmas Pudding* (1932) and a satirical novel about her sisters' political activities, *Wigs on the Green* (1935), followed by *Pigeon Pie* (1940). She is best remembered for the essays and novels about upper-class life in England and France, including *The Pursuit of Love* (1945), *Love in a Cold Climate* (1949), and *The Blessing* (1951).

She wrote four successful biographies about Louis XIV, Voltaire, Madame de Pompadour and Frederick the Great. She helped to popularise 'U'(upper-class) and 'Non-U' usage of language and behaviour, notably in her essay *Noblesse Oblige* (1956).

Nancy married The Hon. Peter Rodd ('Prod') in 1933, the youngest son of the 1st Baron Renner (diplomat, politician and poet). They separated in 1939, but didn't get divorced until 1958. She moved to Paris to be near her amour, Colonel Gaston Palewski, a French soldier and politician. Although this relationship went nowhere, her financial independence enabled her to stay in Paris, enjoying an exciting social and literary life.

She was made a CBE (Commander of the Order of the British Empire) and an officer in the French Foreign Legion of Honour in 1974. She moved from Paris to Versailles, where she died of Hodgkin's Disease.

Wendy RICHARD
Actress
Shepherds Tavern, Shepherd Market — Map Ref 8

Wendy Richard was born Wendy Emerton, the only daughter of Henry William Emerton and Beatrice Reay Emerton (nee Cutter) in Middlesborough in the North East of England. She had a highly successful career of almost fifty years in television, and made number one in the record charts (when it was still called the 'hit parade').

Her parents were publicans, and ran a number of pubs before taking over the Shepherds Tavern in Mayfair, where her Heritage Foundation commemorative plaque is located. She attended St George's Primary School around the corner in Mount Street, and moved schools as her parents changed pubs. Her father died when she was 11, but as he had been a Freemason, Wendy was able to attend the Royal Masonic School for Girls in Hertfordshire. She left at 15 and paid her own way to study at the Italia Conti Stage School, where she changed her name to Richard, and made her first television appearance with Sammy Davis Jnr. at the age of 17.

In 1962 she had her only No 1 hit record (!), *Come Outside* with Mike Sarne, for which she received a fee of £15! Half a million copies were sold: but no royalties for Wendy! However, she had already embarked on a career on television, with her first memorable role in BBC's soap opera, *The Newcomers* from 1965 to 1969. She appeared in iconic television series including *Dad's Army, Up Pompeii,* and *The Likely Lads*, before playing the sexy Miss Brahms in the 1970's sitcom *Are You being Served?* for thirteen years.

From 1985 to 2006, she was viewed as central to the BBC's award-winning soap opera, *EastEnders*, where she appeared in 1400 episodes playing Pauline Fowler, matriarch and heroine. She decided to leave the programme as she disagreed with the future storyline that had been proposed for her. Wendy's last TV role was as Mrs Crump in *Marple: A Pocket Full of Rye* in 2008.

Over the years, Richard appeared in many radio programmes, including the long-running *Just A Minute*, and toured in theatrical productions and pantomimes. She married four times, three of which ended in divorce, was awarded an MBE in 2000, and a British Soap Award for 'Lifetime Achievement'. After many years fighting cancer, she died at the age of 65.

General John BURGOYNE
Soldier

10 Hertford Street **Map Ref 9**

John Fox Burgoyne was born in London, one of four sons of General John Burgoyne and Susan Caulfield. His father was an army officer, politician, and successful playwright. His mother was an accomplished opera singer. He was educated at Eton School and entered the Royal Military Academy in Woolwich.

He was commissioned into the Royal Engineers in 1798, and from 1805 served in Malta, Sicily, Egypt, and with the Duke Of Wellington in the Peninsular War in Spain. He was present at all the sieges as 1st or 2nd in command of the engineers. Only a few months after the Peninsular War, he was Commanding Engineer in the attack on New Orleans, and returned to England in 1815.

Burgoyne was largely employed during the long peace, which followed Waterloo, in other public duties as well as military work. He sat on numerous commissions, and in 1831 he met King William IV, who sought his advice of the defences and fortifications on the south coast of England. For the next fourteen years, Burgoyne was Chairman of a Board of Public Works in Ireland, and in 1845 was appointed Inspector-General of Fortifications.

He was back in Ireland two years later with a brief to organize and conduct the Commission for the relief of the distress caused by the famine.

Richard SHERIDAN also has a plaque on this property and his biography is detailed at his other address in the Mayfair South walk Map Ref 29

When the Crimean War broke out, he accompanied Lord Raglan's headquarters to the East, and was in effect the principal engineer to the English Commander during the first part of the siege of Sebastopol, until he was recalled in 1855, by which time he was 73 years old. In 1838 he had been knighted, and in 1856 he was created a baronet, and promoted to the full rank of General.

In 1865 he was appointed Constable of the Tower of London, and in 1868 Queen Victoria appointed him as the first engineer to be a Field Marshal. He had married Charlotte Rose, the daughter of a Nairnshire gentleman, in 1821. They had one son, Captain Hugh Talbot Burgoyne VC, one of the first recipients of the Victoria Cross, who tragically died whilst in command of HMS 'Captain', which capsized in the Bay of Biscay.

Sir George CAYLEY
Engineer

20 Hertford Street **Map Ref 10**

George Cayley was born in Scarborough in Yorkshire, one of six children, to George – the 5th Baronet – and Isabella. His father headed this important and influential Yorkshire family, and his mother was well-educated and artistic, and descended from the Setons of Darbroath, a wealthy Scottish family. The younger George proved to be a genius of invention, and became known as the Father of Aerial Navigation.

Cayley's father travelled extensively, and his mother took it upon herself to ensure that George had every opportunity to develop the creative talents she recognised in him. He was schooled at home until he was fifteen years old, at which stage he was sent to boarding school in York, followed by being a tutoring-boarder in Nottingham and then Hackney in East London.

He inherited Brompton Hall and its estates on the death of his father, thus becoming the 6th Baronet, and engaged in a wide variety of engineering projects. His wide interests included the development of self-righting lifeboats, caterpillar tractors, seat belts, automatic signals for railway crossings and tension spoke wheels. However, his abiding interest was experimenting with 'flying machines'.

One hundred years before the Wright Brothers, he developed the first proper understanding of the principles of flight. In 1804, he constructed the first man-carrying glider, and he 'encouraged' his coachman to take to the air! He discovered the four aerodynamic forces of flight – weight, lift, drag and thrust – upon which modern aeroplane design is based.

By 1816 Cayley had designed an airship, and was the first to define the principles of mechanical flight, including cambered wings. He realised that control of flight could only be achieved when a lightweight engine had been developed to give the necessary thrust and lift. He designed the first actual model of an aeroplane and also diagrammed the elements of vertical flight.

In a lifetime devoted to science and engineering, he still found time to become the Whig party MP for Scarborough, between 1832 and 1835. Even during this period of his life, his true interests can be illustrated when he became a founder member of the British Association for the Advancement of Science.

Rufus ISAACS (1st Marquess of Reading)
Statesman
32 Curzon Street — Map Ref 11

Rufus Daniel Isaacs was the son of a Jewish fruit merchant at Spitalfields in London, who became a lawyer, politician and diplomat. He was educated at University College School, and joined his father's business at the age of fifteen. He served as a ships-boy, who ran errands for the captain, but in his early twenties he returned to shore to work on the stock exchange.

He was called to the bar in 1887, and practised as a successful lawyer for the next fifteen years, at which time he entered the House of Commons as the Liberal MP for Reading. During his nine years as an MP he served as the Solicitor-General in Campbell-Bannerman's government, and Attorney-General for Asquith. In 1913 he was appointed Lord Chief Justice, a position he held for eight years.

An article in the French newspaper, Le Matin, in 1913 accused high-ranking members of the Liberal government of corruption and insider trading in a contract with the electronics company, Marconi. Isaacs sued the paper for libel, and four days later they printed a complete retraction of the accusations.

Isaacs continued in the role of Lord Chief Justice, even when he spent a year as Ambassador to the United States of America in 1918. In 1921 he was appointed Viceroy of India, where he encountered Mahatma Gandhi, and remained in place until 1931, when he briefly served as Secretary of State for Foreign Affairs.

In 1887 he had married Alice Cohen, and after her death in 1932, he married her secretary, Stella Charnaud. Isaacs had been knighted in 1910, and after being ennobled Baron Reading in 1914 – he lived in Earley, Reading in Berkshire – he rose through the ranks of the peerage, eventually becoming Marquess of Reading in 1926.

Benjamin DISRAELI
Prime Minister and Writer

19 Curzon Street **Map Ref 12**

Benjamin Disraeli was born in London, the second of five children to Isaac D'Israeli, the Jewish author of books on literature and history. His father fell out with his local synagogue, and had Benjamin baptised into the Church of England at the age of 13. He wrote romantic, novels, and served in government for over forty years, was Prime Minister twice, and played a key role in creating the modern Conservative Party.

After a private education, Disraeli trained as a solicitor. He did not enjoy the profession, and at the age of 20 began to invest in South American mining companies. He created The Representative newspaper to promote the mines – losing a fortune in the process. He took the route from 1831 to 1837 that others have followed since, of writing books to recover his finances: the best known being Sybil and Vivian Grey.

In the 1830's he attempted to become an MP, finally capturing the seat of Maidstone in 1839. In 1842 he helped to launch 'Young England', which sought an alliance between the aristocracy and the working class, and his opposition to the attempts to repeal the Corn Laws split the Conservative party. He became Chancellor of Exchequer for two very short periods in 1852 and 1858, and again in 1866 when the new Prime Minister Lord Palmerston also appointed him as Leader of the House of Commons.

Disraeli promoted a new Reform Act (1867), which gave the vote to an additional 1.5million men, and ensured a fairer distribution of parliamentary constituencies. For less than a year in 1868 he became Prime Minister, lost the next election to Gladstone with whom he had a lifelong battle, and then after six years in opposition returned as PM for six years.

During this time, he had a major impact on social conditions, passing legislation for Artisans Dwellings, Public Health, Pure Food and Drugs, Factories, and the Climbing Boys Act. He also passed laws that allowed peaceful picketing, and workers were now able to sue employers if they broke legally agreed contracts.

Aged 35 he had married Mary Anne Lewis, a wealthy widow 12 years his senior. Unlike Gladstone, he got on well with Queen Victoria, who approved of his desire to make Britain the most powerful nation in the world. She granted him the title of Earl Beaconsfield in 1880 when the Conservatives lost the election, and he retired and bought 19 Curzon Street from the proceeds of his book sales.

Fitzroy SOMERSET (1st Baron Raglan)
Soldier and politician

5 Stanhope Gate **Map Ref 13**

Fitzroy James Henry Somerset was born in Badminton, Gloucestershire, the eighth and youngest son of Henry Somerset (5th Duke of Beaufort), and Elizabeth Boscawen. His secondary education was at Westminster School, and he joined the army in 1804 at the age of 16. Within three years he had been sent to Turkey to work with the British Diplomat, Sir Arthur Paget, in his attempts help the Ottoman Sultan extricate itself from its alliance with France.

Later in 1807 he joined Sir Arthur Wellesley (soon to be the Duke of Wellington) as his aide and subsequently military secretary, in his skirmishes in Copenhagen, Portugal and the Peninsular War. He was made a Lieutenant Colonel in 1814, and was secretary of the Embassy in Paris when Napoleon sailed from Elba and re-entered Paris in 1815. Napoleon immediately set about raising an army, which culminated in his final downfall at the Battle of Waterloo, where Raglan lost an arm.

From 1818 to 1820, and from 1826 to 1829 he was elected as MP for Truro. At the same time, he was Wellington's secretary, retaining that position until the latter's death in 1852, when he was raised to the peerage. He was appointed Commander-in-Chief of the British forces in the Crimean War, and showed himself a brave officer and was made Field Marshal after the battle of Inkerman.

He gave an ambiguous order in the Battle of Balaclava that led to the disastrous charge of the Light Brigade under the Earl of Cardigan. Raglan became the scapegoat for the campaign's lack of progress and the inadequate supplies of troops in the winter of 1854-1855. Despite his lack of competence, the British won the battle, and he was promoted to Field Marshal. Before the end of the war, Raglan became ill, and died from disease.

He had married Lady Emily Harriot Wellesley-Pole, the Duke of Wellington's niece, in 1814 with whom he had two sons. His name was applied to the 'raglan', an overcoat in which the sleeves go directly to the neck without shoulder seams, which was probably designed to adapt his coat to the arm he had lost at Waterloo.

Pasquale PAOLI
Statesman

80 South Audley Street **Map Ref 14**

Pasquale was a Corsican patriot, who was exiled from Corsica twice, and took refuge in London. He was born in Haute-Corse in Corsica, the second son of Giacinto Paoli, a physician. Napoleon Bonaparte, who was also born in Corsica, initially admired Paoli, but ultimately fell out with him. When he was born, Corsica was under the rule of Genoa, but the Corsicans were unhappy with the way in which they were governed, and rebelled against their masters. The Genoese called on the French to help them quash the rebels, and in 1739 Corsica surrendered, and aged fourteen, Paoli was taken into exile in Naples by his father: two years later he joined the army, serving under his father.

Paoli worked with other Corsican exiles in Italy to create a Corsican government, and in 1754 an election was held and he was elected General-in-Chief of Corsica. With Paoli leading the resistance, the Corsican people declared themselves a democratic republic in 1755, independent of Genoa, and he was elected President. The Genoese finally decided they'd had enough of Corsica, and in 1764 secretly sold it to France.

Six years later, the French formally declared the island a French Province, and a war between them and the partisans ensued, which resulted in defeat for Paoli and he fled to England.

Paoli became a part of 'The Club' of like-minded liberals in London. King George III gave him a pension on the basis that if he ever returned to Corsica he would support British interests against the French. In 1790, France granted amnesty for exiles, and he returned and was re-elected as President. He acted as a 'secret agent' for British interests in Sardinia, but Napoleon learned of this, declared him a traitor, and attempted to remove him. Paoli and his royalist supporters defeated the French, and he sought British protection, leading to Corsica becoming a British protectorate for a short time.

In 1795, the French recaptured the island, and Paoli was invited to return to exile in London – again with a pension – where he lived for the next twenty-one years until his death. He never married, and left no heirs.

Sir Richard WESTMACOTT
Sculptor

14 South Audley Street Map Ref 15

Achilles by Westmacott on Hyde Park Corner

Richard Westmacott was born in Grosvenor Square, London, the eldest of thirteen children to Richard Westmacott, a sculptor, and Sarah Vardy, daughter of furniture maker Thomas Vardy. At the age of 14 he was apprenticed to his grandfather, Thomas Vardy, and subsequently influenced by his father.

In 1792, 17 years old Westmacott went to Italy with his tutor, and he studied at the Academia di San Luca in Rome. In 1796 he returned to London, firstly to 24 Mount Street in Mayfair and moved South Audley Street in 1818. He established his own studio, and in 1797 he made his debut at the Royal Academy, and by 1811 he was a full member. In 1827 he became Professor of Sculpture at the RA, a role he performed for thirty years.

Westmacott established himself as the leading sculptor of the time of national monuments, including one of the first large-scale bronzes with the 5th Duke of Bedford's monument in Russell Square, London. Amongst other notable pieces he produced were monuments of Lord Nelson in Birmingham, the Duke of Wellington in Hyde Park, George III in Liverpool, and the Duke of York at Carlton House Terrace in London. He also worked on figures at Woburn Abbey in Bedfordshire and Petworth House in West Sussex.

His church monuments were much in favour, and as well as conventional monuments in stone, he also produced statues, busts, and reliefs. In 1811 he was elected to the Society of Antiquarians, which encouraged

the study and knowledge of the antiquities and history of Britain and other countries, and in 1817 to the Society of Dilettanti, a group of elite young men who had met on the 'grand tour' to Italy.

He was knighted by Queen Victoria in 1837, and was called as an expert by the House of Commons in favour of bringing the Elgin Marbles from the Acropolis in Athens. He had married Dorothy Margaret Wilkinson at St. Georges in Hanover Square, with whom he had eight children, and whose eldest son – also Richard – also became a successful sculptor. He continued to exhibit at the Royal Academy until he reached the age of 64, and continued to work until his death.

King CHARLES X of France
Royalty
72 South Audley Street — Map Ref 16

Charles Phillipe, Count of Artois, was born at Versailles, near Paris. He was the fourth child of the son of Louis XV, the Dauphine Louis and Marie Josephe of Saxony. He married Princess Marie Therese of Savoy in 1773 at the age of 16, with whom he had two sons.

He was a disruptive youth at the Court of Louis XVI, but with the fall of the Bastille in 1792 at the start of the French Revolution, he left France and sought asylum in Great Britain. King George III allowed him and his Court to live at Holyrood Palace in Edinburgh, in what is now the residence of the Monarch of the UK in Scotland. From 1805 Charles also lived in the house in South Audley Street.

In 1814 he returned to France, helping to restore the monarchy of Louis XVIII after Napoleon's abdication. Charles took an active political role in foreign matters, legislation and the appointment of ministers. During his 'reign', Louis had spent 23 years in exile, and in 1808 he stayed at Gosfield Hall, near Braintree in Essex, before moving to Hartwell House in Buckinghamshire, which was let to him by its owner, Sir Charles Lee. (Today Hartwell is a luxury 46 bedroom hotel).

Upon the death of Louis XVIII in 1824, who had no children – the last French monarch to die while reigning – the Count of Artois became Charles X. By taking a pragmatic approach to his role, the new King initially won a great deal of favour from the populace.

His rule of almost six years ended in 1830, when he abdicated in favour of his nine-year-old grandson, Henri, Duke of Bordeaux. His impatience and lack of judgement in the choice of advisors lead to the July Revolution and contributed to the overthrow of royalty in France.

Once more he crossed La Manche to escape, and upon his arrival took the pseudonym 'Count of Ponthieu'. The family lived in Lulworth Castle in Dorset, before moving back for a further six years to Holyrood Palace. Charles died whilst on holiday in the Styrian area of Goritz – a Duchy in what is now southern Austria and northern Slovenia.

Constance SPRY
Floral Artist and Author

65 South Audley Street   **Map Ref 17**

Constance Spry was born in Derby, the only daughter and eldest of six children to George Fletcher and his wife Henrietta Maria (nee Clark). He had been a railway clerk, who rose to become Assistant Secretary in the Department of Agriculture in Ireland. The family moved to Ireland, where she studied hygiene and food analysis: she took a health course in London, before returning to Ireland at the age of 22 to become a lecturer at the Women's National Health Association.

In 1910 she married James Heppell Marr with whom she had a son. At the beginning of the First World War she was Secretary of the Dublin Red Cross, and then separated from her husband, returning to England in 1916. She became a welfare supervisor at a Vickers factory, and a year later head of women's staff at the Ministry of Aircraft Production, where she met Henry Ernest Spry. In 1921 she was appointed Headmistress of the Homerton and South Hackney Continuation School.

Constance divorced her husband in 1923 and set up home with Spry, but they never married as he could not bring himself to divorce his wife. In 1927 she received her first commission in flower arranging, from Sidney Bernstein, owner of the Granada Cinema chain, who introduced her to the designer Norman Wilkinson. She arranged flowers for his latest perfumery in Old Bond Street, and her unique style was widely acclaimed. This encouraged her in 1928 to leave teaching, and establish a small shop, *Flower Decoration*, in Pimlico. She attracted fashionable customers and with commissions flooding in, she moved to South Audley Street in 1934 with her seventy staff.

In 1934 Constance published the first of her thirteen books, *Flower Decoration*, and in 1937 travelled to France to decorate the wedding of the Prince of Wales to Wallis Simpson. She undertook a lecture tour of America in 1938 and opened a shop in New York. During the Second World War, Constance lectured all over Britain, encouraging the populace to grow their own food. After the war, she set-up a Cordon Bleu Cookery School with her friend, Rosemary Hume, teaching serious cookery and all aspects of running a home efficiently and making it beautiful.

Spry's first royal commission was to supervise the flowers at Princess Elizabeth's wedding to Prince Philip in 1947, and in 1952 she received her most prestigious 'order' - to oversee the floral decorations for the Queen's coronation. She also volunteered to provide lunch for 300 guests, where she devised the famous Coronation Chicken dish.

Duke of CLARENCE
Royalty

22 Charles Street **Map Ref 18**

H.R.H. The Duke of Clarence
lived here
1826
Later to become King William IV
(The Sailor King)
1830-1837

Christened William Henry (1756 - 1837), he was the first king of the United Kingdom called William, although there had been three previous Kings of England and two Kings of Scotland called William. He was born in what was then called Buckingham House – later Palace – the third son of George III and Charlotte of Mecklenburg-Strelitz. He was the younger brother and successor to George IV.

He was known as the 'Sailor King', having joined the Royal Navy as a midshipman at the age of 13, and spent many years in what became known as the 'senior service'. He served in New York during the War of Independence in America, moved up the ranks to Lieutenant in 1785, and Captain of HMS Pegasus in 1796. He became great friends with Lord Nelson, and worked under his command in the West Indies. He commanded the frigate HMS Andrumida in1778, and was promoted to Rear-Admiral of HMS Valiant in 1789.

In the same year, and in order to stop William becoming a Member of Parliament, George III appointed him to be Duke of Clarence. Despite his many efforts, he never returned to an active role in the navy. In the House of Lords, he spoke vehemently in opposition to the abolition of slavery.

Prime Minister Canning appointed William as Lord High Admiral, in which role he was a reformer, with the abolition of the use of the cat'o'nine tails for offences other than mutiny, improved the standard of gunnery, and enhanced the quality of ships, including the introduction of the first steam warships.

With his elder brother having died, upon the demise of King George III, William became King at the age of 64. In many ways, he was a man of the people and was a reforming monarch. He was seen by some as a buffoon, but the majority view was that he was shrewd and diplomatic, particularly with the relations he developed with America.

William had ten children with his mistress, the actress Dorethea Bland – known by her stage name of Mrs Jordan – but his two legitimate children died before they reached the age of one, and upon his death he was succeeded by his niece Princess Victoria of Kent, who came to the throne as Queen Victoria at the tender age of eighteen.

Beau BRUMMELL
Socialite

4 Chesterfield Street **Map Ref 19**

George Bryan Brummell was recognised as the arbiter of fashion in Regency England. He is an example of how a 19th century man with no title, or illustrious family connections could climb-up in society through education, wit and the right friends. He became known as a 'dandy' – somebody devoted to smartness of dress. He paid great attention to his clothes, and created the fashion of beautifully cut clothes, adorned with an elaborately-knotted cravat. He is credited with introducing the modern-man's suit, worn with a tie.

His grandfather was a shopkeeper in Mayfair, who let lodgings to the aristocracy. Brummell was the son of the private secretary of Lord North, who was Prime Minister between 1770 and 1783, and his father ultimately became High Sheriff of Berkshire. His education was conducted at Eton School, where he was known as 'Buck Brummell', and very briefly at Oriel College, Oxford University, where he preserved his reputation for fashion and added to that of a wit.

His short-lived army career was with the Tenth Light Dragoons, and his friendship with the Prince of Wales (who became King George IV) helped his promotion to Captain. He left in 1799, succeeding to a fortune of £30,000 (£3m in today's money), a bequest from his father. Brummell took the house in Mayfair, and his friendship with the Prince blossomed. After a period of avoiding gambling, he was encouraged by his circle of wealthy friends to spend extravagantly and to gamble.

To be part of Brummell's set was Society's top cachet, and to be cut by him was social death. However, his fortune was eventually exhausted and he quarrelled with the now Prince Regent. With his popularity declining, he fled to Calais in France in 1816 to escape the debtors' prison, where he received help from his friends in England, including Lord Alvanley and the Marquess of Worcester, who used their influence to secure him the post of British Consul in the French city of Caen from 1830 to 1832.

In 1835 he was imprisoned for debts, and was yet again rescued by his friends, However, he soon lost his interest in dress, and his personal appearance became slovenly and dirty. He died penniless and insane from strokes and syphilis in Caen.

Beau Brummell in Mayfair's Jermyn Street, one of the best-known addresses for gentlemens' fashion in London.

Anthony EDEN
Prime Minister

4 Chesterfield Street   **Map Ref 19**

ANTHONY EDEN
Lord Avon
1897 - 1977
PRIME MINISTER
of
GREAT BRITAIN
Lived Here

He was born in Bishop Auckland, County Durham, the fourth of five children. He was educated at Eton School and Christ College, Oxford. He was married twice, first to Beatrice Beckett when she was only 18, by whom he had two sons, but who found being the wife of an ambitious politician unacceptable. His second wife was Clarissa Spencer-Churchill, who was 23 years his junior, which created a frisson in the press at the time.

He served in 21st (Yeoman Rifles) Battalion of the King's Royal Rifle Corps in the 1st World War, reached the rank of Captain and won a Military Cross. After the war, he was elected as MP for Warwick & Leamington in 1923, and the following year, in Stanley Baldwin's Conservative government, he became Personal Private Secretary to the Home Secretary, and then in 1926 to the Foreign Secretary. The Conservatives lost the election in 1929, and Labour was returned without an overall majority.

At 38 he became Foreign Secretary, but resigned in objection to Prime Minister Neville Chamberlain's policy of appeasement against the fascist policies of Germany. He rejoined the government in the 2nd World War as Commonwealth Secretary, and became Secretary of War in the coalition government, setting-up the Home Guard. Churchill promoted him to head the Foreign Office, and Leader of the House of Commons.

After the war, Eden was Deputy Leader of the opposition Conservatives, and when Churchill was returned to power in 1961, he again took the role of Foreign Secretary. His skills as a diplomat and negotiator helped him with the issue of the Cold War and troubles in the Middle East, and he has been widely praised in this role.

He became Prime Minister in 1955 at the age of 57, but his tenure lasted less than two years. His decisions in the Suez crisis to bomb Egypt after they had 'nationalised' the Suez Canal, were seen by many to be ill-judged, and he became ill from the strains, resulting in his resignation in 1957. In 1961 he was ennobled as the Earl of Avon.

Somerset MAUGHAM
Novelist and Playwright

6 Chesterfield Street **Map Ref 20**

William Somerset Maugham was one of the most successful writers of the early 20th century. He was born and raised in Paris, the sixth son of the solicitor to the French embassy, with French as his first language. He was sent to live with his uncle in England at the age of 10 when his parents died, and attended King's School, Canterbury, where he was teased for his poor English. With suspected tuberculosis, he recuperated on the French Riviera, before returning to England to become a medical student at St.Thomas' Hospital in London, and wrote his first novel Liza of Lambeth (1897).

After graduating, he left medicine, living off his inheritance and continued to write plays and novels. In 1908 he had four plays running simultaneously in the West End theatre, including A Man of Honour and Lady Frederick. His breakthrough novel was the semi-autographical Of Human Bondage (1915), followed by The Moon and Sixpence (1919) and Cakes and Ale. Maugham had more works (98) adapted for film and television than any other author, including Of Human Bondage, providing Bette Davis with her first critically acclaimed film role in 1934. In the same year came The Painted Veil, with Greta Garbo in the lead role, and Up at the Villa, a 2000 adaption starring Kristin Scott Thomas and Sean Penn.

He lived at 6 Chesterfield Street throughout the 1st World War, when he worked as an espionage agent for British Secret Intelligence. After an affair in 1916, he married Sylvie Wellcome, the daughter of Dr Barnado. The marriage lasted just 11 years, primarily due to his relationship with his secretary, American Gerald Haxton, who eventually became his lover.

As Haxton was not allowed to live in England, they lived in Cap Ferrat on the French Riviera until the start of the 2nd World War, when they escaped the Nazis to live in Hollywood. Here he worked on the screen adaption of his novel Razors Edge (1944). Haxton died during the war and Maugham returned to his home in France, where he died in 1965.

"I've always been interested in people, but I've never liked them"

5th Earl of ROSEBERY
Prime Minister
20 Charles Street   Map Ref 21

Archibald Rosebery was born in Charles Street, off Berkeley Square, London, to Lord Dalmeny and Wilhelmina, daughter of the Earl of Stanhope. He was educated at Eton College and Christ Church, Oxford. He succeeded to his grandfather's Scottish earldom, and became involved in politics as a Liberal.

Under Prime Minister, William Gladstone, he served as Under Secretary of State for the Home Department, before becoming Lord Privy Seal. Between 1886 and 1894 he became Foreign Secretary, and succeeded Gladstone in 1894 as Prime Minister. He held this role for 15 months.

He was reputed to be homosexual, but this didn't stop him marrying Hannah, who as the only child of the Jewish banker, Baron Mayer de Rothschild, had inherited his fortune, and with whom he had four children. They were married in the synagogue in Mount Street, close to Charles Street in Mayfair, and the marriage was blessed in a Christian ceremony in Christ Church, Down Street, off Piccadilly.

His vast wealth enabled him to indulge his passion for horse racing, owning horses that won all the English Classic Races, the 1000 Guineas, 2000 Guineas, the Oaks, the Derby and the St.Leger. Through marriage and his inherited fortune, he owned a string of houses in England, Scotland and Italy. These included Mentmore Towers in Buckinghamshire, which today is home to the Mentmore Golf & Country Club.

Lord Rosebery had been the richest PM of all time, with his estate being valued at £1.5m when he died (equivalent to £62m in today's money). His Scottish heritage led to him taking a keen interest in Scottish football, becoming Honorary President of the Scottish Football Association. He was elected Rector of no less than four Scottish universities – Aberdeen, Edinburgh, Glasgow and St.Andrews.

Lady Dorothy NEVILL
Horticulturalist

45 Charles Street **Map Ref 22**

Dorothy Fanny Nevill was born the youngest of three sons and two daughters to Horatio Walpole, the 3rd Earl of Orford, and Mary, daughter of William Augustus Fawkener, envoy-extraordinary at St Petersburg. She lived variously in Norfolk, Dorset and Berkeley Square. Although of good stock, the Walpoles were very much on the fringes of society, and Dorothy had no formal education, but was taught Italian, French, Greek and Latin by a governess.

She was introduced to 'society' in London at the age of twenty, and engaged in what were referred to as 'colourful relationships'. Her parents hastily encouraged her to settle down, and in 1847 she married Reginald Henry Nevill, a cousin who was twenty years her senior, with whom she had six children. Nevill had inherited wealth, and in 1851, in addition to owning 45 Charles Street, the Nevill's acquired Dangstein, a substantial estate in Petersfield, in West Sussex. Dorothy took charge of the house and 23 acre gardens.

Dorothy was celebrated in horticultural circles for her exotic plants, and she established a relationship with William Hooker at Kew Gardens, and his son Joseph, by exchanging plants. Dangstein had 34 gardeners and had one of the earliest herbaceous borders, a pinetum, exotic birds and animals, a silkworm farm and a museum. She established a collection of 18th century porcelain and pictures.

Back in London she became famous as a hostess, inviting politicians, writers, artists, scientists and soldiers to Charles Street. She was a close friend of Disraeli, and was a founder member of the Primrose League in 1883 along with Lord Randolph Churchill, an organization aimed at spreading Conservative principles, by combining political propaganda and regular programmes of social activities.

Her husband died in 1878, leaving many of his properties to their children, and she moved her main country residence to Stillyans, near Heathfield in East Sussex. She shared a passion of orchids with Joseph Chamberlain, one of the most important politicians of the early 20th century. and wrote books on silkworms, her Walpole ancestors, and three autobiographies.

Harry SELFRIDGE
Retailer

9 Fitzmaurice Place **Map Ref 23**

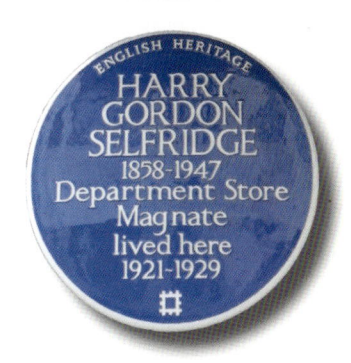

Harry Gordon Selfridge was one of three boys born in Ripon, Wisconsin, USA to Robert and Louis Selfridge. He was visionary in the world of retail, and created the iconic Selfridges store in London. His father ran a general store in Ripon, and when Harry was three, he left to join the army, never to return. The two brothers died, and he and his teacher-mother moved to Jackson, Michigan.

Harry was always an entrepreneur, and at the age of 13 made his first money selling advertising in his own boys' monthly magazine. He left school at 14 and worked in a bank, as a bookkeeper, and in insurance, until he joined Field, Leiter and Co as a stock boy in their Chicago store. Marshall Field owned the shop, and Selfridge worked his way up the company - which acquired more stores and was ultimately bought by Macy's - becoming a partner and amassing a considerable fortune.

He married the wealthy Rosalie Buckingham in 1890, and after selling his share in the business in 1901, contemplated retirement. However, on a holiday in London in 1906, he was unimpressed with the quality of existing London stores, and their antiquated selling methods, and decided to build his own department store. The architect for this flagship shop was Daniel Burnham, who had also designed several of the Marshall Field stores in Chicago, and it opened in 1909.

Selfridge became famous for his innovative marketing ideas, and whilst he set-out to make shopping fun, he also ensured that his shop 'assistants' actually did 'assist' the customer to buy. He promoted the store through paid advertising by suppliers, and it was he who coined the phrase - "The customer is always right". Selfridge recognised that merchandising was a key to success, with such initiatives as placing the perfume counter in the main entrance to the store. He attracted shoppers with unique displays, including the monoplane that Louis Bleriot had flown across the English Channel, and in 1925 was the first to demonstrate television sets.

He enjoyed a busy and lavish social lifestyle, and after the death of his wife in 1918, pursued many liaisons, including a dalliance with Sylvie Barnado Wellcome, who had previously been married to Somerset Maugham. He continued his lavish spending during the Great Depression of the 1930's, and his fortune dwindled and eventually disappeared.

> 9 Fitmaurice Place (see photograph on next page) is the home of the Lansdowne Club, a Private Members Club since 1935 that describes itself as "A haven of tranquility where 18th century grandeur and stylish Art Deco meet 21st century vitality. Perfect for relaxation, recreation and business, the Lansdowne Club offers an unrivalled range of facilities including accommodation, sports and social events."

William PETTY (2nd Earl of Shelburne)
Prime Minister

9 Fitzmaurice Place   **Map Ref 23**

ENGLISH HERITAGE
WILLIAM PETTY
EARL OF SHELBURNE
1st MARQUESS
OF LANSDOWNE
1737-1805
Prime Minister
Supporter of
American Independence
lived here

Born William FitzMaurice, in Dublin in Ireland, the first son of John FitzMaurice, who was the second surviving son of the 1st Earl of Kerry. Lord Kerry had married Anne Petty, the daughter of Sir William Petty, Surgeon-General of Ireland. Upon the death of Anne's brother, the Petty estates passed to William, who changed his branch of the family's surname to Petty.

He went up to Christ College, Oxford, in 1755, joined the 20th Foot Army Regiment in 1757, and was promoted to the rank of Colonel and appointed George III's Aide-de-Camp. He became an MP in the Irish House of Commons for Kerry in 1761, as well as MP for Wycombe in the British House of Commons. He succeeded his father as an Irish peer, Earl of Shelburne, and a British peer, 2nd Baron Wycombe.

Petty had an illustrious, if somewhat chequered history as a politician, with disagreements and mistrust from his colleagues. King George III helped him progress in his career, but when Petty caused him displeasure, forced him to resign from senior office. He held cabinet positions as 1st Lord of Trade (under Prime Minister Grenville), Home Secretary (under William Pitt), and for nine months as Prime Minister (1782 – 1783). He was appointed the 1st Marquess of Lansdowne (in Somerset) in 1784, but never regained high office.

His first marriage to Lady Sophia Carteret, daughter of 1st Earl of Granville (sometime British Ambassador to France and Russia, and Secretary at War) produced one child – John Henry Petty, who sat as MP for 20 years for Chipping Wycombe – and secondly to Lady Louisa Fitzpatrick, daughter of 1st Earl of Upper Ossorey, with whom he had a son and a daughter.

He was known for his enlightened political views and numbered many scientists and literary characters amongst his friends. He died in 1805 at his Berkeley Square home.

George CANNING
Prime Minister

50 Berkeley Square **Map Ref 24**

George Canning was born in London to George Snr, a failed merchant and lawyer from Londonderry, and Mary Costello. His father died when he was one, leaving his family in poor financial circumstances, and his mother became an actress. His mother's brother, Stratford, a successful merchant, became his guardian and paid for him to go to Eton College and then Christ Church, Oxford. After graduating, he practised law for three years, before his uncle Stratford introduced him to influential Whig politicians. He was interested in a political career, but his financial circumstances prevented him from joining the wealthy Whigs, and he became a Tory MP for rotten boroughs, Newport, Isle of Wight in 1793 and Wendover, Buckinghamshire in 1796.

Canning gained an early political following as an excellent public speaker, with wit and intelligence, and he was one of the first politicians to campaign in the country. In 1796 PM William Pitt (the Younger) appointed Canning as Secretary of State for Foreign Affairs, the first of a number of posts, including Commissioner of the Board of Control.

Paymaster-General, and Treasurer of the Navy. When Pitt resigned in 1801, Canning joined the opposition to Henry Addington's government, and especially their refusal to accept Catholic emancipation. He had married Joan Scott in 1800, with whom he had four children, shared all his concerns and trusted her judgement.

In 1807 he was made Foreign Secretary under the Duke of Portland, but in 1809 fell out with War Minister, Castlereagh, over the deployment of troops, which lead to his adversary challenging him to a duel. Canning had never fired a pistol before, completely missed, and suffered a thigh wound. Both protagonists resigned! Canning became Ambassador to Portugal in 1814, but after a year returned to join Lord Liverpool's government as President of the Board of Control. Castlereagh committed suicide in 1822 and he replaced him as Foreign Secretary, and his success in the role is encapsulated in his preventing the French capture South America.

He replaced Liverpool as PM in 1827, and formed a coalition with the Whigs, but his premature death resulted in his holding the record of being PM for the shortest period of time at 119 days. He became a role model for Disraeli, and there was much speculation about what would have happened had he lived.

CLIVE OF INDIA
Soldier and Politician

45 Berkeley Square   **Map Ref 25**

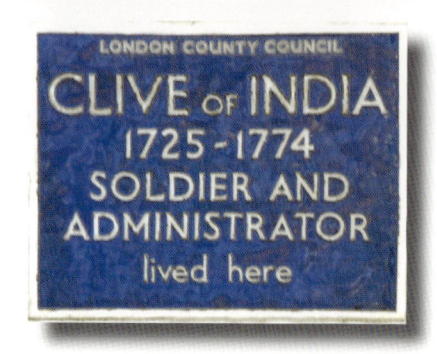

Robert Clive was born in Market Drayton in Shropshire, one of his lawyer father's 13 children. At the age of 3 he was sent to live with childless relatives, who spoiled him rotten, and when he was returned to his parents he was completely out of control. He would now be referred to as a juvenile delinquent, and was expelled from three schools, including Market Drayton Grammar School.

In desperation, his father dispatched him at the age of 17 to India, to work as a clerk with the East India Company in Madras. He was often in trouble with his superiors, but fate stepped in, when in 1746 the French captured Madras and Clive escaped to Fort George 20 miles away. Here he joined the East India Company's private army, and he found his true vocation in life.

Over the next seven years, Clive's reputation for courage and skill in battle in the wars against the French and their Indian allies was established. Many believe that he made the creation of the British Empire possible, and Prime Minister William Pitt described him as a "heaven-born General". In 1753, at the age of 28 he returned to live in London, and married Margaret Maskeylne.

Clive became bored and returned to India in 1756 as a Lieutenant Colonel and Deputy-Governor of Fort St.David. He was immediately thrown into action and re-took Calcutta - with its infamous 'Black Hole' used to hold prisoners – from the French-Indian partnership. The ensuing battle at Plassey, when Clive's army of 3000 men routed the 68,000 strong enemy, removed any opposition to British rule in India.

In 1760 he returned to England, and was elected for Parliament as MP for Shrewsbury: two years later he was ennobled as Baron Clive of Plassey. Corruption had become rife in India, and he went back for a third time in 1765 to restore order. Clive returned to the UK in poor health, and faced a Parliamentary inquiry into allegations that he had accepted lavish gifts from 'grateful' Indian leaders. His reputation, however, remained intact, and he was again returned as MP in 1774.

He was known to be a manic-depressive, there were suggestions that he suffered from mental illness, and had abdominal pains for which he took opium. It is believed that as a result of these innate problems he committed suicide at his home in Berkeley Square at the age of 49.

Bernard SUNLEY
Contractor and Philanthropist

20 Berkeley Square **Map Ref 26**

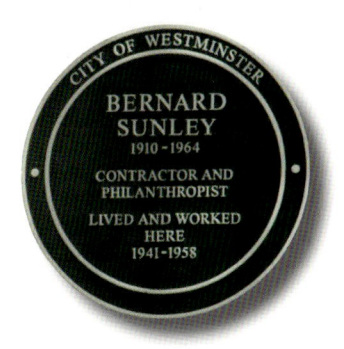

Bernard Sunley was born in London, to his Yorkshire-born father, who was a senior executive with Carters Seeds Landscape Division, and his cockney mother. He left school at the age of fourteen, and followed his father's profession in landscape gardening. During his 20's, he built-up a formidable building and civil engineering business, and then added a major earth-moving equipment company.

Before and during the 2nd World War he was actively involved in the construction of armament factories and airfields, and by 1950 he was controlling two synergistic businesses – the Bernard Sunley Investment Trust and Blackwood Hodge Group. The former included an open-cut mining business, and a major property investment and construction concern: the latter included a substantial housebuilding division in England, and in the 1980's it constructed one of the first purpose-built ski resorts in France, at Isola 2000, which sits above 1500m, with direct access to 120km of downhill skiing.

Blackwood Hodge was primarily an earthmoving equipment operation, which sold and serviced major construction and mining equipment. The business was highly successful in the UK, and expanded throughout Europe and the Commonwealth. Sunley created a new industry in the UK, when he persuaded two substantial American equipment companies to manufacture their products in the UK – the Euclid Road Machinery Co from Ohio, and Cummins Diesel Engine Co from Indiana.

Sunley had a life-long dedicated interest in politics, with the desire to become a Member of Parliament, but he was unsuccessful when he stood for the Ealing West constituency in 1945, and St Pancras in 1947. His lasting legacy was the creation of the Bernard Sunley Charitable Foundation in 1960, which has made grants of over £89m to thousands of charities throughout the world. His overriding desire was to improve people's quality of life, particularly those in need. Sunley was married to Mary, with whom he had three children, and two of their grandchildren are Trustees of he Foundation. He loved to entertain, and from his school days was a keen sportsman. He played table tennis with his lifelong friend, the Wimbledon tennis champion, Fred Perry, and in later life he played golf, tennis and went horse racing.

Terence DONOVAN
Photographer

30 Bourdon Street　　　　　　　　　　　　　　　　**Map Ref 27**

CITY OF WESTMINSTER
TERENCE DONOVAN
1936 - 1996
PHOTOGRAPHER
WORKED HERE
1978 - 1996
OLYMPUS CAMERAS 1999

Terence Donovan was born in Stepney, in London's East End, the only child of a working-class family. His father was Daniel Donovan and his mother Lillian Constance (nee Wright). He is best remembered as a fashion photographer, and his pursuit of perfection places him amongst the legends of British photography.

He was fascinated by photography and left school at the age of 11 years of age to enrol at the London School of Photo-Engraving. He left at the age of 15 to become a photographer's assistant in London, and during his two years National Service, he was given a position as Army photographer. After he was demobbed, he spent a year at John French's Studio between 1957 and 1958, and then at the age of 22 set-up his own studio.

The business was an instant success, with work pouring in and his versatility attracting a wide range of clients. These included leading advertising agencies, and fashion lifestyle magazines – Vogue and Man About Town commissioned his work, and later the influential Nova, Marie Claire and Elle followed. As one of the new generation of fashion photographers he found enthusiastic support for his distinctive style, which became synonymous with the perception of 'Swinging 60's' in London.

Donovan shot mostly in black and white, and his informal and intelligent style set him apart. Nevertheless, he was associated with David Bailey and Brian Duffy as one of the three celebrity photographers who revolutionised the world of magazine and fashion photography. In the early 1970's, he branched out into film production, and it was during this period that he moved his studio to 30 Bourdon Street. By the 1980's he was making award-winning TV commercials and ad campaigns, and he became a pioneer in the production of pop-promo videos, most famously Robert Palmer's Addicted to Love.

He is acknowledged as a dedicated technician who invested his work with wit and intelligence, and he was selected to take photographic portraits of the Royal family, particularly of Diana, Princess of Wales. Donovan committed suicide, after suffering from depression, and shortly before his death, he was appointed as Visiting Professor at St Martin's School of Photography. He had been married twice, and had two sons.

Sir Norman HARTNELL
Fashion Designer

26 Bruton Street **Map Ref 28**

Norman Hartnell was born in south-west London, to parents who owned the Crown & Sceptre public house in Streatham. He was the most famous fashion designer of the 20th century, but despite being awarded Royal Warrants from HM Queen Elizabeth II, and HM The Queen Mother, he wasn't granted a knighthood until he was 76 years old, at which stage the press dubbed him 'The First Fashion Knight'.

He attended Mill Hill School and went to Cambridge University, where he notably designed productions for the Cambridge Footlights revues, which in later years featured such luminaries as Peter Cook, David Frost and Jonathan Miller. After university, he worked for two London designers, before opening his own design business at 10 Bruton Street at the age of 22. Hartnell had a good business partner in his sister, Phyllis, who encouraged him to create practical everyday clothes, as well as designing innovative dresses.

He became famous in Paris and New York as well as London, and attracted young stars of stage and screen, including Gladys Cooper, Gertrude Lawrence and Anna Neagle (q.v). He also designed costumes for a number of films in the 1930's.

His success enabled him to move to a state-of-the-art emporium at 26 Bruton Street, designed by architect Gerald Lacoste in 1934, where he ran his empire for 45 years. It is claimed that at one stage all female members of the Royal Family had designs created by Hartnell, Many members of the Royal Family became regular clients, and amongst his most famous creations were the design of Queen Elizabeth II's Coronation Dress of in 1953, and the wedding dress for Princess Margaret in 1960, who was the darling of the press, which gave him even more international publicity.

He enjoyed a high-profile life through the media, and was always looking for original publicity to maintain his position. He was still working and designing collections until his death at 77, by which stage his range of merchandise sold across the world included cosmetics, bags, jewellery, and menswear.

Lord Henry BROUGHAM
Statesman

5 Grafton Street **Map Ref 29**

Henry Peter Brougham was one of the Britain's leading politicians of the 19th century, and became Lord Chancellor, Head of the Judiciary. He was born in Edinburgh, the eldest son of Henry and Eleanora, an influential family from Cumberland, and was educated at the High School and University of Edinburgh. His work on scientific papers led to him being elected a Fellow of the Royal Society at an early age.

He chose law as his profession, and in order to pay for his studies became a journalist, helping to found the Edinburgh Review at the age of 24. He left Scotland for London, and as a result of his reputation was appointed secretary to a diplomatic mission to Portugal, to counter-act the anticipated French invasion of Portugal. He was called to the English Bar in 1808, and quickly became recognised as a skilled lawyer. In 1810 he was elected as MP to the rotten borough of Camelford, and later for Winchelsea, and gained a reputation for his work for the cause of education and law reform.

Brougham continued his legal career and became famous for his defence of Caroline Brunswick in her successful battle with her estranged husband, George IV. In 1827 he was made a King's Counsel, and Lord Chancellor in 1830, creating him as Lord Brougham and Vaux of Westmoreland. The support he gave to the Reform Act of 1832 and the Slavery Abolition Act of 1833 ensured that they were passed, but his conflicts with the government led to him losing office in 1834, as his ideas were considered too radical

"A lawyer is a gentleman that rescues your estate from your enemies, and then keeps it to himself."

He remained committed to further political reform, and his belief in equal rights for women led to the passing of the Matrimonial Causes Act in 1857. He was a writer on scientific, historical political and philosophical themes, but his eccentricity damaged his influence. He had married Mary Spalding at the age of 43, with whom he had two daughters. He was instrumental in developing the French Riviera city of Cannes, where he spent his last days.

The 'Brougham' was a light, 4-wheeled horse-drawn carriage that was invented for Brougham, and became the pre-curser of today's taxi cabs.

Sir Henry IRVING
Actor
15a Grafton Street — Map Ref 30

SIR HENRY IRVING 1838-1905 ACTOR lived here 1872-1899

Irving was born John Henry Brodribb in Somerset to Samuel, a travelling salesman, and Mary. He became one of the most successful actor-managers of the 19th century, and gained a reputation as the greatest English actor of his time. At the age of 4, his parents moved to Bristol and his maternal aunt, Sarah, in Penberthy, Cornwall, brought him up.

At the age of 11 Irving joined his parents in London, and he attended the City Commercial School. At 13 he became a clerk in an office, but fell in love with the theatre, and against his Methodist mother's wishes began to tread the boards at 18.

He took the stage name, Henry Irving, and over the next ten years toured the provinces and played over 600 parts. By 1866 he was established in London, but it took him another five years before he found 'overnight fame' in Leopold Lewis' The Bells. For the next thirty years he was to be at the centre of Victorian Society, culminating in his becoming the sole manager of the Lyceum Theatre in London between 1878 and 1899.

Irving formed a partnership with the actress Ellen Terry, and with her as his leading lady, revived the classic Shakespeare plays of Hamlet and The Merchant of Venice. He invited leading figures of the cultural world to contribute to his productions, including actors, composers and authors such as Pinero, Tennyson and Conan Doyle. He made eight major tours across North America between 1883 and 1904, and regularly took his productions to major cities in the UK. The quality of Irving's performances and his stage management skills led him in 1895 to become the first actor in Britain to receive a knighthood. Irving was also a man of letters and received honorary doctorates from Cambridge, Dublin and Glasgow Universities. He became financially successful, socially popular and internationally famous.

Irving had married Florence O'Callaghan in 1869, with whom he had two sons, but they separated after two years. They never divorced, and she called herself 'Lady Irving'. Elder son, Harry, successfully followed in his father's footsteps as an actor-manager, and younger son Laurence became a dramatist.

George BASEVI
Architect

17 Savile Row   **Map Ref 31**

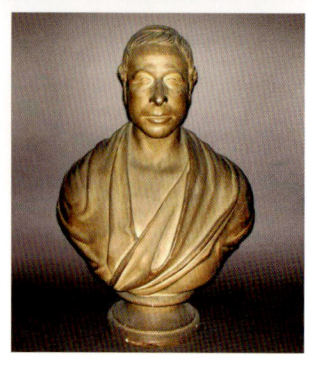

Elias George Basevi was a Jewish-Italian born in London to George and Maria, who was the sister of Isaac d'Israeli, whose second child became the future Prime Minister, Benjamin Disraeli. He was educated at Dr. Burney's School in Greenwich, southeast London, and at the age of 16 he became a pupil of Sir John Soane.

Soane holds a unique position in English architectural history and is regarded as one of the greatest architects of the late 18th and 19th century. He had the reputation as 'the most original British architect since Vanbrugh'. His commissions included the Bank of England, and he was appointed Professor of Architecture at the Royal Academy in 1806. He was active in the founding of the Royal Institute of British Architects (RIBA).

In 1816, on the expiry of his articles, Basevi began a three-year tour of Italy and Greece. Upon his return, he began to exhibit at the Royal Academy, and in 1821 he became Surveyor to the Guardian Assurance Company. He was probably the most brilliant of Soane's many pupils, and he upheld in Victorian England the classical tradition in which he had been trained.

His Gothic churches show little sympathy with the revivalists, and his most successful works were all in the handsome Graeco-Roman style of the corner houses of Belgrave Square, London, and the Fitzwilliam Museum in Cambridge.

He designed buildings at Balliol College, Oxford, and in association with Sydney Smirke - the son of portrait painter and architect Robert Smirke, and another pupil of Soane – the Conservative Club House in St.James Street. In addition to public buildings in the Gothic style, he gained fame for his churches, including St.Jude and St.Saviour in Chelsea, Foxhills in Surrey, and the house that Queen Elizabeth II was to give her daughter Anne on her marriage to Mark Phillips, Gatcombe Park in Gloucester.

He died while inspecting the western bell tower of Ely Cathedral, when he fell through an opening in the floor as he was inspecting repairs, and died on the spot.

Richard SHERIDAN
Playwright, Poet and Politician

14 Savile Row   **Map Ref 32**

Richard Brinsley Sheridan was born in Dublin, Ireland, to Thomas, an actor-manager, and Frances, a playwright and novelist. He wrote plays that are still being performed two hundred and fifty years later. The family moved to London when he was seven, and at the age of eleven he was sent to Harrow School. After six years at Harrow, he went to live with his father in Bath, where he had become an elocution teacher.

In 1772 Sheridan fought two duels with Captain Thomas Matthews, after he had defamed the character of his intended, Elizabeth Linley. Sheridan was seriously wounded, but recovered and the couple married in 1773. They lived in grand style on her dowry, and Sheridan began to write plays. His first play was poorly received initially, but after a revision, The Rivals, ran with great success at London's Covent Garden Theatre in 1775.

The following year, Sheridan joined with his father-in-law to buy the Theatre Royal Drury Lane, and became its manager. In 1777 he produced his most popular comedy, The School for Scandal, which was an immediate success, and guaranteed him fame and fortune.

In 1776 he met Charles Fox, the leader of the Whigs in the House of Commons, and despite only being 25 years old, he decided to abandon his writing in favour of a career in politics. In 1780 he became MP for Stafford, and quickly gained a reputation as one of the best orators in Britain. In 1782 the Prime Minister, Lord Rockingham, appointed him as Under-Secretary for Foreign Affairs, and over the next thirty years he held a number of junior posts.

Sheridan held radical political beliefs and strong views on a number of issues. He supported the French Revolution, an uncensored press, argued against attempts to use the libel laws to prevent criticism of the government and he opposed the Act of Union with Ireland.

At the latter end of his political career, he had serious financial problems and in 1813 was arrested for debt. He was rescued by his wealthy friend, Samuel Whitbread MP, the son of the noted brewer, and released from jail. Sheridan became ill and died in great poverty.

George GROTE
Historian and Politician

12 Savile Row   **Map Ref 33**

George Grote was born in Beckenham, Kent, the eldest of eleven children, to George Snr. and Selina Peckwell, whose father was a church minister. His grandfather, descended from German ancestors, was a founding partner in the London banking house, Prescott, Grote & Co. He was educated at first by his mother and then Sevenoaks Grammar School and finally Charterhouse School.

He was not allowed to go to university, and at the age of 16 he joined his father's banking business as a clerk. In his twenties, he began to collect material for what would become his seminal work, the History of Greece. Whilst working at the bank, he began to take an interest in politics, and was strongly influenced by David Ricardo, the political economist, financial speculator and friend of James Mill and Jeremy Bentham – prominent members of the 'Philosophical Radicals'. Ricardo believed in low wages to discourage population growth of the working class.

Grote published a number of political works in the 1820's, and from 1826 he worked with J.S Mill and Henry Brougham on creating a new 'university' in Gower Street, London. In 1830 he went abroad, and spent some time with French liberal leaders. His father's death hastened his return to England, and he became the manager of the bank. He published Essentials of Parliamentary Reform in 1831, and the following year was elected Member of Parliament for the City of London, and until he resigned in 1841, was principally committed to the promotion of 'vote by ballot'.

After a trip to Italy in 1842, he severed his connection with the bank, and dedicated himself to literature, and by 1846, the first two volumes of his History were published, and the remaining ten volumes followed in rapid succession, with the final volume being published in 1856. He continued to write, and in 1865 he published Plato and the Other Companies of Socrates.

He had married Harriet Lewin in 1820, and his only child died a week after its birth. In the latter part of his life, he was heavily involved in the management of University College London, and the British Museum.

Richard BRIGHT
Physician

11 Savile Row   **Map Ref 34**

Richard Bright was born in Bristol, to a wealthy intellectual family. He was the third son of Richard Bright, a successful banker and merchant, and his wife Sarah. From an early age he was interested in science, and became one of the leading physicians of his time. After attending private school, he went up to the University of Edinburgh in 1808 to study philosophy, economics and mathematics, and only switched to medicine in his second year.

Whilst in Edinburgh, Bright learned that the famous geologist, Sir George Steuart Mackenzie was planning an expedition to Iceland. Bright and his friend Henry Holland joined Mackenzie on this mission to study the volcanic geology of Iceland. The journey to Iceland profoundly affected Bright, and when he returned in 1810 he began his medical studies at Guy's Hospital in London and in Edinburgh. He graduated in 1813 with a thesis on Erysipelas, a disease of the skin, in which he stressed its contagious nature.

By 1814 he was on his travels again, and toured Europe, resulting in a 762-page book, Travels from Vienna through Lower Hungary that was published in 1818. The book covered many subjects as well as medicine, including history, art, archaeology, religion, law, social conditions, the people and the countryside.

Bright was appointed assistant physician at Guy's Hospital in 1820. He worked alongside other celebrated medical pioneers, and his research into the causes and symptoms of kidney disease led to his identifying what became known as 'Bright's Disease' and he was recognised as the 'father of nephrology'. Until the passage of the Apothecaries Act in 1815, which ensured a more rigorous standard of qualification for surgeons in the form of written examinations, the Physical Society had an important role to play in filling the gaps left by often inadequate medical education and the absence of medical journals.

Richard Bright, along with other leading medicos such as Sir Astley Cooper, Thomas Addison and Thomas Hodgkin were leading lights of the Society. They were instrumental in creating the impressive reputation of Guy's Medical school during the first half of the 19th century. Bright had two sons; the younger also became a physician and the elder an historian. At the age of 69, he died of heart disease in London.

Allen LANE
Publisher

8 Vigo Street **Map Ref 35**

Lane was born in Bristol, christened Allen Lane Williams, the first of four children of Samuel Allen Gardiner Williams, an architect, and his wife Camilla Matilda (*nee* Lane). He attended Telesford House School and then Bristol Grammar. Lane's uncle, John Lane, owned the publisher Bodley Head, which he had founded in 1887. He encouraged his nephew to move to London and learn the business, which had grown with the help of notable authors such as Oscar Wilde and Aubrey Beardsley, and he proved to be particularly adept at dealing with authors and customers.

John Lane died in 1925, and Allen Lane became a director at the age of 23, and within five years was appointed chairman. Bodley Head was a staid business, and Lane had to fight to ensure they published James Joyce's *Ulysses*. The board had feared that they would be prosecuted, even though an American court in 1933 had ruled that the book was not obscene, and eventually in 1936 it was published to public acclaim.

He conceived the idea of marketing a series of inexpensive, but high-quality paperback books at the price of 6d, and reluctantly the board agreed. Their view of the venture was reflected by other publishers, such as Jonathan Cape, who sold Lane the rights to a number of their books at very low prices. The first ten titles under the *Penguin Books* nomenclature were published in 1934, with simple, eye-catching orange and green covers, from authors such as Dorothy L Sayers and Agatha Christie. Volume sales would be needed to be successful, and an initial order from Woolworths guaranteed wide exposure for the books. Over 1 million *Penguins* were sold in the first twelve months, and in 1936 Lane established *Penguin Books* and left Bodley Head to run the new venture.

In 1937, Lane met William Emrys Williams, who suggested that there was a market for non-fiction books with an educational purpose. The result was the launch of *Pelican Books*, also priced at 6d, with the first title George Bernard Shaw's *The Intelligent Women's Guide to Socialism*. Lane continued to innovate and launched *Penguin Specials, Puffin Books*, a series for children, *The Armed Forces Book Club* during the 2nd World War, and in 1945 *Penguin Classics*. His innovative approach and willingness to take a risk was illustrated by his decision to launch a complete set of D.H. Lawrence's works, including *Lady Chatterley's Lover*, which had been judged as 'high-toned' pornography. A high profile prosecution followed in 1960, which *Penguin* won, ensuring enormous publicity and sales of over 3 million copies.

Lane had married Lettice Lucy Orr, a psychiatric social worker, in 1941, with whom he had three daughters. He was knighted in 1952, and created the Allen Lane Foundation in 1966, which has a policy of funding projects deemed 'unpopular' in society.

Ziggy STARDUST
Rock Persona
23 Heddon Street   Map Ref 36

The plaque is unique in this book, as it is the only one dedicated to a fictional character. The only other such plaque in London is at 221b Baker Street to celebrate the 'home' of Conan Doyle's detective, Sherlock Holmes. This is the first plaque sponsored by the Crown Estate, which is owned by the Sovereign, and is a diverse property business that manages a wide range of properties across the UK.

The Crown Estate was keen to commemorate the fortieth anniversary in 2012 of the seminal record album, *The Rise and fall of Ziggy Stardust and the Spiders from Mars*. that launched Ziggy Stardust. Ziggy was created by the enigmatic David Bowie, as his 'glam rock' alter-ego. Bowie was born David Richard Jones in Brixton, south London in 1947, and came to prominence in 1969, when his record, Space Oddity reached #5 in the UK Singles Charts.

Three years later, Bowie had morphed into the flamboyant, androgynous Ziggy Stardust. This iconic creation, dressed in a striking costume, his hair dyed red, was launched at the less than glamorous Toby Jug pub in Tolworth, south London. His attire as a space Droog was a boiler suit he'd had stitched together after seeing the recently released *A Clockwork Orange*.

> "He'd like to come and meet us, but he thinks he'll blow our minds".

Heddon Street is where Ziggy was said to have landed from space, and the photograph on the front cover of the album was taken by Brian Ward. Ward had been taking photographs of the band in his studio in Heddon Street. He persuaded Bowie to step outside to continue the shoot, but the other members of the band thought it too cold to venture out, and declined to join him for the picture. Wearing a green jumpsuit on this cold January night, with his foot resting on the step of number 23, Bowie posed for the photograph.

The plaque was unveiled by Gary Kemp, the Spandau Ballet singer, who commented that "Ziggy was the ultimate messianic rock star, and with him Bowie successfully blurred the lines, not just between boy and girl, but himself and his creation". Bowie toured as Ziggy for eighteen months before a theatrical retirement in 1973 at London's Hammersmith Odeon. He has continued to make music, forever changing his style, playing a wide range of instruments, and adding a successful career in films.

James YEARSLEY
Surgeon

32 Sackville Street Map Ref 37

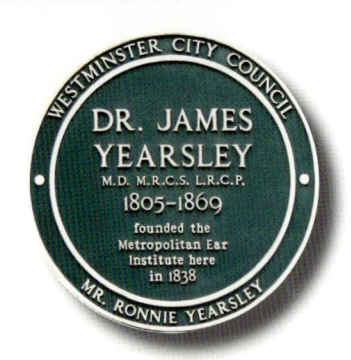

DR. JAMES YEARSLEY M.D. M.R.C.S. L.R.C.P. 1805-1869 founded the Metropolitan Ear Institute here in 1838 — MR. RONNIE YEARSLEY

James Yearsley was born to Moses Yearsley and his wife, Jane, a north-country family who had settled in Cheltenham. Little is known of his early education, and the first we hear of him is as an apprentice at the age of 17 to Ralph Fletcher, a surgeon based in Gloucester. Two years later, in 1824, he became a student at St Bartholomew's Hospital in London, where he qualified in 1827 with the Diploma of Membership of the Royal College of Surgeons.

After practising for a short while in Cheltenham, in 1829 he moved to Ross-on-Wye, Herefordshire, as a general practitioner. He moved to Paris to study diseases of the ear, before settling in London in 1837, where he began to practise as an aural surgeon in Savile Row. In 1838 he founded the Institution for Curing Diseases, and what became the Metropolitan, Ear, Nose and Throat Hospital.

In 1840 Yearsley published his first book, *Improved Methods of Treating Diseases of the Ear*, which confirmed his understanding of the influence of conditions of the nose and throat on the ear. Contributions to *Aural Surgery* followed in 1841, and in the same year he published a book on stammering, in which he claimed a cure, which was later found to be fallacious. He returned to the study of ear, nose and throat, writing articles in magazines such as *The Lancet*.

He co-founded the *Medical Directory* in 1845, which recorded the names of recognized practitioners, and ultimately lead to the Medical Registration Act of 1858. In 1846 Yearsley became surgeon to the Royal Society of Musicians, and in 1852 he originated *The Medical Circular*, which incorporated four years later with the *Dublin Medical Press*, and morphed into *The Medical Press Circular*.

The *Circular* was said not to have achieved its full potential, as Yearsley pursued a previously popular aggressive approach, which was no longer in vogue. He continued to publish treaties on ears, including *Deafness Practically Illustrated* in 1854, and became known for removing tonsils as an aid to recovery from deafness, a practise he began to realise was not as effective as he originally thought.

Yearsley had married Hanna Eliza, one of the daughters of his old master Ralph Fletcher, with whom he had three children. He is remembered as probably the first clinician to practise as an ear, nose and throat specialist, and his memory is perpetuated in the annual Yearsley lecture, held at the Royal College of Surgeons of England.

MAYFAIR NORTH W1
CITY OF WESTMINSTER

JIMI HENDRIX
1942–1970
Guitarist and Songwriter
lived here
1968–1969

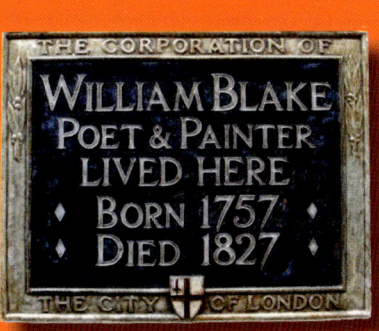

GEORGE FRIDERIC HANDEL
1685–1759
Composer
lived in this house
from 1723
and died here

THE CORPORATION OF
WILLIAM BLAKE
POET & PAINTER
LIVED HERE
BORN 1757
DIED 1827
THE CITY OF LONDON

In This Building
Were Located The Headquarters
of
General of the Army
Dwight D. Eisenhower
Commander in Chief
Allied Force
June – November 1942
Supreme Commander
Allied Expeditionary Force
January – March 1944

CITY OF WESTMINSTER
THE BEE GEES
BARRY, ROBIN & MAURICE GIBB
COMPOSED AND STAYED HERE
1968–1980
THE HERITAGE FOUNDATION

MAYFAIR NORTH W1
CITY OF WESTMINSTER

Mayfair as it is today came about through the foresight and development of just a few families, who created their own estates, and this walk covers the part of the area north of South Street up to Oxford Street.

The largest estate is the Grosvenor Estate. Sir Thomas Grosvenor set about a building programme on the 100 acres of fields and farmland that the family owned in 1770. He laid out well-designed streets, with Grosvenor Square becoming the centrepiece of his plans to attract the fashionable set. The head of the Grosvenor Estate today is the Duke of Westminster, one of the richest men in Britain.

Hyde Park is one of London's historic landscapes, and its 350 acres border the western side of this walk. One of the key features of the park is the Serpentine Lake. At the northeast end is Speakers Corner, the cradle of free speech. Visit on a Sunday and you will most likely catch speakers delivering their passionate views. This is one of the Royal Parks, and is open from 5.00am to midnight all the year round, and hosts various events in the summer months. There are subways at Green Street and Alford Road, which allow you to cross Park Lane to our walk.

The Serpentine in Hyde Park

The major shopping streets of Oxford Street and the up-market New Bond Street border two sides of the walk. Oxford Street houses a number of major department stores, including John Lewis, Marks & Spencer, Debenhams, House of Fraser and Selfridges. Luxury abounds in New Bond Street, and includes Aspreys, Fenwick, Guccii, Armani and Versace. And look out for the Roosevelt and Churchill bench on the pavement where Old Bond Street meets New Bond Street.

As you view the houses, there are scores of interesting yards, mews and alleys along the way, ready to be explored, as well as luxury hotels such as Grosvenor House, The Dorchester and Claridges. Whilst on the walk you can rest awhile in one of

The Selfridges Clock

the gardens. Enjoy the six acres of the Grosvenor Square Garden, around which originally fifty large houses were built, initially nearly all occupied by MP's. The square has strong connections with the USA, with the American Embassy dominating the western side, and a statue of Roosevelt in the gardens. It is planned to move the Embassy to Battersea, and the present building is likely to become an hotel.

A smaller garden in Hanover Square is just off New Bond Street, which was developed in the early 1700's, and features a statue of William Pitt the Younger. Tucked away between the Grosvenor Chapel and the Church of the Immaculate Conception is Mount Street Gardens, an oasis of peace and quiet, and yet so close to the hustle and bustle of the nearby shops. This is the former burial ground for the parish of St. Georges, and is known for the large variety of birds that frequent the gardens.

All the gardens are open to the public all year round, but it is best to check opening hours, as they vary throughout the year. (Contact Parks & Gardens on 0207 839 3969)

The churches on the walk are worth a visit. The Parish Church of St George Hanover Square, built in 1721, became an important part of the lives of Shelley, Disraeli, John Buchan, George Eliot and John Galsworthy, as they were all married there. A famous regular was Handel, who was a warden for a number of years, and as a result the church hosts the annual Handel Festival. (The church is open from 8.00am to 4.00pm Monday to Friday, and 8.00am to 12.00pm on Sundays).

Wellington Arch at Hyde Park Corner

The Grosvenor Chapel in South Audley Street was built in 1730, and has a strong reputation for music, including the performance of free lunchtime recitals. Close by is the Jesuit Church of the Immaculate Conception, in Mount Street, which was built in 1849, and just south of Oxford Street, in Binney Street, is the Ukrainian Cathedral.

The Dorchester Hotel in Park Lane

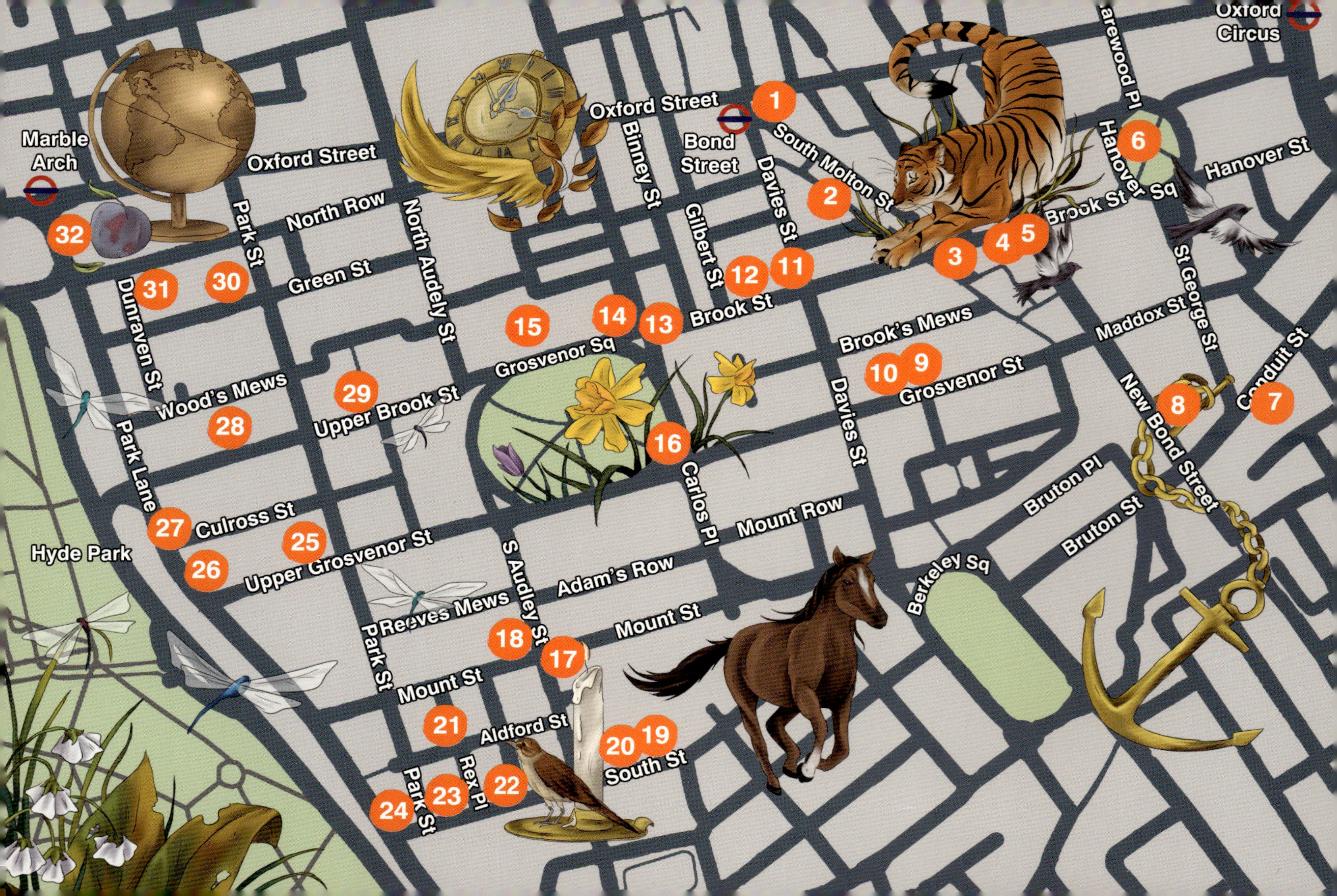
Oxford Circus
Hanover St
St George St
Conduit St
7
8
New Bond Street
Bruton Pl
Bruton St
Hanover Sq
6
Brook St
Maddox St
5
4
3
Oxford Street
1
Bond Street
South Molton St
2
Davies St
11
12
Gilbert St
Brook St
Binney St
13
14
15
Grosvenor Sq
Brook's Mews
9
10
Grosvenor St
Davies St
16
Carlos Pl
Mount Row
Berkeley Sq
Adam's Row
Mount St
S Audley St
17
18
19
20
South St
Aldford St
21
22
Rex Pl
23
Park St
24
Reeves Mews
Park St
Mount St
Marble Arch
32
Oxford Street
North Row
Park St
30
31
Green St
North Audely St
Dunraven St
Wood's Mews
28
29
Upper Brook St
Park Lane
27
Culross St
25
26
Upper Grosvenor St
Hyde Park

MAYFAIR NORTH WALK GUIDE

Page	Ref	Person	Place
58	1	Ernest BEVIN	34 South Molton Street
59	2	William BLAKE	17 South Molton Street
60	3	Sir Jeffry WYATVILLE	39 Brook Street
61	4	Jimi HENDRIX	23 Brook Street
62	5	George Frideric HANDEL	25 Brook Street
63	6	Prince TALLEYRAND	21 Hanover Square
64	7	Charles ROLLS	14 Conduit Street
65	8	Lord Horatio NELSON	147 New Bond Street
66	9	Ann OLDFIELD	60 Grosvenor Street
67	10	Sir Alexander KORDA	21-22 Grosvenor Street
68	11	The BEE GEES	67 Brook Street
69	12	Colen CAMPBELL	76 Brook Street
70	13	John ADAMS	9 Grosvenor Square
71	14	Walter PAGE	7 Grosvenor Square
72	15	Dwight D. EISENHOWER	18 Grosvenor Square
73	15	Sir Frederick HANDLEY PAGE	18 Grosvenor Square
74	16	Charles PECZENIK	48 Grosvenor Square
75	17	James PURDEY	57/58 South Audley Street
76	18	Jack BUCHANAN	44 Mount Street
77	19	Lord ASHFIELD	43 South Street
78	20	J Arthur RANK	39 South Street
79	21	Gilbert WINANT	7 Aldford Street
80	22	Catherine WALTERS	15 South Street
81	23	Florence NIGHTINGALE	10 South Street
82	24	Dame Anna NEAGLE	63, 64 Park Lane
83	25	Sir Robert PEEL	16 Upper Grosvenor Street
84	26	Benjamin DISRAELI	93 Park Lane
85	27	Sir Moses MONTEFIORE	99 Park Lane
86	28	Leo BONN	22 Upper Brook Street
87	29	Sir George SEFERIS	51 Upper Brook Street
88	30	Sir Thomas SOPWITH	46 Green Street
89	31	P.G. WODEHOUSE	17 Dunraven Street
90	32	Keith CLIFFORD HALL	140 Park Lane

Distance : 2.4 miles (3.9 Km)
Starting Point: Bond Street Underground Station — Central / Jubilee

Finish Point: Marble Arch Underground Station — Central

Ernest BEVIN
Statesman
34 South Molton Street — Map Ref 1

Ernest Bevin was a plain-speaking man, who became a key Labour politician. He was born in Winsford, Somerset, to Diana Bevin, who had described herself as a widow since 1877. His father is unknown, and his half-sister's family brought him up when his mother died when he was eight years old. He had little formal education, and went to work at the age of 11 as a labourer. He became a lorry driver in Bristol, which led him to joining the Bristol Socialist Society. He gave up his role as a Baptist lay-preacher, where he had honed his oratorical skills, when he became Branch Secretary of the Dockers' Union, and in 1914 its National Organiser.

Bevin was one of the founders of the Transport & General Workers Union in 1922; elected General Secretary in 1925 until 1945, in what was to become the UK's biggest trades union. He joined the Labour Party, was strongly opposed to communism, and preferred negotiation to strike action, which he considered to be a last resort.

He was elected MP for Wandsworth in 1940, and when PM Winston Churchill formed an all-party coalition government during the 2nd World War, he was appointed Minister for Labour and National Service. He had complete control over the nation's labour force, and was responsible for diverting 48,000 soldiers to work in the coal industry, who became known as the 'Bevin Boys'.

In 1945 Clement Atlee became Prime Minister of the newly elected Labour government, and he appointed Bevin as Foreign Secretary. He was a strong supporter of the United States during the early years of the Cold War against Russia, and backed British involvement in the Korean War. His efforts contributed to the creation of NATO (North Atlantic Treaty Organization), and the Marshall Plan for financial aid in post-war Europe.

Bevin favoured the creation of an Arab state in Western Palestine, but failed to stop the plans of the Zionists and the United Nations in creating a Jewish state. In 1951, with his health deteriorating, he was persuaded to resign from the role of Foreign Secretary and became Lord Privy Seal for a short time before his death.

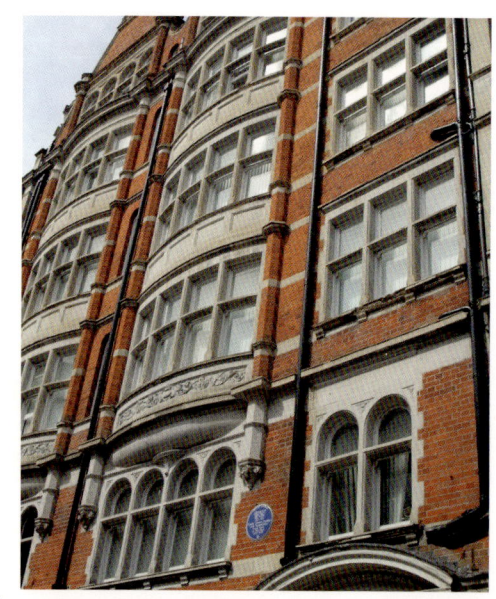

William BLAKE
Poet, Painter and Engraver

17 South Molton Street   Map Ref 2

William Blake was born in Soho to James and Catherine, the third of seven children. His creativity was largely unrecognised in his life, but many have described him as a disturbed soul. His father was a successful haberdasher and hosier, and like his brothers and sisters, William was educated at home by his mother. This was probably due to their strong religious beliefs as members of the 'Dissenters', a group that had broken away from the Church of England in the 16th century, and who opposed State interference in religious matters.

At the age of 14, Blake became apprenticed to James Basire, an engraver, and he spent seven years learning the profession. In 1779, at the age of 22, he became a student at the Royal Academy, where he eschewed the fashionable painters such as Rubens, in favour of the classical style of Michelangelo and Raphael.

From a young age, Blake claimed to have seen visions. They were often associated with beautiful religious themes and imagery, and may have inspired him further with spiritual works and pursuits. He believed he was personally visited and encouraged by Archangels to create his artistic work.

Blake married Catherine Boucher in 1782, and over the ensuing years created a unique form of illustrated verse. He developed a revolutionary method of etching, which he used to accompany his literary and artistic offerings. He moved briefly to Sussex in 1800, before returning to London four years later, where he worked on his most ambitious work, *Jerusalem*.

His appeal has been wide and varied, with decades of schoolchildren learning his poem *"Tiger Tiger burning bright, In the forests of the night…"* from *The Songs of Innocence and Experience;* he wrote the popular hymn - *"And did those feet in ancient time…"* His literary works included The Canterbury Pilgrims and Book of Job, upon which Vaughan Williams was to base his ballet, *Job: A Masque for Dancing*. Blake was still working on engravings for Dante's *Divine Comedy* up to the time of his death.

"He whose face gives no light, shall never be a star"

Sir Jeffry WYATVILLE
Architect

39 Brook Street Map Ref 3

Jeffrey's original surname was Wyatt, and following a high profile career as an architect and landscape gardener, and after receiving a knighthood, he decided to 'gentrify' his name to Wyattville. He lived and died at number 39, and is regarded as the most successful member of the large Wyatt family, which included several of the major architects of the 18th and 19th centuries: his uncles, the highly rated architects, Samuel and James Wyatt, mentored him.

His garden designs were many and varied, including the mediaeval Chillingham Castle in Northumberland, Windsor Great Park, Buxton Pavilion Gardens, and the Royal Botanical Gardens at Kew.

He was generally regarded as the leader in neo-gothic architecture, sometimes referred to as 'Romantic Gothic'. He revived mediaeval styles in contrast to the classical styles that prevailed at the time. He worked with his Uncle James at Ashridge House in Hertfordshire, which was a private house until the 1920's and today is a popular country house venue for weddings. After James' death in 1813, Jeffrey worked on the house for a further six years.

He is particularly remembered for his work at Chatsworth House, in Derbyshire, home of the Dukes of Devonshire, where Mary Queen of Scots was imprisoned, and where he supervised the alterations and interior refurbishment. His most important commission was probably the remodelling of Windsor Castle, and one that won the acclamation of King George IV. This work encouraged a public appreciation for the Gothic.

At the height of his career, the leading portraitist, Sir Thomas Lawrence, painted him with the silhouette of Windsor Castle looming in the distance, and plans for its Round Tower beside him on a table. Wyattville was invited to undertake architectural work in America, and the only museum of Americana outside the United States – the American Museum in Bath - is housed in Claverton Manor, the Georgian mansion designed by him.

Jimi HENDRIX
Rock Star

23 Brook Street   **Map Ref   4**

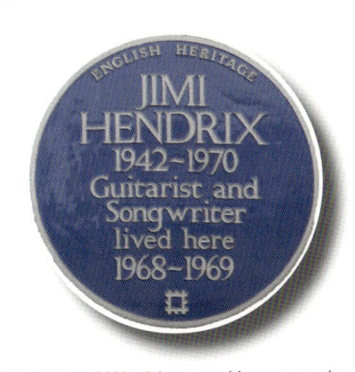

Jimi was born Johnny Allen Hendrix in Seattle, on the east coast USA state of Washington. He was a shy and sensitive child, reflecting the guilt he felt about his poor upbringing. In his short life – he died aged 27 – he achieved superstar status as a songwriter, singer and rock and blues guitarist.

After a brief spell in the army – rather than go to jail for stealing cars – he played in various groups in Tennessee, Nashville, American southern states, and then moved to New York in 1964. He revolutionised the playing of the electric guitar, favouring a Fender Stratocaster, famously using a right-handed guitar and turning it upside-down to play left-handed, he popularized the wah-wah pedal, and constantly sought new sound effects.

His career took off when he was spotted by ex- Animals bass player, Chas Chandler, in a New York night club. Chas encouraged him to move to London in 1966 and record as a solo act. Thus the Jimi Hendrix Experience was born. *Hey Joe, Purple Haze,* and *The Wind Cries Mary* all made the Top Ten in 1967. Surprisingly, he only recorded three studio albums, *Are You Experienced'* (1967), Axis: Bold As Love (1967), and *Electric Ladyland* (1968). After success in Europe, he returned to the USA, receiving acclaim at the Monterey Pop Festival, and he headlined at the iconic Woodstock Festival in 1969. Later, he disbanded The Experience, formed the Band of Gypsies, recording a live album with them, starring at the 1970 Isle of Wight Festival, before re-forming The Experience again.

He was famous for his Afro hairstyle, his unique clothes, scarves, and hats (replaced later by bandanas). His final public appearance was an informal jam session at Ronnie Scott's Club in Soho with ex-Animal Eric Burden's band, War. Nobody seems able to agree about the direction the music of the father of heavy metal and psychodelia was heading in his final months. He died from drug-related complications in 1970, and was posthumously inducted into the US Rock and Roll Hall of Fame in 1992, and the UK Music Hall of Fame in 2005.

His house adjoins that in which Handel lived 200 years before, and which is now a museum.

George Frideric HANDEL
Composer

25 Brook Street **Map Ref 5**

He was born in Halle in 1685 in the Duchy of Magdeburg, a province of Brandenburg-Prussia, to Georg and Dorothea (nee Taust) Handel. By seven he was already a skilful performer on the harpsichord and pipe organ, and on his 7th birthday his Aunt Anna gave him a spinet. His father wanted him to study law, but his mother encouraged his musical skills, and he studied musical composition and keyboard technique.

Upon the death of his father, he honoured his desires, and briefly studied law, but quickly returned to music, moving to Hamburg in 1703, playing in the opera house orchestra. He produced the first of his 42 operas in 1705, Almira and Nero, and in 1707 moved to Italy, where he composed sacred music, including Dixit Dominus. His first all-Italian opera, Rodrigo, was produced in 1707, followed by Agrippa in 1709.

In 1710, he became Kapellmeister (the person in charge of music-making) to George, Elector of Hanover - who became George I of Great Britain in 1714. Handel moved to London in 1712, receiving an income from the monarch Queen Anne, and he began to write choral compositions, including the twelve Chandos Anthems.

In 1717 his Water Music was performed, and in 1723 he moved into 25 Brook Street, Mayfair. His opera Scipio was performed in 1726, he became a naturalized British subject in 1727, and in the same year he was commissioned to write four anthems for the coronation of George II, including Zadok the Priest.

Handel was Director of the Royal Academy of Music between 1720 to 1728, followed by joining the management of the King's Theatre from 1729 to 1734. After suffering a stroke, he took spa treatment in Aachen, Germany, and upon his recovery began to concentrate on composing oratorios, including Messiah (one of 29), which was first performed in 1742. In 1749 he wrote Music for the Royal Fireworks.

He maintained a long association with the Royal Opera House in London's Covent Garden. He never married, and despite losing a fortune in operatic management, upon his death he left an estate of £20,000 (over £3 million in today's money).

His house is now the Handel House Museum, which is open every day except Mondays. There is free entrance for children on Saturdays and Sundays.

Prince TALLEYRAND

Diplomat

21 Hanover Square   **Map Ref   6**

PRINCE TALLEYRAND 1754–1838 French Statesman and Diplomatist lived here

Charles Maurice de Talleyrand-Perigord – Prince of Beneventum – was born of aristocratic, albeit not wealthy, parents in Paris. He was noted for his capacity for political survival, and as one of the most influential European diplomats, he lived through the old regime, the French Revolution, the Directory, the rise-and-fall of Napoleon Bonaparte, the restoration of the monarchy and the Revolution of 1830.

The man, who was to become the most astute statesman that Europe has ever known, was ordained a priest in 1779, and the following year was elected to represent he French clergy as 'Agent-General. He was created Bishop of Auton in 1789. and was known as the 'Bishop of Revolution', by calling for the confiscation of church property to fund the government. The Pope excommunicated him in 1790, and he was sent to England as an envoy in 1792. He returned briefly to France, but was expelled during the Reign of Terror, moving to the United States from 1794 to 1796. Back in France in 1797 he served as Foreign Minister, but was forced to resign in 1799 for involvement in bribery scandals. He astutely backed Napoleon, and again became Foreign Minister between 1799 and 1807.

His relationship with Napoleon was intriguing, and they had a mutual respect and admiration for each other. Napoleon granted him the Italian town of Beneventum in 1806, with the title of Prince. Talleyrand helped to foster the career of Napoleon, but opposed his expansionist foreign policy, and committed near-treason by colluding with Austria and Russia against him. Talleyrand arranged Napoleon's marriage to Marie-Louise of Austria, but actively supported his enemies, and encouraged the restoration of the Bourbon monarchy as a preferable alternative.

In 1814 he was elected Foreign Minister to Louis XVIII, and in what many regarded as his finest moment, he represented France at the Congress of Vienna, where his skills steered the proceedings to allow France to remain an integral part of the concert of Europe. Talleyrand was a womaniser, and was considered by his enemies as a money-grabber. Nevertheless, he held major French government posts – including for a brief period Prime Minister – for nearly four decades. He became involved in the July Revolution in 1830, and lived again in England for four years, when he was appointed as Ambassador to Britain, at the age of 76 in 1830.

Talleyrand was not above playing both sides of the political street to be assured of coming out on top. Through bribes and speculation he amassed a huge fortune.

Charles ROLLS
Motoring and Aviation

14 Conduit Street **Map Ref 7**

Charles Stewart Rolls was born in Berkeley Square, London, the third son among the four children of John Allan Rolls and his wife Georgiana Marcia (nee Maclean). His father was MP for Monmouthshire and in 1892 was raised to the peerage as the 1st Baron Llangattock. Charles attended Mortimer Vicarage Preparatory School in Berkshire and Eton College, before entering Trinity College, Cambridge to study mechanical and applied sciences.

Rolls was the fourth man in England to own a motor car, when he imported a 3.75hp Peugeot from France in 1896, which cost £225. On his first journey he violated the Locomotive Act of 1878, which limited self-propelled vehicles to 4mph, and required the display of a red flag. He was a founder member of the Automobile Club of Great Britain (which became the RAC), and took part in numerous 'goggles and dust' trials and races, during which he broke the land speed record several times. From 1896 to 1906 these activities sifted the possibilities of the three types of propulsion – petrol, steam and electricity.

To fund his racing, Rolls created a car sales company in Fulham in 1902, which led to a meeting in 1904 with the engineer Henry Royce, and Rolls becoming the sole agent for Royce. His 'Grey Ghost' car was exhibited at the first Olympia Motor Exhibition in 1905, and Rolls-Royce was registered in 1906. By 1908 the company had a purpose-built factory in Derby, and output rose from under six a month to over three hundred a year by 1910. Much play was made of the quietness and smoothness of the Rolls-Royce, and Rolls visited the USA to promote the cars.

Rolls became increasingly interested in aeronautics: He was a founder member of the Royal Aero Club in 1903, and he was one of the first people to fly solo in Wilbur Wright's newly invented aeroplanes. In 1909 he suggested to the Rolls-Royce board that they should acquire rights to manufacture Wright aeroplanes, which was rejected. In June 1910 he made the headlines by becoming the first man to fly non-stop across the Channel and back. The following month his passion for adrenaline finally caught up with him, and at the age of 32 he was killed during a flying display at Bournemouth.

The plaque commemorating Rolls' life was unveiled on the centenary of his death by Lord Montagu of Beaulieu, the founder of the National Motor Museum. The building was the West End headquarters of Rolls-Royce, and Roll's place of work from 1905 to 1910.

Lord Horatio NELSON
Admiral of The Fleet

147 New Bond Street   **Map Ref   8**

NELSON.
LIVED HERE IN 1797.
BORN 1758.
FELL at TRAFALGAR 1805.

Viscount Nelson of the Nile was born in Burnham Thorpe in Norfolk, the sixth of eleven children, to Reverend Edmund and Catherine Nelson. She was related to Robert Walpole, (Prime Minister in the early 1700's) but died when he was only nine years old. He became the greatest hero in British naval history, reaching the rank of Vice-Admiral, winning many battles, saving the country from invasion and giving it maritime supremacy.

Nelson attended grammar schools in North Walsham and Norwich, in Norfolk, but influenced by an uncle, he left school at 12 years old to join the navy as a Midshipman on HMS *Raisonable*. Within a few years he had served in an Arctic expedition, spent three years in the East Indies and saw active service in North America during the War of Independence. He rose rapidly through the ranks, and by the age of 20 took command of his first ship, HMS *Badger*.

He won critical victories at sea, and was courageous in combat, which was demonstrated at the Siege of Calais in 1791- when he lost his right eye, at the Battle of Santa Cruz de Tenerife – where he lost his right arm, and at the Battle of Trafalgar in 1805 against the Franco-Spanish fleet, where he was mortally wounded on his ship, HMS *Victory*.

His aggressive and unorthodox tactics earned him insults as well as praise, but with his record of victories he became a popular hero. Despite his flawed personality, with his vanity, mood swings, and insecurities, he led from the front and had a strong grasp of tactics. He was a shrewd judge of his opponents, and inspired his men, bringing out the best in them. Nelson's legacy can be illustrated by the publication in recent years of management books based on his style of leadership.

He was married to Frances Nisbet, a widow whom he had met in the Caribbean, and who had a son from her marriage, but in 1799 he began a notorious affair with Lady Emma Hamilton. She had married the much older Sir William Hamilton, British Envoy to Naples. She hero-worshiped Nelson, which led to their infamous love affair, and together they had a daughter, Horatia in 1801. He was knighted in 1797, and made a Viscount in 1801, and has been judged as one of Britain's greatest military heroes along with the Dukes of Wellington and Marlborough.

"Thine island loves thee well, thou famous man, the greatest sailor since the world began" **TENNYSON**

Ann OLDFIELD
Actress

60 Grosvenor Street **Map Ref 9**

Anne Oldfield was one of the leading actresses of the 18th century. She was born in London, the daughter of a soldier. In her early life she worked as a seamstress. George Farquar, the Irish dramatist – an actor turned writer of plays, such as *The Recruiting Officer* and *The Beaux' Stratagem* – fortuitously heard her reciting some lines from a play when she was working as a barmaid at the Mitre Tavern in Fleet Street, London. This was a favourite haunt of lexicographer Dr Samuel Johnson and his friends, including Oliver Goldsmith, the Anglo-Irish playwright.

Farquar arranged for her to audition for theatrical roles, and John Vanbrugh, architect and writer of such plays as *The Relapse* (1696) and *The Provok'd Wife* (1697) gave her her first Drury Lane Theatre role. Anna's looks were the key to her initial success, but the innate acting ability she brought to the parts she played helped to make her the best actress of the time.

Whether she played comedy or tragedy, she was deemed to be the queen of the theatre. It was said that on many occasions, the success of a play was as much to do with her performance, as to the quality of the piece. She was noted for the clarity of her speaking voice.

Amongst Anne's major successes were her performances in Colley Gibber's *The Careless Husband* (1704) – in which she played the ever-tactful wife - and *The Provoked Husband* (1728) again at the Theatre Royal, Drury Lane. She also played the leading ladies in Ben Johnson's *Epicoene* and *Volpone*, which had been written a hundred years earlier.

She married twice, first to Arthur Mainwaring, by whom she had a son, and then to Lieutenant-General Charles Churchill, by whom she also had a son. She was only 47 when she died, and as reflection of her fame and the respect in which the theatre-going public held her, she was buried in Westminster Abbey.

Sir Alexander KORDA

Film Director

21-22 Grosvenor Road   **Map Ref 10**

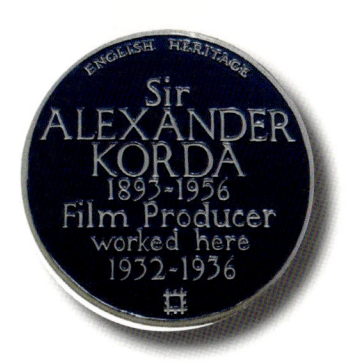

The prolific film-maker, Alexander Korda, was born Sandor Laszio Kellner in Turkeye, Hungary, the oldest of three boys to a Jewish-Hungarian family. His father died when he was a young teenager, and he was sent to Budapest to study. By the age of 15 he had become a journalist, but became interested in filmmaking, and by the time he was 20 he was writing screenplays, which was soon followed by directing films.

The Hungarian government collapsed in the aftermath of World War I, and Korda was selected as one of the leaders of the new democratic government. However, he fell foul of the battles between the Communists and anti-Communists, and was jailed, only to be rescued and released through the efforts of his wife, Maria, who was a popular actress.

He moved to Vienna in 1919, followed by Berlin, and then Hollywood, making films all the while. The late 1920's was the end of the era of silent movies, and Maria's strong Hungarian accent was not appealing for the new "talkies", and she quickly fell from grace. Paris was Korda's next port of call in 1931, before he headed for London.

He created London Film Productions in 1932, built Denham Film Studios, Buckinghamshire, and became a British citizen in 1936. The business became a leading British film maker, producing films such as *Private Lives* (1933) and *Rembrandt* (1936) – both of which starred Charles Laughton – the action-adventure *Four Feathers*, and the fantasy-film *Thief of Baghdad*. In 1940 he returned to the USA, but was back in England again two years later. In 1949 he produced *The Third Man*, probably his most famous picture, which was directed by Carol Reed and starred Orson Welles.

Korda had divorced Maria in 1930, and married Merle Oberon in 1939. She was an Indian-born British actress, who initially worked under the name of Queenie O'Brien. He divorced her and his final marriage was to Alexandra Bovau, until his death in 1956. He received a knighthood during the Second World War, at the recommendation of Winston Churchill's government.

The BEE GEES
Pop Artists

67 Brook Street **Map Ref 11**

THE BEE GEES
BARRY, ROBIN & MAURICE GIBB
COMPOSED AND STAYED HERE
1968-1980
CITY OF WESTMINSTER – THE HERITAGE FOUNDATION

The Bee Gees was one of the major recording acts of the 1970's and 1980's, known as the 'gods of the disco', and one of the most celebrated songwriting teams of all time. They sold over 200 million records, and over 2000 artists have recorded their compositions. Barry Gibb was born on the Isle of Man in 1946, as were the twins Robin and Maurice Gibb in 1949. They began performing when Barry was nine and the twins were six at a local cinema in Manchester. The Gibb family immigrated to Australia in 1958, and the young Gibbs became regulars on TV, and had a string of minor hits.

The brothers returned to England in 1967, and were signed-up by Robert Stigwood, who had recently joined Brian Epstein's NEMS Enterprises. They enjoyed nine Top 20 singles over the next 5 years including two number 1's with *Massachusetts* in 1967 and *I've Gotta Get A Message To You* the following year.

The turning point in their lives was when Stigwood commissioned them to write songs for his film *Saturday Night Fever* in 1977. Songs such as *Night Fever* and *Stayin' Alive* became disco classics, and the soundtrack sold over 40 million copies. As well a string of hit singles in the late 70's, they penned and produced the title song for the movie *Grease*.

Through the late 70's and 80's they became famous for writing songs for other artists to perform, including *Chain Reaction* for Diana Ross, *Woman in Love* for Barbra Streisand, and *Islands in the Stream* for Kenny Rogers and Dolly Parton. In 1978 the Gibb brothers had five songs in the US Top 10 at the same time. They are the fifth most successful recording artists of all time, and have won 8 Grammy Awards, received a Lifetime Achievement Award from the British Music Industry, and were awarded a star on the Hollywood Walk of Fame. In 1994 they were inducted into the Songwriters Hall of Fame, were awarded CBE's, and in 2006 were only the third pop writers to receive the 'Fellowship of the British Academy of Songwriters and Composers'.

Their music continues to live on, despite the deaths of Maurice at 53 with a heart attack in 2003, and Robin at 62 from colorectal cancer in 2012 Robin was the longest serving president of the Heritage Foundation from 2008 to 2011, the plaque sponsors mentioned in the Introduction.

Colen CAMPBELL
Architect

76 Brook Street **Map Ref 12**

No picture of Campbell is available: this is one of his finest designs, Houghton Hall in Norfolk

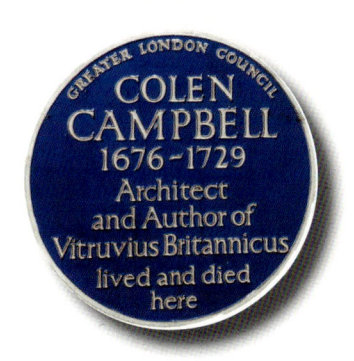

COLEN CAMPBELL 1676-1729 Architect and Author of Vitruvius Britannicus lived and died here

Very little is known of the early life of this Scot, born in Nairnshire. He was born the eldest of four children to Donald Campbell, Laird of Boghole and Urchary, and Elizabeth, daughter of Sir Robert Innes of Muirton Moray. He was trained as a lawyer but changed his allegiance to the study of architecture.

He first appears in England as the 'agent' of William Benson, the successor to Christopher Wren – designer of St Paul's Cathedral amongst other notable works – as Surveyor General. Benson appointed Campbell as Chief Clerk of the King's Works and Deputy Surveyor, but shared in Benson's disgrace in 1719 and lost both his offices. Benson had sacked his ablest staff, infuriated the Treasury and brought upon himself the wrath of the House of Lords, when he falsely insisted that their Lordships' Chamber was in imminent danger of collapse.

However, he created one of the most influential architectural texts of the 18th century – *VITRUVIUS BRITANNICUS* – a three-volume book on Neo-Palladianism. The book extolled Neo-Palladianism as the dominant style of architecture of 18th century Britain. It featured the designs of the famous architects of the 17th century, including Inigo Jones and Christopher Wren, as well as contemporary buildings.

Campbell found a new patron in Richard Boyle, the third Lord Burlington, after he had read the book and employed him. He commissioned Campbell as the architect for the *Royal Academy* – Burlington House – in Piccadilly, which had been built originally in 1668 for the 1st Lord Burlington. Boyle had studied Roman architecture inspired by Italy's classical inheritance, especially the work of Andrea Palladio. These influences were reflected in the changes made to the façade and interiors. The building today houses one of the capital's most prestigious art exhibitions.

Campbell was heavily influenced by James Smith, a Scottish architect, who pioneered the Palladian style in Scotland, and is described in Campbell's book as "the most experienced architect of that Kingdom". Campbell designed and built the house in Brook Street, and his most important architectural commissions included *Wanstead House* in Essex, designed for Sir Richard Child – an English Member of Parliament and Irish Peer - *Stourhead* in Wiltshire, built for banker Henry Hoare, and *Mereworth Castle* in Kent, commissioned by John Fane (7th Earl of Westmoreland), an English nobleman and MP for over 17 years.

John ADAMS
President of the United States of America
9 Grosvenor Square   **Map Ref 13**

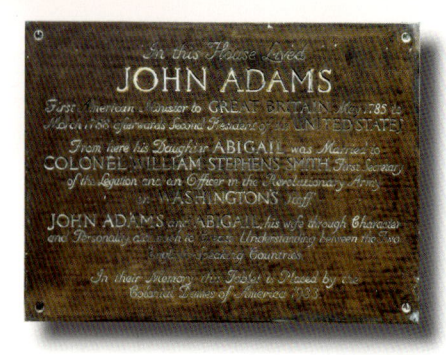

John Adams was born in Braintree, Massachusetts, America, the eldest son of 'Deacon' John Adams, a farmer and shoemaker, and Susanna (nee Boylston). Adams was descended from early-seventeenth English emigrants through both his parents, and he wanted to follow his father working on the land. His father wanted him to become a church minister, and at 16 he studied at Harvard University. A bitter dispute between his hometown's minister and his parishioners confirmed Adams' view that the church was not for him.

He became a lawyer, and by his early thirties he had become the most successful attorney in Massachusetts. He had always been interested in politics, and from the mid-1760's Adams increasingly began to oppose British legislation in its American colony. Despite his hostility to the British government, in 1770 he defended the British soldiers involved in the Boston Massacre, which made him unpopular but marked him out as a man of high principles. Adams joined Congress and persuaded other colonists of the need for opposition to Britain, and then of the cause for independence. In 1776 he was appointed to the committee to draft the Declaration of Independence, and during the Revolutionary War he ran the Board of War, raising and equipping the army and creating a navy. In 1778, Adams was sent to Paris on a diplomatic mission, and in 1783 was one of the three Americans to sign the Treaty of Paris, which ended the American War of Independence.

In 1785 he served as America's first Minister to the Court of St James's – Ambassador to Britain – but returned to Massachusetts in 1788 after failing to persuade the Pitt ministry to negotiate a commercial treaty with America. On his return to America, he was elected the first Vice-President under George Washington, and in the presidential campaign of 1796, which was the first to be contested by political parties, Adams sided with the Federalist Party and was elected President. Relations with France deteriorated which led to a naval war, and in 1798 Adams signed the Acts that limited rights to free speech, which were opposed throughout America. At the same time, he faced opposition from his party, resisting their demands for all-out war with France, and lost the 1800 election to Thomas Jefferson.

Adams had married Abigail Smith in 1764, who gave him strong support throughout his career, and who bore him five children. Their eldest son, John Quincy, became the sixth President.

Walter PAGE
Diplomat, Publisher and Journalist
6 Grosvenor Square **Map Ref 14**

Walter Hines Page was an American born in Cary, North Carolina. The 28th President, Woodrow Wilson, appointed him as the American Ambassador to Great Britain in 1913.

Page was educated at Trinity College, North Carolina, then at Randolph-Macon in Virginia, and in 1876 he became a Fellow at Johns Hopkins University. He decided that he did not want to spend his life reading Greek classics, and at the age of 23 he began his journalistic career as a 'cub' reporter on the *St.Joseph Gazette*, in Montana, soon becoming its editor.

Within a year he had left, and travelled throughout the southern states, writing about the social and economic problems he encountered, some of which appeared in the *New York World*. He hoped to modernize the region, but his editorial promotion of social and political reforms in the *Raleigh State Chronicle* aroused animosity, and he returned to New York. There as editor of the *Forum, Atlantic Monthly* and *World's Work* he became known as a leader of reform. He helped develop Doubleday, Page & Company in 1899, which became one of the great publishing houses of the 20th century, and included Rudyard Kipling amongst its writers.

As Ambassador, he rapidly won the respect of the British political leaders, and caused a rift with Woodrow Wilson with his advocacy of diplomatic and economic assistance to Britain and its allies at the beginning of World War I in 1914. He promoted British policies to Wilson, and helped to garner support with the President and the American people. When America eventually entered the war in 1917, he urged extensive naval and financial assistance for the war effort.

In his latter days, his extensive correspondence was dismissed by Washington as 'Anglophile propaganda'. He was plagued with ill health, but stuck with his Ambassadorial role until four months before his death in December 1918.

Dwight D. EISENHOWER
Soldier. President of United States of America

18 Grosvenor Square   **Map Ref 15**

'Ike' was born David Dwight Eisenhower in Denison, Texas, and brought up in Abilene, Kansas, USA. He was the third of seven sons to David Jacob Eisenhower, a small farmer, and Ida Elizabeth (nee Stone), who between them had German, English and Swiss ancestry. At school he proved to be a star athlete, excelling in baseball and American football. He left school in 1909 and took a job as a night foreman at a creamery, but swiftly moved on, and trained for four years at West Point Military Academy in New York, despite his parents' misgivings based on their religious beliefs.

After graduating in 1915, he served in the infantry, although he saw no combat in the 1st World War. He married Marie Geneva Doud in 1916, with whom he had two sons. He took a keen interest in tank warfare, but his career stagnated until he was posted to the Philippines in 1935, to assist in advising their government. Eisenhower returned to the USA in 1939, and after the Japanese attack on Pearl Harbour, he was responsible for creating the war plans to defeat Japan and Germany. In 1942, he was transferred to London as Commanding General European Theater of Operations. He held senior posts in the fight against the Nazis, culminating in his taking supreme command of all Allied forces in 1944, and was subsequently promoted to General of the Army.

"Leadership is the art of getting someone else to do something you want done because he wants to do it".

Eisenhower disagreed over strategy with British PM, Winston Churchill and the leader of the British Army, Field Marshal Montgomery, but this did not stop him working with them and the other key allies, Marshal Zhukov of Russia and General de Gaulle of France. Following the defeat of Germany, he became Chief of Staff of the US Army, and was appointed Military Governor of the US Occupation Zone in Berlin, Germany. In 1948 he returned to the USA, becoming President of Columbia University, to where he returned in 1952 for a year, after two years as Supreme Commander of NATO.

The Republican Party encouraged him to seek the presidency, and with the irresistible slogan – "I like Ike" - he was elected in 1952 as the 34th President of the United States of America. During his eight years as President, he oversaw the cease-fire of the Korean War, began the Interstate Highway System - which he saw as vital to American security during the Cold war with Russia – launched the Space Race, and enlarged the Social Security programme.

After two terms as President, he endorsed the candidacy of his Vice-President, Richard Nixon, who lost narrowly to Democrat John F Kennedy in 1961. Upon leaving the White House, he returned as a 5-Star General in the Army, and continued his lifelong love of golf.

Sir Frederick HANDLEY PAGE

Aircraft Manufacturer

18 Grosvenor Square — **Map Ref 15**

Frederick Handley Page was one of the major influencers in the development of the aircraft industry in the 20th century. He was born in Cheltenham, Gloucester, the son of Theodore Page, a furniture maker, and married Uma Thynne with whom he had three daughters. He studied electrical engineering at college in London, and after graduating he joined a small electrical manufacturer, soon becoming their chief designer. He taught himself about aviation, starting his own business in the proverbial 'shed at the bottom of the garden', founding Handley Page Ltd in 1909 in Barking, Essex, where he built, bi-planes and monoplanes. In 1912 he established a factory and an airfield at Cricklewood, in north London.

During the 1st World War they produced heavy bombers for the Royal Navy. A number of these planes were modified after the war for passenger use, and flew under the Handley Page Transport brand from London to Paris. In 1924, they merged with two other regional airlines to create Imperial Airways, the first UK airline service. The company built eight 4-engine bi-planes known as the Atlantic, which Imperial Airways flew throughout Europe and to such exotic locations as South Africa, India and the Far East between 1924 and 1939.

With the threat of another war, Handley Page was active in the 1930's in bomber design, and their twin-engined Hampden aeroplane took part in the first British raid on Berlin. They had bought Radlett Aerodrome in Hertfordshire in 1929, where the four-engined Halifax bomber was built. It was considered to be a superior aircraft to its rival, the Lancaster, and it is estimated that 7000 Halifax bombers were employed in the 2nd World War.

He was knighted in 1942, and after the war, Handley Page became involved in the development of 'V' jet bombers to carry nuclear deterrents. The last plane the company made was the 'Jetstream', which was a small turbo-prop commuter aircraft, designed particularly for the American market, holding 12 to 18 passengers. During his life, he was committed to research, and the company is recognised to be the first to install its own wind-tunnel for in-house experiments. Handley Page's company couldn't compete in a world where large companies prevailed, and went into voluntary liquidation in 1970.

Charles PECZENIK
Architect

48 Grosvenor Square   **Map Ref 16**

No picture of Peczenik is available: this is Negrin as detailed below

Charles Edmund Peczenik 1877-1967 Architect Lived here

Charles Edmund Peczenik was born in Paris, and although not much is known of his life, the privately-placed plaque in Grosvenor Square recognises the fact that he lived and was involved in re-building the square from the 1930's to 1950's. We believe he was educated at Trinity College, Cambridge University, where it is understood he read engineering.

He studied architecture under the noted French architect, Rene Sergent in Paris. Sergent had studied at L'Ecole Speciale d'Architecture, establishing his own practice in 1902, and he was noted for the integration of modern concepts into an imposing classical style. The majority of his commissions were in France, but he also worked on landmark hotels in London, including the Savoy and Claridges.

Peczenik became an estate developer in the UK, working mainly in London, and particularly in Grosvenor Square. The square had originally been laid-out by the Grosvenor family in the early years of the 18th century, but represented different architectural styles, and as such lacked uniformity. In the 1930's, the 2nd Duke of Westminster, head of the Grosvenor Estate, proposed a coherent scheme of re-building.

He had employed Detmar Blow, the London-born architect and friend of Lutyen, as his Private Secretary and Manager of the Estates in 1916. Blow asked his former business partner, Fernand Billerey, who had been 'Beaux-Arts' trained, specialising in the neoclassical style, to prepare designs. In turn, Billerey called in Peczenik, and it is interesting to note that the re-design came from two French-trained architects, with Peczenik being seen as the first and most faithful executor of Billerey's design.

Peczenik occupied his flat in Grosvenor Square in the 1940's and 1950's, although it is believed that the occupant in 1941 was Juan Negrin, (photograph above) the Republican Prime Minister of Spain, who fled to England from Paris, where he had attempted to maintain a government in exile from Franco's anarchists, until the Germans invaded.

James PURDEY
Gunmakers
57-58 South Audley Street — Map Ref 17

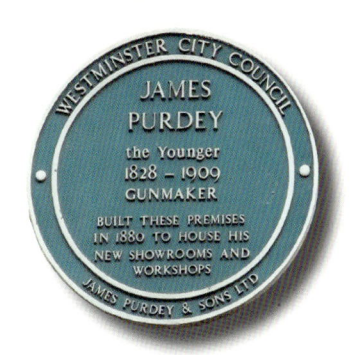

Purdey is one of the most famous gunmakers in the world. It is one of the world's oldest sporting brands, and has been known internationally for top quality, innovation and excellence for almost two hundred years.

The founder, James Purdey, began a seven-year apprenticeship with leading gunmaker Joseph Manton in 1798, before leaving in 1814 to establish his own business in the west end of London. The company moved into Manton's premises in Oxford Street twelve years later, where it stayed for the next fifty-six years.

The founder's son, James, took over the company in 1858. In 1880 Purdey moved to their present premises, which incorporated the factory for making guns, rifles and cartridges, offices and a showroom, on the corner of South Audley Street and Mount Street. As the company grew, the factory moved and today they build between 70 and 80 bespoke guns and rifles a year at their premises in Hammersmith, west London.

James the Younger was always at the forefront in the design of their products, and he filed many patents for technical innovations, many of which were adopted by other gunmakers. In 1900 Athol succeeded his father, continuing its growth and adding the manufacture of gun parts for use in World War I. His sons, James and Tom, joined the company in the 1920's and took over from their father.

Purdey & Sons has always enjoyed royal patronage, starting with Queen Victoria buying a pair of pistols in 1838, to being granted their first Royal Warrant in 1868 by the future King Edward VII, and they continue to hold Royal Warrants from Queen Elizabeth II, the Duke of Edinburgh, and Prince Charles today.

In the aftermath of the difficult market conditions after World War II, Purdey's was sold in 1946. However, a Purdey remained involved in the company until 2007 when Richard Purdey, from the sixth generation, stood down as Chairman. The business is today owned by the luxury goods Richemont Group, and continues to prosper.

Jack BUCHANAN
Actor, singer, dancer

44 Mount Street **Map Ref 18**

JACK BUCHANAN Actor-Manager 1890-1957 lived here

Walter John Buchanan was born in Helensburgh, Scotland, named after his father, an auctioneer, and Patricia, (nee McWatt). He was educated at the Glasgow Academy. He was compared with Fred Astaire, with whom he cornered the top-hat-and-tail style of musical film.

His father's gambling habits left the family poor, and it is believed that his deprived childhood affected his health, which made him medically unfit to join the army. After a brief attempt to follow his father's profession, he became a music-hall comedian as Chump Buchanan. Caught up in the world of amateur dramatics while he was an office worker in London, making his stage debut in 1911 and he first appeared on the West End stage the following year in the comic opera *The Grass Widow*.

He appeared successfully in West End plays during the war, and was described by The Times as 'the last of the knuts' - a fashionable or showy young man. In 1915 he starred in the long-running play *Tonight's the Night*, and followed this in 1921 in the revue *A to Z* with Gertrude Lawrence. Amongst the numbers in the show was Ivor Novello's *And Her Mother Came Too*, which became his signature tune. The show transferred successfully to Broadway in New York in 1924.

In 1917 he made his silent film debut in *Auld Lang Syne*, and he appeared in over thirty films: once the talkies appeared, his cultured British voice was much in demand in Hollywood. By the mid 1920's he was an established star with his own production company and so successful that in 1930 he built his own theatre, the Leicester Square Theatre. He continued to be busy on the stage and in musicals during the 1930's, but by the 1940's his film career had run into the sand, he lost money on the show *Top Hat and Tails* and his theatre burnt-down.

Despite this, Buchanan provided financial backing for a fellow son of Helensburgh, John Logie Baird, in his quest to develop the television. One of his last movies was in 1953, when he appeared with Fred Astaire in the musical *The Band Wagon*, which included a scene were Buchanan and Astaire were joined by Nanette Fabray in baby bonnets as the 'Triplets'.

76

Lord ASHFIELD
Transport Pioneer

43 South Street **Map Ref 19**

Albert Henry Stanley was the son of Henry and Elizabeth Knattriess (nee Twigg), in Normanton, Derbyshire. He became a very successful railway operator, created what became the London Underground, and for a short time held political office.

His father worked for the coachbuilder, Pullman Company, and in 1880 the family immigrated to America, to work for the parent company. The family changed its surname to 'Stanley' in the mid-1890's. Albert was keen to become an engineer, and at 14 started work with Detroit's horse-drawn tram company. He continued to study at technical college, and his abilities and ambitions were recognised, and he rose rapidly through the company.

Stanley joined the Street Railway Department of New Jersey in 1903. Much of the finance and equipment for the newly created Underground Electric Railways Company of London (UERL) had come from America, and his reputation helped to secure him the job of General Manager in 1907, and Managing Director in 1910. Stanley began to grow the business by increasing passenger numbers, extending the tracks, and acquiring other underground rail companies, to create the Underground Group.

Stanley resigned in 1915 to join the Government under Prime Minister, David Lloyd George, first as Director-General of Mechanical Transport at the War Office, and then having being elected as MP for Ashton-under-Lyne 1916, as President of the Board of Trade. Despite his managerial strengths outside Parliament, he was not a successful politician, and returned to the UERL in 1919.

He became Chairman in 1921 and continued to pursue an integrated, non-competitive system of public transport across London. With support from Transport Minister, Herbert Morrison, he played a major part in the formation of the London Passenger Transport Board (LPTB) in 1933. The Labour government of Clement Atlee nationalized all public transport systems, and Stanley joined the British Transport Commission in 1948.

J Arthur RANK
Industrialist and Film Producer
39 South Street Map Ref 20

J. ARTHUR RANK 1888–1972 Industrialist and Film Producer worked here

Joseph Arthur Rank was born in Kingston-Upon-Hull, the youngest of three sons and sixth of eight children to Joseph Rank and his wife, Emily (nee Voase). His father was born in a cottage attached to the family windmill, built a substantial flour milling business, and was an exemplary influence throughout Arthur's life. Arthur was considered a dunce at The Leys, Cambridge, the Methodist boarding-school he attended from 1901 to 1906. He joined Joseph Rank Ltd from school and became a director in 1915. In 1914, he enlisted in an army ambulance unit, and was promoted to sergeant in charge of twenty ambulances, before becoming a signalling expert, and reaching the rank of Captain in the Royal Field Artillery. After the First World War, Arthur worked in the milling side of his father's business, taking charge of its diversification into production and the sale of branded animal feeds. The company was floated in 1933, and he became joint managing director.

Rank shared his father's commitment to Methodism, buying the *Methodist Times* in 1925, and teaching at Sunday School. He would make no decision without talking to God, and believed his decisions were sanctioned by a higher force. Rank founded the Religious Films Society in 1933, to promote films with a religious and moral message. When his newspaper complained about the negative influences that films were having on family life, he took up the challenge, creating his first films, *Mastership*, Tolstoy's *Let There Be Love*, and *St Francis of Assisi,* starring Donald Wolfit and Greer Garson. Along with the young film producer, John Corfield, and Lady Bute, he created the British National Films Company in 1934.

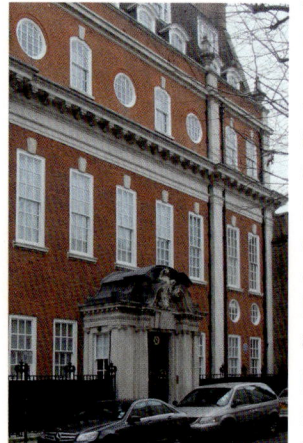

Their first film *The Turn of the Tide* (1935) was declined by the Hollywood-dominated distributors, and they realised that they needed to handle their own distribution and own their own cinemas. By 1942, the Rank Organization owned 619 cinemas, including the Odeon, Gaumont and Paramount cinema chains, as well as Pinewood and Denham Film Studios. They produced a string of successful films, including Henry V (1944), *The Red Shoes and Hamlet* (1948), and a trio of great films in 1949, *Passport to Pimlico, Whisky Galore* and *Kind Hearts and Coronets.*

Following the death of his only surviving brother in 1952, Rank was obliged to concentrate on the family milling business. As Chairman, during the 1950's the company bought over a hundred businesses, which were consolidated into British Bakeries, the agricultural division extended its interests, in 1962 Hovis-McDougall was acquired, and a grocery division was created in 1968 with the acquisition of Cerebos.

In 1917 he had married Laura Allen, and they had one son, who died at birth, and two daughters. Throughout his life Rank strove for unity between the Methodist church and the Church of England. In 1957, he was ennobled as Lord Rank of Sutton Scotney.

Gilbert WINANT
Politician and Ambassador

7 Aldford Street   **Map Ref 21**

Gilbert Winant was born in New York City, who spent a lifetime in public service as a teacher. He was a member of a wealthy family, and attended prep school at St Paul's in Concord, New Hampshire, as well as Princeton University. After graduating, he returned to St Paul's in 1913, and stayed there for four years as a history teacher, during which time he was elected as a moderate Republican to the New Hampshire House of Representatives.

In 1917 at the age of twenty eight, he joined the United States Army Air Service, where he trained as a pilot, rising to the rank of Captain, and commanded the 8th Aero Squadron in France during the 1st World War. In 1919 he returned to St Paul's School, and the following year he was elected to the New Hampshire Senate. He was elected as Governor of New Hampshire from 1925 to 1927, and again later from 1931 to 1935.

President Franklin D. Roosevelt appointed Winant to the International Labour Office (ILO) in Switzerland in 1935, but called him back after a few months to be the first Head of the Social Security Board. He remained there for two years, before returning to the ILO, where he was elected to the top job in 1939.

Roosevelt appointed him to the position of Ambassador to Great Britain during the 2nd World War in 1941, when he replaced Joseph Kennedy, and where he remained until 1946. He was with the British Prime Minister, Winston Churchill, when the Japanese attacked American battleships at Pearl Harbour, with the loss of hundreds of lives. He helped to plan the Three Powers Foreign Ministers Conference in Moscow in 1943.

In 1946, President Harry S. Truman appointed him as the U.S. representative to the Economic and Social Council of the United Nations (UNESCO). In 1947, Winart became only the second American citizen, after Dwight Eisenhower, to be made an honorary member of the Order of Merit, an order recognising distinguished service, and remains the personal gift of the British monarch. In 1947 Winant committed suicide, although it is not revealed as to what drove him to take his own life.

Catherine WALTERS
Courtesan

15 South Street   **Map Ref 22**

CATHERINE WALTERS (Skittles) "The last Victorian Courtesan" lived here from 1872 until 1920

Catherine 'Skittles' Walters was born in Toxteth in Liverpool, the third of five children to Edward Walters, a customs officer in the Liverpool docks, and Mary Ann Fowler. Before she was twenty years old, she moved to London and became a fashion trendsetter and courtesan.

Her nickname came from stories that either she worked as a child in a skittle alley behind a pub in Liverpool, or that she worked at a skittles alley near to Park Lane in London. She was obviously a very beautiful lady, and this, along with her skills as a horsewoman, made her a very attractive proposition to wealthy young bucks.

In her early twenties, she reached an agreement with the owner of a livery stable in London to act as a demonstrator of his horses. The sight of her riding through Hyde Park apparently drew huge crowds of sightseers, and she was reputedly naked under her tight-fitting riding habit. Despite her questionable profession, her fashion-sense helped her to become a trendsetter, and this along with her ability to hold her own in conversation, enabled her to become a more than acceptable member of society.

She counted amongst her lovers Napoleon III, the Prince of Wales (later King Edward VII), and the Marquess of Hartington (later the 8th Duke of Devonshire). Her relationships often lasted for years, and due to the pressure on young aristocrats to conform probably to their mothers' social position, the young lovers often had to resort to intensive correspondence as part of their liaison.

During her life as a courtesan, her trustworthiness and discretion with her benefactors became a vital factor in maintaining her role in Victorian London. Despite many rumours about her being involved with specific well-heeled men, she always remained totally discreet. This made her a very attractive proposition to her suitors, and gave a long life to her career. She retained a position in high society, looking the part at the theatre and race meetings, and she retired a very wealthy lady.

Florence NIGHTINGALE
Nurse and Statistician

10 South Street **Map Ref 23**

Florence Nightingale is remembered as 'The Lady of the Lamp' for her work as a nurse in the Crimean War, as a result of her making rounds at night to tend injured soldiers. She was born in Florence, when her wealthy parents William and Frances, were touring Europe. He was born Shore, but assumed the name Nightingale when he inherited his Uncle Peter Nightingale's estate.

Her early education, along with that of her sister Parthenope, was in the hands of governesses. After a battle with her parents, she was allowed to be tutored in mathematics, which was to play an important part in her life. Religion was also significant for her, and at 17 she believed she received a calling from God, which lead to her entering nursing in 1845. Nursing was not considered to be a suitable profession for a well-educated lady, but she ignored her parents' protestations.

Florence toured Europe in 1849, and began to study different hospital systems, later publishing her findings. On returning in 1853, she took a job at the Institute for the Care of Gentlewomen, in London. One year later the Crimean War started, and after severe criticism of British medical facilities, Sidney Herbert, the Secretary for War, asked her to oversee the introduction of nurses to military hospitals, and she left for Turkey with 38 nurses.

She used statistical data to improve hospital conditions, where injured soldiers were seven times more likely to die from diseases than on the battlefield. Upon her return to England in 1856, she used statistics to show the need for sanitary reform in all military hospitals. Her work gained the attention of Queen Victoria, and resulted in a Royal Commission on the Health of the Army, and election to be a Fellow of the Royal Statistical Society.

Her work enabled her to make nursing a responsible and respectable profession for women, and in 1860 her Training School for Nurses was opened at St.Thomas' Hospital in London. She had contracted a serious illness in the Crimea, but despite being bedridden, she continued to campaign for improved health standards. She received the Royal Red Cross and became the first woman to receive the Order of Merit. She never married.

Dame Anna NEAGLE
Actress

63, 64 Park Lane **Map Ref 24**

> **Dame Anna Neagle (1904 - 1986)**
> Due to building work at this address her plaque had been moved when going to press

Florence Marjorie Robertson was born in Forest Gate, East London to Herbert, a merchant navy captain, and Florence (nee Neagle). She won several awards as Britain's favourite actress for her many stage and film appearances. Anna attended St Alban's High School for Girls, and made her professional stage debut as a dancer at the age of 13. She appeared in numerous choruses in revues staged by the impresario, C B Cochran, and understudied Jessie Matthews in many roles. Film producer and director, Herbert Wilcox, discovered her when she starred with the actor Jack Buchanan in the hugely successful West End Musical, *Stand Up and Sing* (1931), which ran for almost two years.

Wilcox cast her in a starring role, again alongside Jack Buchanan, in the 1932 film Goodnight Vienna, which became a big box office hit. She starred in *The Flag Lieutenant* with Henry Edwards, who both directed and starred in the movie. After this, she worked exclusively with Wilcox, including Noel Coward's musical *Bitter Sweet* in 1933, and the following year with her first major success as *Nell Gwyn*. She continued to make a film each year, until she returned to the London stage in 1938, playing the title role in *Peter Pan*.

Anna Neagle and Herbert Wilcox continued to make films together, with a number made in Hollywood, including *No, No, Nanette* in which she sang 'Tea for Two'. Their final American film was *Forever and a Day* in 1943, the year in which they married. For the next 14 years, Neagle continued to star in films, making the occasional appearance on the stage. Her favourite film is believed to be *Odette* (1950), co-starring Trevor Howard and Peter Ustinov, her last box-office hit *My Teenage Daughter* (1956), and her final film appearance was in *The Lady is a Square* in 1957.

Her husband went bankrupt in 1964, but Neagle revived his fortunes with a string of successes on the stage. She starred in the West End musical *Charlie Girl*, which ran for an incredible six years. She continued to tread the boards well into her eighties, when she appeared as the Fairy Godmother in the pantomime *Cinderella* at the London Palladium.

The couple lived in a top floor flat at Aldford House, and the plaque was sponsored by Sir Cameron Mackintosh, who was very fond of her, and she appeared as Mrs Higgins in his first production of *My Fair Lady* (1979). It was unveiled as part of the centenary celebrations for British cinema by HRH Princess Anne.

Aldford House as it was when Anna Neagle lived there

Sir Robert PEEL
Prime Minister

16 Upper Grosvenor Street **Map Ref 25**

Robert Peel was born in Ramsbottom, Lancashire, to the industrialist, Sir Robert Peel, 1st Baronet. He went to Hipperholme Grammar School, before attending Harrow School and then Christ Church College, Oxford, where he read classics and mathematics.

He became MP for the Irish rotten borough of Cashel, Tipperary, Ireland, at the tender age of 21 where he had been sponsored by the future Duke of Wellington, the Chief Secretary for Ireland. He changed seats on three occasions – firstly Chippenham, - another rotten borough - he then represented Oxford University, and finally Tamworth.

Peel's first major political appointment was in 1822 as Home Secretary, in which role he pursued many reforms in criminal law, including reducing the number of crimes that were punishable by death. In 1829 he famously established the Metropolitan Police Force in London, and the constables were nicknamed 'Bobbies' or 'Peelers'. By 1857 all cities in the UK had to have their own police force, following the success of cutting crime in London.

When George Canning replaced Prime Minister Lord Liverpool he resigned as Home Secretary, but returned under the premiership of the Duke of Wellington. He succeeded him as PM for a year in 1834, before returning after a period of political turmoil in 1841. Peel's first Budget re-introduced Income Tax, which had been removed at the end of the Napoleonic War, in order to raise money during the economic recession.

Known as a reforming Prime Minister, he most notably introduced The Factory Act in 1844, which restricted the number of hours that women and children could work, and set basic safety standards for machinery. He repealed the Corn Laws, which had restricted grain imports, although this ultimately led to his political downfall in 1846. Nevertheless, he continued to have influence, particularly in areas of economic free trade.

Peel had married Julia, youngest daughter of General Sir John Floyd, 1st Baronet, in 1820, with whom he had seven children. He died after his horse fell on him whilst riding, and his position amongst the hierarchy of politicians is reflected in his statue in Parliament Square, London.

Benjamin DISRAELI
Prime Minister and Writer

93 Park Lane — **Map Ref 26**

Benjamin Disraeli (1804 -1881) is one of the few individuals who has more than one plaque commemorating the houses in which they lived in London.

"Though I sit down now, the time will come when you will hear me"
Maiden speech in the House of Commons 7th December 1837

"No government can be long secure without a formidable Opposition"

"I was told that the Privileged and the People formed Two Nations"

"Everyone likes flattery; and when you come to Royalty you should lay it on with a trowel"

"An author who speaks about his own books is almost as bad as a mother who talks about her own children"

"Read no history: nothing but biography, for that is life without theory"

"A Conservative government is an organized hypocrisy"

"Finality is not the language of politics"

"When I want to read a novel I write one"

"The blue ribbon of the turf" (The Derby)

"Every woman should marry – and no man"

"Man …..is a being born to believe"

"Little things affect little minds"

"London is a modern Babylon"

"Youth is a blunder; Manhood a struggle; Old Age a regret"

Benjamin Disraeli's biography appears under his other residence at 19 Curzon Street, which is Map Ref. 7 in Mayfair – South Walk.

Sir Moses MONTEFIORE
Financier

99 Park Lane   **Map Ref 27**

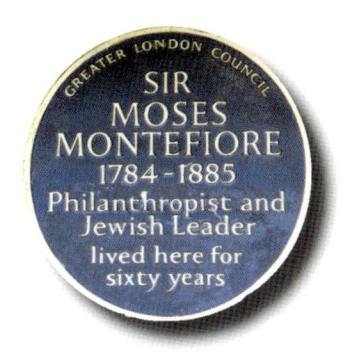

SIR MOSES MONTEFIORE 1784-1885 Philanthropist and Jewish Leader lived here for sixty years

Moses Haim Montefiore, one of the most famous Jews of the 19th century, was born in Livornon near Pisa, on the west coast of Italy. In his first job he was apprenticed to a firm of grocers and tea merchants. He emigrated to England and went into business as a stockbroker with his brother Abraham.

At the age of 28, he married Judith Cohen, the daughter of Levi Barent Cohen. Her sister, Hannah, married Nathan Rothschild, who headed the family's banking business in England. Montefiore's firm acted as their broker, and the two brothers-in-law built a business together. His investments included the supply of gas for street lighting to European cities, established Alliance Life Assurance, and the Provincial Bank of Ireland.

His successes enabled him to retire at he age of 39, a very rich man.

He now devoted his life to helping Jews across the world, and his passion to alleviate the persecution of minorities in the Middle East led him to travel extensively including time spent in Turkey, Italy, Russia, Morocco, and Romania. Back in England he campaigned tirelessly to abolish slavery, he was appointed President of the Board of Deputies of British Jews, and bought a large country estate in Ramsgate, Kent, where he invested a considerable amount of time and money.

Montefiore was elected as Sheriff of the City of London in 1836, knighted by Queen Victoria the following year, and granted a baronetcy in 1846. In addition to his other philanthropic work, he donated considerable energies and money to a wide range of projects in Palestine, with the objective of ensuring that the Jews had their own safe homeland.

He died at the age of 100, and his strict observance of the Jewish faith and philanthropy lead to many public buildings and synagogues to be commemorated to him.

Leo BONN
Banker and founder of RNID

22 Upper Brook Street　　　　　　　　　　　　　　**Map Ref 28**

Leo Bonn was a successful and wealthy banker in the City of London, who developed hearing problems, and became deaf in his sixties. In addition to trying to address the issues of his own deafness, he became interested in the cause of deaf people generally.

He was recommended to see a lady called Mary Hare, who taught lip reading. Mary Hare is now the nomenclature of a national charity, and she founded the Mary Hare School, which became a special school providing for profoundly and severely deaf children and young people from all over the UK. Each pupil's Local Education Authority would pay their fees.

Her legacy is that she believed that there were better ways for deaf people to communicate without relying solely on sign language, and she used an auditory/oral approach. Bonn picked-up this philosophy and visited a Mr Storey, who ran a school for deaf children in Stoke-on-Trent. Mr Storey was enamoured by Bonn's enthusiasm, and agreed to begin a clearing-house to help the interests of deaf people.

This activity culminated in Bonn creating the National Bureau for Promoting Welfare of the Deaf in 1911, and its first meeting took place in Bonn's dining room at 22 Upper Brook Street. The Bureau swiftly became an advocate for encouraging a more sympathetic approach to the causes of deafness, and seek the means of preventing it.

Bonn became the President and Chairman of the Bureau during its formative years, and in 1924 it was re-named Royal Institute for the Deaf. (RNID). The RNID's vision is expressed as a world where deafness or hearing loss does not limit or determine opportunity, and where people value their hearing. Its present President is Lord (Jack) Ashley of Stoke, the UK's first totally deaf MP: he has been a tireless campaigner for the disabled, particularly the deaf and the blind.

Sir George SEFERIS
Poet and Diplomat

51 Upper Brook Street **Map Ref 29**

Born Georgios Seperades in the Greek town of Urla, in what is now Izmir, Turkey. He was the son of Stelios, who became Professor of Law at Athens University. The family had moved to Athens when he was 14 where he finished his secondary education. Four years later he moved to Paris to study law at the Sorbonne for seven years.

He returned to Athens in 1925, joined the Greek Ministry of Foreign Affairs, and subsequently held many key diplomatic positions. He had posts in England, Albania - and after the 2nd World War - Turkey, London (again), and the Middle East. In 1957 he returned to London rising to the position of Royal Greek Ambassador to the United Kingdom, at a time when the two countries were disputing the future of Cyprus.

He had married Maria Zanou in 1941, on the eve of the Nazi invasion of Greece. In addition to being a highly successful career diplomat, he was know as an essayist, diarist, novelist, and received the Nobel Prize for Literature for his poetry. Much of his writing was inspired by his love of Cyprus, and he continued to fight for a resolution to the dispute between UK, Greece and Turkey about the island's future.

In 1967, the nationalist 'Colonels' conducted a coup d'etat and took power in Greece. Seferis took a stand against the regime, culminating in making a well-publicised statement demanding that "this anomaly must end". He didn't live to see the junta come to its end in 1974.

51 Upper Brook Street was originally built in 1730 – 1731.

With no bathrooms or hot water builder John Garlick was allowed to rebuild in 1905 – 1906 to a design by architect R.G.Hammond, Since 1730 occupants have included Judges, MPs, Barons and, currently, the Greek Legation / Embassy.

Sir Thomas SOPWITH
Aeroplane Designer

46 Green Street   **Map Ref 30**

Thomas Octave (he was the 8th child!) Murdoch Sopwith was born in London, and became a pioneer of the aviation industry. He came from a reasonably well-off family, established for several generations in engineering. He did not distinguish himself at school, but at 17 started a business with a friend in the motor trade, which grew into a successful Rolls Royce dealership.

He enjoyed ballooning and sailing yachts and was a pioneer air pilot, a racing car driver, and motorboat champion. At 18, whilst auto-racing at Brooklands, in Surrey, he became interested in flying, and soon after bought his first aeroplane, which he crashed. Wishing to recoup expenses from his expensive hobby, he sought prize money from endurance flights, including winning the 'de Foret' prize for the longest flight, of 161 miles in three hours, to the European continent in 1910.

After two years touring in America, showing-off his skilful flying feats, he returned to England and established a flying school, and the first authoritative test pilot school in the world. Amongst his students was Lord (Major) Trenchard, who became known as the 'father of the Royal Air Force'. In 1912 he formed the Sopwith Aviation Company, and during the 1st World War made more than 16,000 aircraft, most famously the Sopwith Camel, the airplane that finally brought down the Red Baron, Manfred von Richtofen.

After the war, the company attempted to produce aircraft for the civil market, but the wide availability of war-surplus aircraft at knock-down prices meant this was never economic. They tried unsuccessfully to diversify into motorbikes and cars, but the company collapsed in 1920. Upon its demise, Sopwith with Harry Hawker (his former chief test pilot) formed Hawker Aircraft, that would later become Hawker Siddeley, and of which he was Chairman between 1935 and 1963. The company built Hurricane fighters and Lancaster bombers during the 2nd World War, and later the Harrier Jump Jet, which was used successfully in the Falklands War. In 1977 the company was nationalized, and became part of British Aerospace Group.

Sopwith had always been a man with many interests, and in 1934 and 1937 had raced yachts – albeit unsuccessfully - in the Americas Cup. In 1953 Sopwith was knighted, and long after his retirement he continued to enjoy his pursuits, and was still active at the venerable age of 92.

P.G. WODEHOUSE
Novelist, playwright and lyricist

17 Dunraven Street **Map Ref 31**

Pelham Grenville Wodehouse is regarded as the greatest humorous writer of the 20th Century. He wrote more than 70 novels, 200 short stories, had articles published in more than 80 magazines, and wrote lyrics for musical comedies. At one time, he had five musicals running on Broadway.

Rarely addressed by his Christian names, he was known as 'Plum' to his friends and family. He was born in Guildford in Surrey, the third youngest son of Eleanor and Henry Earnest Wodehouse, a British judge in Hong Kong. At the age of three, he was placed in the care of a nanny, and spent all his formative years in English boarding schools, culminating in Dulwich College, where he became a prefect and succeeded in sport and drama. He was expected to go to university, but his father's financial problems forced him to take a job with what is now the HSBC bank.

He did not enjoy banking, and after two years, he became a full-time writer, contributing to a variety of newspapers and magazines, including Punch and The Globe. From his early thirties Wodehouse split his time between England and the USA. He married Ethel Rowney, an English widow, in New York in 1914.

He is best known for his stories centred on English upper-class society, starring Lord Emsworth and Blandings Castle, and Bertie Wooster and Jeeves. He is renowned for creating the hilarious situations in which Bertie finds himself, and how his trusty valet Jeeves solves them, as well as inventing perfect hangover cures for his master. In 1934, at the age of 53, he moved to France in order to avoid paying double tax on his earnings in both England and America He got caught up in the German invasion of France, and was interned in 1940. He was accused of being a traitor, which was strongly refuted and later confirmed by the authorities, but the criticism hurt him and led to his moving permanently to New York.

He became an American citizen in 1955, and the lingering resentment about his supposed links with the Nazis, meant that his major contribution to literature was not recognised by the British authorities until he was 93, when he was given a knighthood. recognised by the British authorities until he was 93, when he was given a knighthood.

Keith CLIFFORD HALL
Contact lens pioneer

140 Park Lane **Map Ref 32**

Keith Graham Clifford Hall was born in Cambridge and educated in Surrey. He became one of the world's leading contact lens specialists, and his pioneering work in optometrics lead to a library being named after him at the College of Optometrists in London.

He left school at 17 and took a job as an optician's apprentice in Bracknell, Berkshire. He studied for his Spectacle Makers Certificate at night school, and qualified four years later in 1931. Hall became enthusiastic about the development of contact lenses, which although very much a product of the 20th century, had been a brainwave of Leonardo da Vinci, which, along with helicopters, was way beyond the means of his time to actually do much about!

A E Fick, a Swiss physiologist had developed the first true contact lenses in the late 19th century, and over the ensuing years eye specialists pursued the perfect materials for lenses. Clifford Hall began fitting contact lenses in 1934, but the major breakthrough came in 1938 when Obrig and Mullen in the USA made the first plastic contact lenses. He visited contact lens laboratories and clinics in Germany, Brazil and Russia, and met Theodore Obrig on many occasions, learning various methods of contact lens fitting.

He established the first UK specialist contact lens practice during 1945 at 139 Park Lane, and moved to larger rooms next door at 140, where he saw patients from all over Britain, as well as other parts of the world. His consulting rooms on the sixth floor were also visited by scores of visiting specialists, and in 1946 he collaborated with Frank Dickinson on the first UK book on contact lenses.

As well as London, he also opened practices in Norway and Denmark, and inspired many in the industry with his enthusiasm at his lecture tours all over the world. Clifford Hall predicted the advent of both soft lenses and disposable contact lenses as early as 1948. He was a founder member of the Contact Lens Society, becoming its President in 1947 and 1963, and was awarded the International Society of Contact Lens Specialists' Gold Medal in 1958.

MARYLEBONE WEST W1
CITY OF WESTMINSTER

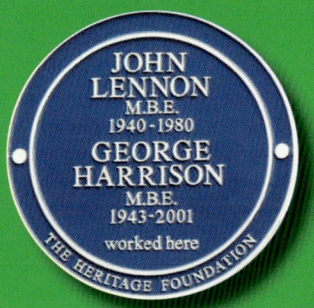

JOHN LENNON M.B.E. 1940-1980
GEORGE HARRISON M.B.E. 1943-2001
worked here
THE HERITAGE FOUNDATION

MICHAEL FARADAY MAN OF SCIENCE, APPRENTICE HERE. B·1791. D·1867.

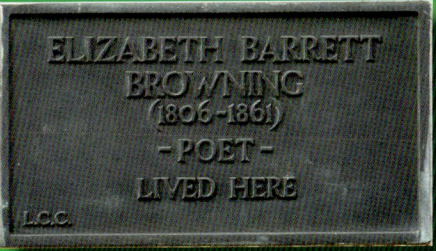

ELIZABETH BARRETT BROWNING (1806-1861) – POET – LIVED HERE
L.C.C.

LONDON COUNTY COUNCIL
WILLIAM WILKIE COLLINS 1824 – 1889 NOVELIST lived here

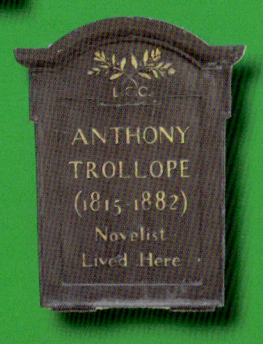

L.C.C.
ANTHONY TROLLOPE (1815-1882) Novelist Lived Here

MARYLEBONE WEST W1
CITY OF WESTMINSTER

Marylebone owes its name to the Parish Church which is dedicated to St Mary, and its original site in 1200 was by the Tyburn (Burn or Bourne being a word for 'stream'). St Mary by the Bourne got shortened to Marylebone. The Marylebone area can be defined as that banded by Oxford Street in the south, Marylebone Road in the north, Edgware Road to the west, and Portland Place to the east. At the heart of Marylebone is the buzzy Marylebone High Street, with its eclectic collection of shops and excellent cafes, bars and restaurants.

Amongst the beautiful churches is St Mary's in Bryanston Square, which has recently been restored to its original Georgian splendour. It was designed by Sir Robert Smirke (1781-1867), most famous for designing the British Museum in London. The church was built as the first of the Commoners' Churches', intended for the needs of the rapidly growing population following the end of the Napoleonic Wars. The Church of the Annunciation at 34a Bryanston Street is an Edwardian Gothic-style building designed in 1911 by Sir Walter Tapper, and is open every day except Mondays.

The Wallace Collection

The Parish Church of St Marylebone is one of Marylebone's major landmarks. Designed by Thomas Hardwick and consecrated in 1817, where the poets Robert Browning and Elizabeth Barrett were secretly married after Elizabeth had scandalously eloped from her strict family home in nearby Wigmore Street. The Crypt and Goose chapel café is open from Monday to Friday.

In George Street is St James's Catholic Church, with a secondary title from the street called Spanish Place. It goes back to after the restoration of Charles II, when the Spanish Embassy was re-established at Hartford House in Manchester Square, and a chapel was built on the corner of Spanish Place and Charles Street (now George Street). Hartford House is where the Wallace Collection is now housed. It is a beautiful museum and the collection was accumulated between 1802 and 1875 by three generations of the Hertford family and Sir Richard Wallace. Sir Richard was the protégé of the 4th Marquis of Hertford, an ardent Francophile, and Sir Richard was the sole heir of his collection. In 25 galleries there are displays of treasures comprising paintings, furniture, porcelain and armoury bequeathed in 1897 by his widow Lady Wallace.

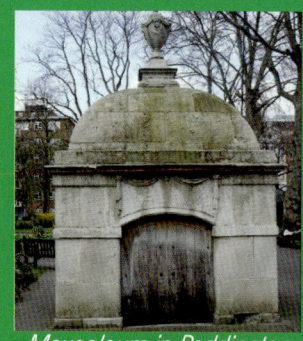

Mausoleum in Paddington Street Gardens

The house was built by 4th Duke of Manchester in 1778 and is a rare example of a London townhouse occupying the whole north side of a garden square. The museum is open seven days a week from 10am to 5pm, with free entry, and there is a restaurant in the Sculpture Garden, which is situated in the enclosed central atrium.

On the north side of Marylebone is the iconic Madame Tussauds, the attraction containing wax models of famous people, which has been blending history and celebrities since 1884. Numerous galleries include the Pirates of the Caribbean, World Leaders, the Royal Family and the History of London. Interactive tasks are available for all the family and you can have your photograph taken alongside an A-list celebrity!

Madame Tussauds

There are a number of attractive gardens on the walk, although all but one falls into the 'you can look but you can't touch' category – Portman Square, Bryanston Square, Montagu Square and Manchester Square are all 'for residents only'. The only one in which we can eat our sandwiches, along with the local office workers and shop assistants, is Paddington Street Gardens. The gardens have a dedicated children's play area, and were formed during the 18th century as an additional burial ground for the old St Marylebone Parish Church. There are probably 80,000 graves here: the gardens are still consecrated ground.

In 1885 the gardens became a recreational area, and most of the tombstones have been removed, apart from the Mausoleum, which was left because of its exceptionally fine design. It was erected by the Hon. Richard Fitzpatrick to the memory of his wuife, Susanna, who died in 1759 at the age of thirty. Her daughter, Baroness de Robeck was also buried there in 1829.

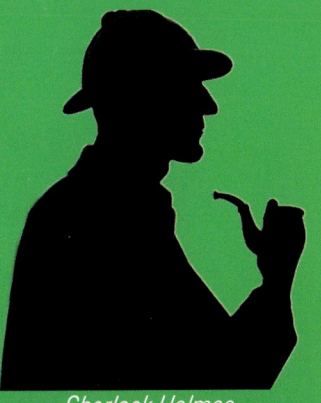

St Marys Church

There are a number of Beatle's legacies in the area, including the infamous Apple Boutique at 94 Baker Street (viz the John Lennon and George Harrison feature at Ref 19 in this walk), and on this walk is Ringo's flat, where John and Yoko lived for a while at 34 Montagu Square (Ref 6) and the original Apple Corps head office at 95 Wigmore Street.

Baker Street is, of course, also the home of the fictional detective Sherlock Holmes between 1881 and 1904, according to the stories by Sir Arthur Conan Doyle. The world's most famous address, 221b Baker Street, was a lodging house up to 1936, and is a couple of hundred yards north of Marylebone Road, and houses the Sherlock Holmes Museum. The famous 1st floor study is faithfully maintained as it would have been in Victorian times. The museum is open every day except Christmas Day, between 9.30am and 6.00pm.

Sherlock Holmes Silhouette

Harley St
Weymouth St
Harley Pl
Queen Anne St
Wimpole Mews
Wimpole St
Wigmore St
Devonshire St
New Cavendish St
Devonshire Pl
Westmoreland St
Marylebone Ln
Stratford Pl
Bond Street Tube
Marylebone st
Bentinck St
James St
Mandeville Pl
Thayer St
Hinde St
Duke S
Marylebone High St
Spanish Pl
Manchester Sq
Garbutt Place
Moxon St
Aybrook St
Wigmore St
Nottingham Pl
Manchester St
Robert Adams St
Fitzhardinge St
Paddington St
Paddington St Gdns
Chiltern St
Portman Sq
Orchard St
Baker St
Baker Street Tube
Blandford St
George St
Portman Close
Dorset St
Rodmarton St
Crawford St
Baker St
Marylebone Rd
Bickenhall St
Gloucester Pl
Gloucester Place Mews
Seymour St
Upper Berkeley St
Montagu Sq
Montagu St
Upper Montagu St
Grt Cumberland Pl
Marble Arch Tube 100 yards
Balcombe St
Wyndham Pl
Bryanston Sq
George St
Bryanston Pl
Enford St
York St
Seymour Pl
Marylebone Tube
Crawford St
Homer St
Harcourt st
Molyneux St
Cato St
Brendon St
Edgware Rd
Old Marylebone Rd
1
2
3
4
5
6
7
8
9
10
11
12
13
14
15
16
17
18
19
20
21
22
23
24
25
26
27
28
29
30
31
32
33
34

MARYLEBONE WEST WALK GUIDE

Page	Ref	Person	Place
96	1	Michael BALFE	12 Seymour Street
97	2	Edward LEAR	30 Seymour Street
98	3	Elizabeth Garrett ANDERSON	20 Upper Berkeley Street
99	4	Mustapha RESCHID	1 Bryanston Square
100	5	John LENNON	34 Montagu Square
101	6	Anthony TROLLOPE	39 Montagu Square
102	8	Jacqueline du PRÉ	27 Upper Montagu Street
103	8	Sir Alfred AYER	51 York Street
104	9	Emma CONS	136 Seymour Place
105	10	Sir Gerald KELLY	117 Gloucester Place
106	11	George RICHMOND	20 York Street
107	12	Tony RAY-JONES	102 Gloucester Place
108	13	Elizabeth BARRETT BROWNING	99 Gloucester Place
109	14	Wilkie COLLINS	65 Gloucester Place
110	15	Benedict ARNOLD	62 Gloucester Place
111	16	John GODLEY	48 Gloucester Place
112	17	Thomas MOORE	85 George Street
113	18	Sake MAHOMED	102 George Street
114	19	John LENNON and George HARRISON	94 Baker Street
115	20	William PITT (The Younger)	120 Baker Street
116	21	Charles KEMPE	37 Nottingham Place
117	22	Leonard STOKOWKSI	63 Marylebone High Street
118	23	Octavia HILL	2 Garbutt Place
119	24	Charles BABBAGE	1a Dorset Street
120	25	Sir Henry SEGRAVE	St Andrews Mansions, Chiltern Street
121	26	Michael FARADAY	48 Blandford Street
122	27	Sir Francis BEAUFORT	51 Manchester Street
123	28	Lord Alfred MILNER	14 Manchester Square
124	29	Simon BOLIVAR	4 Duke Street
125	30	John JACKSON	3 Manchester Square
126	31	Sir Julius BENEDICT	2 Manchester Square
127	32	George GROSSMITH	3 Spanish Place
128	32	Captain Frederick MARRYAT	3 Spanish Place
129	33	Dame Rose MACAULAY	11 Hinde Street
130	34	Sir Paolo TOSTI	12 Mandeville Place

Distance : 3.7 miles (6 Km)
Starting Point: Marble Arch Underground Station

Finish Point: Bond Street Underground Station

Central
Jubilee
Central

Michael BALFE
Composer and Singer

12 Seymour Street   **Map Ref 1**

Michael William Balfe, whose father was a dancing master and violinist, was born in Dublin, Ireland. The family moved to Wexford when he was a child, and the precocious Michael played violin for his father's dancing-classes between the age of 6 and 7. The only teaching he received was from his father, and he made his violin solo debut at the age of eight. In the next year he composed the ballad, *The Lovers' Mistake*, which was sung by many of the leading singers of the time, and performed in the opera *Paul Pry* by London-born Lucia Bartolllozzi, the opera singer known as Madame Vestris.

Balfe's father died when he was fifteen, and shortly after he was taken to London, where he got a job playing violin in the orchestra at the Theatre Royal, Drury Lane, eventually becoming leading violinist. He had by now developed a fine baritone voice, and two years later in 1825 he began his career as an opera singer. Whilst travelling via Paris to Italy where he met the Italian-born Cherubini, composer of operas and sacred music. In Italy he studied under Filippo Galli, the famous bass for whom Rossini had composed. After his sojourn in Italy, Balfe returned to Paris where met and became a protégée of Rossini: at the age of 19 he starred as Figaro in *The Barber of Seville* in Paris. Balfe had begun to compose music, and Rossini suggested that he should pursue this route vigorously, which resulted in his writing his first opera, *I Rivali di se Stessi*, in 1829 in just 20 days.

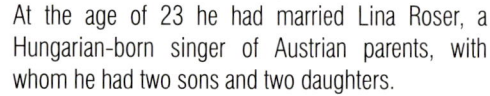

At the age of 23 he had married Lina Roser, a Hungarian-born singer of Austrian parents, with whom he had two sons and two daughters.

Balfe returned to Italy, where he both sang and composed many of his 38 operas. Over the next fifteen years he frequently visited England, and in 1843 produced his most successful opera, *The Bohemian Girl,* (which included the famous *I Dreamt I Dwelt In Marble Halls*) at the Theatre Royal, Drury Lane. From 1846 to 1852 Balfe was Musical Director and Principal Conductor for the Italian Opera at Her Majesty's Theatre in London, where he produced Verdi operas and conducted for the Swedish opera singer, Jenny Lind.

Edward LEAR
Author, Poet and Artist

30 Seymour Street Map Ref 2

EDWARD LEAR 1812 – 1888 Artist and writer lived here — London County Council

Edward Lear was born in Holloway, North London, the 21st child to Jeremiah and Ann Lear. His father was a stockbroker who went bankrupt, and when the family fell into financial problems, his sister Ann, who was 21 years his senior, set-up house with four year-old Edward. He was self-educated and she encouraged his natural talent for drawing and painting. Lear earned money from his artistic talent, but is best known for his 'Nonsense Rhymes'.

He suffered from health problems from an early age, and from the age of six he suffered from epileptic fits, a condition with which he was ashamed, and which caused him to be a depressive. By the age of 16 he was earning money from drawing, and was employed by the Zoological Society and the Earl of Derby, who became his patron. He had published his first book by the age of 19, and for much of his life, Lear travelled extensively in France, Italy, Egypt, and Greece, recording the landscapes. He gave drawing lessons to Queen Victoria after she had been attracted by his first publication, two volumes of *Illustrated Excursions in Italy*, and through his life he made a good living from his paintings and drawings.

Lear had considerable talent as an artist, and is credited with inventing the Limerick, which he wrote to amuse the children of his wealthy clients. In 1846, when he was 32, he published *A Book of Nonsense*, a volume of limericks. As well as limericks, he wrote other nonsense rhymes such as *The Owl and the Pussycat* in 1867 for the children of the Earl of Derby, and created other characters such as Jumblies, Quangle-Wangles and Pobbles.

In his fifties, he settled in his favourite country, Italy, where he bought a villa in San Remo. He had managed to keep his epilepsy so secret that hardly anybody knew about it until after his death. He never married.

> "They dined on mince, and slices of quince
> Which they ate with a runcible spoon;
> And hand in hand, on the edge of the sand,
> They danced by the light of the moon".
> The Owl and the Pussycat

Elizabeth Garrett ANDERSON
Physician
20 Upper Berkeley Street — Map Ref 3

ELIZABETH GARRETT ANDERSON 1836-1917
The first woman to qualify as a doctor in Britain lived here

Elizabeth Garrett was born in Whitechapel, in east London, the second of twelve children of Newson Garrett, a pawnbroker, and Louise (nee Dunnell). Her father later became a successful businessman as a grain merchant and maltster in Aldeburgh, Suffolk, enabling him to send his children to good schools. After school, she was expected to marry well and live the life of a lady, but she met the feminist Emily Davies and Elizabeth Blackwell, the first American woman physician, who convinced her that she should become a doctor.

She applied to Middlesex Hospital, London, and a number of other medical schools, but her attempts to study medicine were denied. She enrolled as a nursing student at Middlesex, and attended classes intended for male doctors, but was barred after complaints from other students. Many of the major medical examining bodies, including the Royal Colleges of Physicians and Surgeons refused to allow her to take their examinations, but The Society of Apothecaries did not forbid women, and in 1865 she passed their exams to become a doctor.

With her father's backing, she established a dispensary for women in 1866, and in 1870 was made a visiting physician to the East London Hospital. She remained determined to obtain a medical degree, so she taught herself French and went to the University of Paris, where she successfully obtained her degree. The British Medical Register refused to recognise her qualification! In 1872 Anderson founded the New Hospital for Women in London, which she staffed entirely with women, and appointed her mentor, Elizabeth Blackwell as Professor of Gynaecology.

In 1873 she gained membership of the British Medical Association, and remained the only woman member for 19 years. Anderson's determination paved the way for other women, and in 1876 an Act was passed which permitted women to enter the medical professions. In 1874 she had helped to found the London School of Medicine, and oversaw its expansion when she was appointed Dean in 1883.

She met James Anderson, a successful businessman with the Orient Steamship Company, at the East London Hospital, married him in 1871 and with whom she had three children. At 66 she retired to Aldeburgh, were her father's business was based, and six years later she became the first female Mayor in England. She was a member of the suffragette movement, and her daughter Louisa was a prominent suffragette.

Mustapha RESCHID
Statesman

1 Bryanston Square **Map Ref 4**

Plaque: MUSTAPHA RESCHID PASHA 1800-1858 Turkish Statesman and Reformer lived here as Ambassador in 1839

Koca Mustafa Resid Pasha (Pasa) was born in Constantinople (now known as Istanbul), and became a reformist Ottoman statesman and diplomat with a Western mindset. His father taught him to read and write, and upon his father's death he completed his education in a Madrasah, a religious school. These schools were Islamic centres for spiritual learning, and were usually built as part of a Mosque complex. (US President Obama attended such a school in Indonesia).

He entered the Turkish public service at an early age, and rose rapidly through the ranks, becoming Ambassador to Paris in 1834 and then to London in 1836. In London he became a member of the Freemasons, and friends with Lord Stratford de Redcliffe, an established diplomat, who represented Britain in Turkey, and who sat in Parliament between 1828 and 1841. Upon returning to Turkey in 1837, Reschid was promoted to Minister for Foreign Affairs, but returned in 1838 to London, where he called upon Britain to help to resolve Turkey's issues with Egypt. Later that year he signed a commercial treaty with England and this lead to the Ottoman Empire becoming an open market for Britain. He returned briefly to Istanbul before being re-appointed as Ambassador in Paris in 1841, at which time he assumed the title "Pasha", the equivalent to the British title of Lord.

In 1843 he served as Governor in the western Turkey city of Erdirne, which had been the Empire's capital in the 14th and 15th centuries, before once again returning to Paris as Ambassador. From 1845 he was back in Istanbul, as the Grand Vizier, which was the highest Minister for the Sultan, with absolute power over the other Viziers. Reschid became one of the most influential statesmen of his time, and under Sultan Mahmud II and his son Abdulmecid who succeeded him, he was the principal author of the legislative remodelling of 'Tanzimat'.

This period of reformation encouraged Ottomanism among the diverse groups of the Empire, and stemmed the tide of nationalist movements. The strategy was to integrate non-Muslims and non-Turks into Ottoman society by enhancing their civil liberties and granting them equality throughout the Empire. After Reschid's first marriage to Ermine Serife Hanim, the daughter of Ibrahim Efendi in Egypt, with whom he had a son, ended in divorce, he married Adile Hanim and had four more sons.

John LENNON
Singer/Songwriter

34 Montagu Square **Map Ref 5**

The plaque was unveiled by Yoko Ono in 2010 at the flat she shared with her husband John Lennon from July 1968. This is only the second English Heritage plaque for a rock star, the first being in Brook Street at the former home of Jimi Hendrix (Mayfair North: Map Ref 4).

The basement and ground floor duplex flat in the 19th century townhouse was bought by Beatle's drummer, Ringo Starr in 1965. and he lived there with his fiancée Maureen Cox. After his marriage, the couple moved to the country, and Paul McCartney moved in to create a home studio in the flat. It is believed that he began the creation of *Eleanor Rigby* and *Tomorrow Never Knows* whilst in residence. The studio was also used by the American author, William Burroughs, who recorded his experimental *Hello, yes, hello* tapes there.

When McCartney gave up the flat, it stayed empty until Starr rented it to Jimi Hendrix in December 1966, along with his manager Chas Chandler of The Animals. Hendrix wrote his classic song *The Wind Cries Mary* at the flat and launched his career.

Over the next few years, Starr lent the flat to friends and Lennon's mother-in-law, Lillian Powell, used to stay there when she came down from Liverpool to visit her daughter, Cynthia.

When Lennon got together with Yoko Ono in 1968, they lived in the flat during the time the Beatles were recording *The White Album* at the studio in nearby Abbey Road. The couple shot the famous 'Two Virgins' album cover at the flat, with its notorious nude photograph.

Later that year, the police raided the flat with the London Drug Squad, and the couple were arrested. In order to protect Ono, Lennon pleaded guilty to possessing hashish. The landlord sought an injunction against Starr, which resulted in the decision that only Starr, or a member of his family, could live in the flat. He eventually sold the lease in 1969.

John Lennon can also be found on this walk at Map Ref 19

Anthony TROLLOPE
Author

39 Montagu Square Map Ref 6

Anthony Trollope was born the third of six children in London to Thomas Anthony Trollope, a barrister, and Frances, the daughter of a parson. Thomas wanted his sons to have the best education, but his legal practice collapsed, an anticipated legacy never materialised, and a venture proved him to be a hopeless farmer. Anthony attended Harrow School as a day-boy from three years old to the age of seven, boarded at Winchester for three years, before returning to Harrow as a day-boy so as to reduce costs.

He was always the 'odd child out', was bullied, and when he was 12, his mother moved to America for four years with Anthony's three youngest siblings. Four years later she returned and earned a good income as a writer. His father's affairs caught up with him, and in 1834 the family was forced to flee to Belgium, to avoid Thomas being arrested for debt, and they lived off France's earnings. After his father died in 1835, his mother got Trollope a job with the Post Office in England, and he returned alone. For seven years he lived in seedy digs in Marylebone, indulged in bouts of rowdy behaviour with his fellow clerks, smoking and drinking in sordid pubs, with night after night of solitary reading.

Ireland changed his life. In 1841, a Post Office Surveyor in Ireland needed a clerk, a job that nobody wanted, despite its £400 a year salary, and he applied for the role and got it. Within three years, he had discovered organizational skills, horses and hunting, some self-esteem, and a wife, Rose, the daughter of a Yorkshire bank manager. His job entailed long train trips and brought him into contact with Irish people, and he began to write. He would write for three hours every morning from 5 o'clock and then go to work: he paid a servant £5 a year to wake him up with a cup of coffee! His early novels met with little success, but once back in England in the 1850's, Trollope's *Barchestershire* and *Pallisers* novels installed him as a literary success.

Trollope was one of the most widely travelled men of his day, with his Post Office work taking him across the world, and everywhere he went, he wrote. He completed 47 novels and several other genres, and is known as one of the great Victorian writers.

He is credited with introducing the ubiquitous red pillar-box in Britain (although the first one was in Jersey, and was hexagonal and green!)

"We always want that which we can't get easily"
From Trollope's novel Orley Farm

Jacqueline du PRÉ
Musician

27 Upper Montagu Street **Map Ref 7**

1945 - 1987
Cellist
JACQUELINE du PRÉ
lived here
1967 - 1971

Jacqueline Mary du Pre was born in Oxford to Derek du Pre, and Iris (nee Greep). He was born in Jersey, where his family lived for generations and after working for Lloyds Bank for 11 years, became assistant editor and then editor of *The Accountant* magazine. Her mother was a piano teacher and taught at the Royal Academy of Music in London. Jacqueline is recognised as one of the greatest cellists of the 20th century.

She grew up in Purley, south London, and at four was fascinated after hearing a cello on the radio, and on her fifth birthday was given a cello. At six du Pre took lessons at the London Cello School, and at seven performed for the first time in public, and began seven years of tuition at the Guildhall School of Music under William Preeth, the London-born son of a Polish émigré family and one of the greatest cellists of the time. During this period she moved to Croydon High School for Girls, in south London, and at twelve performed in BBC Radio concerts in London.

Her cello education included time with the 'masters' - six months with Paul Tortelier in Paris, Pablo Casals in Switzerland, and Mstislav Rostropovich in Russia. At the age of sixteen she was given her first Stradivarius by an unknown admirer, and made her debut in the Wigmore Hall, London with the London Symphony Orchestra (LSO) conducted by Sir John Barbirolli. In 1964, du Pre at nineteen made her first appearance at the Proms, the world's greatest classical music festival, held at the Royal Albert Hall, and she performed every year until 1969.

In 1965 du Pre made her debut at Carnegie Hall in New York, and she recorded the Elgar Concerto with the LSO under Barbirolli, which brought her international fame. Late in 1966 she met pianist Daniel Barenboim, and within six months she had converted to Judaism and they married in Jerusalem. She continued to travel the world playing with the major orchestras and conductors, until 1971 when she was diagnosed with multiple sclerosis, and her ability to play the cello declined rapidly. Her last public concerts were in New York in 1973, and she turned to teaching until her death aged forty-two in 1987. Her relationships and those of her husband and sister were covered in depth in the highly successful 1998 film, *Hilary and Jackie*, much to the dismay of many of her friends.

Sir Alfred AYER
Philosopher

51 York Street　　　　　　　　　　　　　　　　　　　　**Map Ref 8**

Alfred Ayer was born in London and was known as A.J. or 'Freddie' to his friends. He was the most important philosopher of his generation, who was born of wealthy parents: his father, Jules Ayer, a French-speaking Swiss financier who worked for the Rothschild's, and his mother, Rene (nee Citroen), from the Dutch-Jewish family who founded the French Citroen car company.

He was educated at a preparatory school in Eastbourne, east Sussex, attended Eton College, and then went up to Christ Church, Oxford, where he gained a First in Classics. For no particular reason Ayer's involvement in philosophy seems to have come about suddenly, and his first book *Language, Truth and Logic* was published when he was 26, and remained the foundation of his thinking. The book became regarded as the basic English language work on logical positivism.

Ayer's philosophy held that statements in principle that could not be verified by experience were meaningless, and sought to apply the exactness and methods of the natural sciences and mathematics to the work of philosophers. He believed enormously in the value of conversation, and was a well-known social figure, who counted amongst his friends many famous writers – including Graham Greene, George Orwell and Iris Murdoch, and politicians – notably Hugh Gaitskell, Roy Jenkins and Michael Foot.

During the Second World War he served as an officer in the Welsh Guards, and was a member of Churchill's Special Operations Executive, who organized and carried out acts of sabotage in Europe. After the war, he was appointed as a Professor of Philosophy at University College, London, and in 1959 he became Wykeham Chair, Professor of Logic at Oxford University, where his persuasive lecturing style attracted large audiences.

Sir Alfred wrote many important philosophical works, including two on his friend the philosopher, Bertrand Russell. He was closely associated with the humanist movement, and lectured at American universities. He was knighted in 1970, and was a great sports lover, playing cricket to a high standard, and was an avid Tottenham Hotspur football fan. Ayer married four times, including to Nigella Lawson's mother, Vanessa, and the writer Dee Wells, who as Lady Ayer, sponsored the erection of the commemorative plaque.

Emma CONS
Social Reformer
136 Seymour Place **Map Ref 9**

EMMA CONS 1837-1912 Philanthropist and founder of the Old Vic lived and worked here

Emma Cons was born in London, the second daughter of seven children to Frederick Cons, a piano case maker for Broadwood of London, and Esther (nee Goodier), the daughter of a Stockport mill owner. She went to a school run by the mother of the painter Henry Holiday (an established stained glass artist and whose most important painting – *Dante and Beatrice* – sits in the Walker Art Gallery in Liverpool). She attended Art School until the age of 14, and then joined the Christian-Socialist Ladies' Co-operative Guild, who trained girls in glass painting.

Whilst at the Guild she met Olivia Hill (housing reformer and founder of the National Trust), John Ruskin (social revolutionary and art critic) and Charles Kingsley (novelist and parson), and was drawn into volunteer work in social reform, notably in the management of working-class projects. Ruskin employed her to work on the restoration of illuminated manuscripts.

She was at the forefront of ensuring the employment of women, including a watch engraving business, where she encountered hostility from male competitors. Again, she faced conflict with male employees in her next job, when she worked on the restoration of stained-glass windows. At the same time, she continued her volunteer housing project work, which lead to Ruskin funding her to buy and manage properties in London.

Cons was an active member of the temperance movement, which encouraged her to open a 'Coffee Tavern', which lead to a chain of fifty across London, which offered pub facilities without the alcohol. In 1879 she created the Coffee Music Hall Company, and the following year opened what is now known as the Old Vic Theatre, providing 'wholesome entertainment and alcohol-free refreshments'. Although her desires were not met with great public demand, nevertheless she encouraged wealthy supporters to buy the theatre, and she pursued the first part-time educational institution for working men and women in London.

She was active in many other fields, and her eclectic interests included opening the first Women's Horticultural College, developing a Silk Factory for Armenian refugees in Cyprus, becoming an alderman on the London County Council, and creating the London Society for Women's Suffrage. When her health began to deteriorate she encouraged her niece, Lillian Baylis, to take over the management of the Old Vic, who transformed its repertoire.

Sir Gerald KELLY
Portrait painter

117 Gloucester Place **Map Ref 10**

Gerald Festus Kelly was one of the 20th century's leading British artists. He was born in Paddington, London, the youngest of three children and only son to Frederic Festus Kelly and Blanche (nee Bradford), both of whom were of Irish descent. His father was a curate in nearby Paddington, and became vicar of St Giles, Camberwell, London, where he served for thirty-five years. From an early age, Gerald Kelly's loves were cricket, and paintings, which led to his trying his hand at watercolours. He attended Eton College, and in 1897 went up to Trinity Hall, Cambridge, before deciding to become a painter, despite having had no formal training.

In 1901 he moved to Paris, and helped by his innate charm and unflagging determination, he met Old Masters and Impressionists, including Monet, Renoir, Degas, Rodin and Cézanne, His painting was much influenced by James McNeil Whistler, the American tonalist painter. He made friends with Walter Sickert, the German-born English impressionist painter, and Singer Sargent, the American painter and leading portrait painter. Another friend was Somerset Maugham, who used Kelly as the basis for characters in a number of his novels.

He exhibited at the Salon d'Automne in 1904, and was a founder member of the Modern Portrait Painters Society in 1907 and the National Portrait Society in 1910. He was an enthusiastic traveller, visiting among other countries Spain, America, South Africa, and Burma, where he was encouraged to paint a series of Burmese girls, for which he became famous. His artistic breakthrough was when the great contemporary collector, Sir Hugh Lane, bought two of his paintings in 1908. By the outbreak of the 1st World War he was an established portraitist, and continued to attract significant sitters throughout his career, including T.S.Eliot, Harold Macmillan, Vaughan Williams, and Somerset Maugham.

Kelly joined the Intelligence Department of the Admiralty during the 1st World War, and in 1920 he married a young model, Lilian (whom he always called Jane), and who he never tired of painting. He became a favourite painter of the Royal Family, and painted state portraits of King George VI and Queen Elizabeth II. He was elected to the Royal Academy in 1930, and was the Academy's Keeper between 1943 and 1945. He was a member of the Fine Arts Commission between 1938 and 1943, and in 1949, at the age of seventy, he was elected President of the Royal Academy, where he devoted much of his time to organizing loan exhibitions.

George RICHMOND
Painter

20 York Street **Map Ref 11**

GEORGE RICHMOND 1809-1896 Painter lived here 1843-1896 (London County Council blue plaque)

George Richmond was born in London, the fifth son to Thomas Richmond, a miniature painter, and Ann (nee Coram). His great-grandfather was a painter, and with his artistic family background, and a gift for drawing from an early age, it was not surprising that he pursued an artistic career. He had limited elementary education, but regularly visited the British Museum to draw, and at the age of fifteen he entered the Royal Academy School. Within a year he had exhibited his first academy work. At sixteen Richmond was introduced to William Blake, the poet and painter, who inspired and acted as a mentor to him and a group of young artists. Together the 'Ancients', as they called themselves, met regularly, reading poetry, playing music, and putting the world to rights. The group's central figure was Samuel Palmer, a prolific writer, who was ranked as one of the most important landscape painters of the Romantic era.

From 1826 to 1829 Richmond visited France, and supported himself by painting miniatures, and engraving, drawing and painting landscapes. He fell in love with Julia Tatham, and when her father tried to discourage the relationship, they eloped to Gretna Green in Scotland in 1831. They had fifteen children, whose demands provided enough incentive for Richmond to pursue his painting career. In the 1830's he began to extend his social life, and through the Tory politician Sir Robert Inglis he met such luminaries as William Wilberforce, the social reformer. Painting Wilberforce's portrait proved to be a turning point in his career, and by 1836 he was earning over £1000 a year, and enjoying considerable popularity.

In 1837, Richmond and his wife visited Italy, where he sought his old fellow-student, Joseph Severn, who later became British consul, and he became friends with John Baring, of the banking dynasty, who commissioned him to paint landscapes. The Richmond's spent two years in Italy, before returning to England where his portrait commissions multiplied. He went back briefly to Rome in 1840, and when he returned to England was inundated with portrait commissions, which pushed his earnings to over £2000 a year. In 1844, Prime Minister Gladstone appointed him to the School of Design Council, and in one year – 1847 – he painted nearly one hundred portraits.

He enjoyed an active social life, with membership of prestigious London clubs, and although occasionally he turned to sculpture, he continued to paint both landscapes and portraits for the rest of his life.

Tony RAY-JONES
Photographer

102 Gloucester Place   **Map Ref 12**

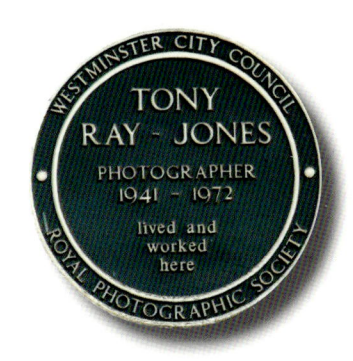

Tony Ray-Jones was born in Wells, Somerset, the youngest son of Raymond Ray-Jones, an engraver whose work was collected in the British Museum and Victoria and Albert Museum. He died before Tony was a year old, and his mother, Effie Irene (nee Pearce) who worked as a physiotherapist, moved her three sons in with her parents in Kent. His work spanned just a decade, but he helped change the face of British photography, with his arresting images of the British at play.

Ray-Jones went to school at Christ's Hospital, West Sussex, and then enrolled on a graphic design course at the London School of Printing. Here he was influenced by Rolf Brandt, the influential photographer and photo-journalist, who encouraged his photography. Ray-Jones won a scholarship to train as a graphic designer at Yale University in America, but was lured away from the drawing board by the call of street photography and he began to receive commissions from American magazines, and advertising agencies.

He returned to England in 1966 and found the beach and the seaside a fertile territory for his documentary photography. He came across a *Country Life book of Old English Customs*, with descriptions of traditional rural pastimes, and saw the possibilities of a photographic record of English life. Ray-Jones met Anna Coates, an art student from St Helens, and they bought a VW camper van and started to make weekend trips. In the late 1960's, before the boom in cheap flights to the beaches of the Spanish Costa's, England's seaside resorts were filled with families taking their holidays. Ray-Jones captured the chaos of these groups – pensioners wrapped-up against the wind, chips and ice cream, beer and litter, children admiring their sandcastles before the sea destroyed them.

Ray-Jones was the first contemporary British photographer to have a one-man touring exhibition, *The English Seen*, organized by the Institute of Contemporary Arts. There was a steady stream of visitors to 102 Gloucester Place, where he lived and worked, including the Director of Photography at the Museum of Modern Art in New York, who bought prints for their permanent collection. In 1971 he accepted a teaching post at the San Francisco Art Institute, but continued working for magazines and the Sunday Times. He died in England of leukaemia at the age of 30.

Elizabeth BARRETT BROWNING
Poet

99 Gloucester Place   **Map Ref 13**

Elizabeth Barrett was born in Durham, the eldest of twelve children to Edward Barrett Moulton Barrett and Mary (nee Graham-Clarke). The family, some of whom were part Creole, had lived for centuries in Jamaica where they owned sugar plantations, but they chose to raise the children in England. She was one of the most famous poets of the Victorian age, educated at home with one of her brothers, and by the age of twelve had written her first 'epic' poem.

Two years later, Barrett developed a lung ailment that plagued her for the rest of her life, and then whilst saddling a pony she suffered a spinal injury. Despite her ailments, her education flourished, teaching herself Hebrew so that she could read the Old Testament, reading the Greek classics, and she had a passionate enthusiasm for her Christian faith.

At the age of 20 she anonymously published *An Essay on Mind and Other Poems*, followed by her translation of *Prometheus Bound*, by the Greek dramatist Aeschylus. Her work gained notoriety in the 1830's, with *The Seraphim and other Poems* in 1838 and *Poems* in 1844. The latter gained the attention of the poet, Robert Browning, who was six years her junior. They exchanged 574 letters over the next two years, which was immortalised in the play *The Barrett's of Wimpole Street*.

Her father opposed the relationship, and after they eloped to Florence in 1846 where she had a child, he never spoke to her again. Elizabeth's *Sonnets from the Portuguese*, dedicated to her husband and written before their marriage, was published in 1850. Political and social injustices embody her later work, including the child labour mines and mills of England, the oppression of the Italians by the Austrians, the slave trade in America and the restrictions placed on women.

Despite the Browning's move to their summer villa in Siena in the 1850's, her health continued to fade, although it is unclear what sort of affection she had. The opium that she was reportedly prescribed probably made it worse, although the presence of Browning almost certainly lengthened her life. Browning returned to England upon her death in 1861.

Wilkie COLLINS
Novelist

65 Gloucester Place   **Map Ref 14**

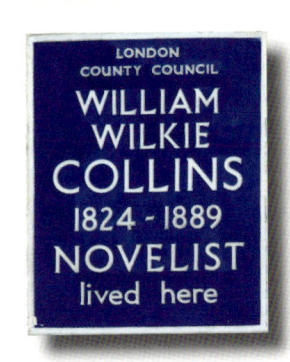

LONDON COUNTY COUNCIL
WILLIAM WILKIE COLLINS
1824 - 1889
NOVELIST
lived here

William Wilkie Collins was born in Marylebone, London, where he lived more or less continuously for 65 years. He was the elder son of William Collins, a celebrated landscape artist and portrait painter, and named after his godfather, Sir David Wilkie. His schooling began at Maida Vale Academy, interrupted at the age of 12 by two years, when he accompanied his parents to France and Italy, and upon returning to England, his schooling continued at Cole's Boarding School. He was hugely popular during the Victorian era, and wrote scores of novels, short stories and plays.

Collins left school at 17, and was apprenticed to the tea merchants, Antrobus & Co in the Strand, London. Collins began to write, and two years later his first story *The Last Stage Coachman* appeared in the Illuminated Magazine. In 1846 he became a law student at Lincoln's Inn, and whilst studying his father died. He wrote his first published book, *The Memoirs of the Life of William Collins, Esq., R.A*, and although he was called to the bar, he never practiced his profession.

Although he published novels in the early 1850's, his main income was derived from journalism, including his contributions to Charles Dickens' weekly magazine, *Household Words*. A firm friendship developed between the two writers, who frequently travelled together on the Continent, and Collins wrote a number of plays that Dickens' theatrical company performed. Collins joined the permanent staff of Dickens' magazine in 1856, and during the 1860's he achieved enduring fame with his four major novels, *The Woman in White, No Name, Armadale*, and *The Moonstone*. T.S.Eliot described the latter as 'the first and greatest of English detective novels', established detective fiction as a genre, and influenced successors from Trollope and Conan Doyle onwards.

Collins lived an unconventional, Bohemian lifestyle, loved good food and wine to excess, wore flamboyant clothes, travelled abroad frequently, and took vast quantities of opium to relieve the symptoms of ill health. He also formed long-term relationships with two women, but married neither. He lived for the best part of thirty years with Caroline Graves, who was probably the real life 'woman in white' – a widow with a young daughter. Martha Rudd was the other woman, with whom he had three children, and although they never married, to give their liaison respectability they assumed the identities of Mr and Mrs Dawson.

Benedict ARNOLD
Soldier

62 Gloucester Place **Map Ref 15**

MAJOR GENERAL BENEDICT ARNOLD AMERICAN PATRIOT RESIDED HERE FROM 1796 UNTIL HIS DEATH JUNE 14, 1801

Benedict Arnold V (1741-1801) was born in Norwich, Connecticut, America, the second of six children to Benedict Arnold III, and Hannah Waterman (nee King), a wealthy widow. He became an American Revolutionary General and America's most famous traitor. He was named after his great-grandfather, an early Governor of Rhode Island, and his brother Benedict IV, who died in infancy. Arnold was a descendant of John Lothropp, an ancestor of several US Presidents, including F D Roosevelt and the George Bush's. He attended private school until his family fell upon hard times, and his mother persuaded his cousins Daniel and Joshua Lathrop for him to become an apprentice at their apothecary business. Arnold left a couple of times to join the army during the French and Indian war, but he remained in their employ for years. He married Margaret Mansfield in 1759, and they had three sons.

Before the outbreak of the American Revolution in 1775, he became a Captain in the Governor's 2nd Company of Guards, and when war broke out Arnold marched to Massachusetts, where he was made a Colonel, and with Ethan Allen's soldiers captured Ticonderoga. He led a force to invade Canada - a march that remains a military classic. Linking up with the American force under Richard Montgomery, he led an unsuccessful attack on Quebec, but was promoted to Brigadier-General for his courage.

Arnold had a brilliant career in the Continental Army, including fighting a series of naval battles in 1776 that helped delay a British invasion from Canada, and forcing the British to surrender in Saratoga in 1777. He became an embittered man, resentful towards Congress for not promoting him to higher rank, and now a widower, he threw himself into a wild social life. His second marriage to Margaret Shippen (with whom he had five children), the daughter of a Loyalist in 1779, aroused suspicions.

His bitterness, and a need for money, led Arnold to negotiate with the British, and he conceived a plan to betray the post he commanded. His attempted treachery was revealed and he escaped to enemy lines and was commissioned a Brigadier-General in the British army. He served George III with the same skill and daring he had shown in the Patriot cause. Arnold went to England in 1781 and turned to trade: he returned briefly to America, but settled in London permanently in 1791.

John GODLEY
Statesman
48 Gloucester Place
Map Ref 16

John Robert Godley, the eldest son of John Godley and his wife, Katherine (nee Daly), was born in Dublin. His father owned country estates in County Leitrim and County Meath in Ireland. He was educated at Harrow School and Christ Church, Oxford, where he obtained a BA in Classics. He was called to the Irish bar in 1839, but because of his on-going illnesses, rarely practised.

Godley was deeply religious and was sympathetic to the Oxford Movement, a group of High Church Anglicans, who argued for the restoration of lost Christian traditions of faith. When he was 28 he travelled to North America, where he developed his interest in the governing of colonies, and he published *Letters from America* in two volumes in 1844. He was appointed High Sheriff of Leitrim, and unsuccessfully proposed state-funded mass emigration of Irish to Canada, to alleviate the devastation of the potato famine.

He began to collaborate with the like-minded Edward Gibbon Wakefield, who served as a King's Messenger, carrying diplomatic mail around Europe. Wakefield promoted the idea of colonisation, as he believed that many of the social problems in Britain were caused by overcrowding and overpopulation. Wakefield owned the New Zealand Company and asked Godley to found a colony in New Zealand that would follow the beliefs of the Church of England. The 'Canterbury Association' was duly created in 1848, with committee members including the Archbishop of Canterbury, MP's and members of the peerage, and land bought in what is now Christchurch.

In 1846 Godley had married Charlotte Griffith Wynne of Denbighshire in Wales, with whom he had a son and three daughters. The family left for New Zealand in 1849, followed by a fleet of four ships the following year, carrying pilgrims and supplies. For the next two years he served as leader of the settlement, with his view of colonial management stated as "I would rather be governed by a Nero on the spot than a board of angels in London". With the passing of the New Zealand Constitution Act in 1852, Godley had realised his desire for Canterbury to become a self-governing province, and he returned to England.

On his return, he worked as a columnist for several newspapers, continuing to write on colonial reform, and acted on immigration issues as an agent of the Canterbury government. He was appointed Commissioner of Income Tax in Ireland, and from 1885 Assistant Under-Secretary at the War Office, where he continued to advocate self-reliance for colonies in the arena of defence policy.

Thomas MOORE
Poet and singer
85 George Street　　　　　　　　　　　　　　　　　　**Map Ref 17**

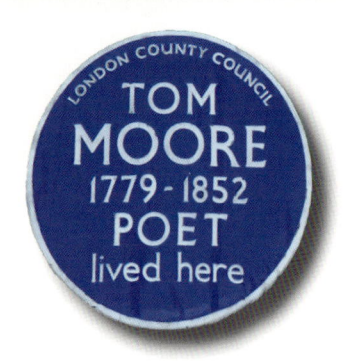

Thomas Moore was born in Dublin, Ireland, and whose father has been variously described as a grocer, shoemaker, or wine merchant (!), and Anastasia Codd (nee Moore) from Wexford. He attended grammar school, and at the age of 16 he entered Trinity College, Dublin, which had recently allowed entry to Catholic students.

At university, Moore met members of the United Irish Society, who enflamed his devotion to the Irish cause. One of his friends was Robert Emmet participated in the United Irishmen Uprisings of 1798 and 1803, and was captured, tried and hanged. He and Moore had been members of a debating society, the "Hist", the Historical Society at Trinity. Again, at college, Moore was introduced to Edward Bunting's collection of traditional Irish music, upon which much of his early work was based.

After graduating from Trinity, Moore studied law at the Middle Temple in London. However, it was as a singer and poet that he found fame, and his first book, Odes of Anacreon was a success, which enabled him to travel to Bermuda, the West Indies and the United States. He returned to London in 1804, and lived there for the rest of his life.

> *Tis the last rose of summer,*
> *Left blooming alone;*
> *All her lovely companions*
> *Are faded and gone*
> *The Last Rose of Summer*

Moore was a noted society figure in London, and despite his vocal Irish national politics, he was popular; a friend of Lord Byron and P B Shelley and he counted the Prince Regent, (later George IV), among his patrons. His ten volume work, Irish Melodies, published between 1807 and 1834, consisted of 130 poems set to music, notably The Minstrel Boy and The Last Rose of Summer. The latter sold more than a million copies in the United States alone, and his works were so popular that he earned £500 annually for more than 25 years from his publications.

His career was not without controversy, and despite being considered Ireland's National Bard, he turned down the post of "Irish Poet Laureate", because he felt it required toning down his politics. Although a Catholic, Moore married a Protestant actress, Elizabeth 'Bessy' Dyke, whom he had met at the Kilkenny Theatre Festival in 1808 when she was 14, and their five children were raised as Protestants.

Sake MAHOMED
Restaurateur
102 George Street
Map Ref 18

Sake Dean Mohamed opened the Hindoostane Coffee Shop in 1810, which was in effect the first Indian restaurant in Britain. The plaque is unusual in that it is located inside the front entrance of Carlton House, at 102 George Street, the present building on the site of the original restaurant. Mohamed was a Muslim born in Patna in India, and related to the Nawabs of Bengal and Bihar, who had ruled large proportions of the Indian subcontinent. In 1769, at the age of 11, he joined the East India Company Army, where he saw active service in a number of campaigns and rose to the rank of Captain.

In 1782, he resigned from the army, choosing instead to accompany his 'best friend' Captain Godfrey Baker and his family, immigrating to Cork in Ireland, via Dartmouth, and became his house manager, He married Jane Daly, the daughter of a wealthy Irish family and wrote a travel book, *The Travels of Dean Mahomet*, and in doing so became the first Indian to write a book in English and have it published. Mahomed moved to London in 1810, where he worked as an assistant to Sir Basil Cochrane, a wealthy former employee of the East India Company, and is reputed to have introduced shampoo to England, whilst working at Sir Basil's 'vapour bath' in Portman Square. Close by in George Street is where he opened his restaurant, which was described as 'a place for the nobility and Gentry, where they may enjoy the Hookha with real Chilm tobacco and Indian dishes of the highest perfection'.

The venture failed and he was declared bankrupt in 1812, and forced to advertise himself as a 'valet to wealthy gentlemen'. In 1814 the Mohameds, with their six children, moved to Brighton, where they successfully opened special treatment baths, where he became "shampoo surgeon" to the dandyish Prince of Wales, George IV and then William IV. He published another book in 1822, *Shampooing or benefits Resulting from the use of Indian Medical Vapour Bath*, which became a best seller.

He was probably at least a century ahead of his time, as the growth of Indian restaurants has moved from six in Britain in 1939, to 3500 in 1982, and today there are now over 8500 in the UK. Reputedly there are more 'Indian' chefs in London than in Delhi!

John LENNON and George HARRISON
Beatles

94 Baker Street Map Ref 19

Although the plaque highlights John Lennon and Geroge Harrison, they did not live at 94 Baker Street. It was the location of one of the first Beatles' ventures outside the world of music, where the ill-fated 'Apple Boutique' was born. Paul McCartney described it as "a beautiful place where you could buy beautiful things". The building began its life in the 19th century as a 4-storey residential house. During the early 60's, three Dutch designers who had run an initially successful boutique called The Trend in Amsterdam landed in England, where they joined up with Simon Hayes and Barry Finch. Together, they became known as "The Fool", and in September 1967 the Beatles gave them £100,000 to design and stock the Apple Boutique.

The Fool had already created the psychedelic design for John Lennon's Rolls Royce, and employed art students to paint a huge psychedelic mural on the front and side of the store. The mural was erased after local traders complained! The store opened in December 1967, managed by Jenny Boyd, the sister of George Harrison's wife Pattie, along with Pete Shotton, John's closest childhood mate, who had played washboard in the Quarry Men. Only John and George turned up to the opening. The boutique was a financial disaster, and closed eight months later, when the staff were told to give everything away!

Apple Corps was the holding company for the Apple Boutique, which the Beatles' manager, Brian Epstein, had created as a tax avoidance device. His unexpected death in 1967 hastened the creation of a stable of companies under the Apple nomenclature, which was based at 3 Savile Row (the street is featured in our 'Mayfair South' Walk), and is where *Let It Be* was recorded on the roof. These companies included Apple Films, which had produced the TV film *Magical Mystery Tour*, Apple Studio, a recording studio in the basement, Apple Publishing and Apple Records.

John Lennon can also be found on this walk, Map Ref 5

As well as Baker Street and Savile Row, John's other connections with the area include the time he lived at 34 Montagu Square, five doors down from Trollope's house, featured earlier in this Walk. Ringo Starr owned the lease, and when he married Maureen Cox and moved into his 'proper' house in Weybridge, he sub-let it to friends, including Jimi Hendrix. Lennon moved in with Yoko Ono in July 1968, but Ringo sold the lease in early 1969 after a police drug-raid ended with Lennon in court for possession.

William PITT (The Younger)
Prime Minister
120 Baker Street — Map Ref 20

William Pitt was born in Hayes in Kent, the second son, and fourth of five children, of William Pitt the Elder, who had been British Prime Minister between 1766 and 1768. He was almost born to be prime minister, being immersed in political life from an early age. Due to ill health he was educated at home, but studied political philosophy at Pembroke College, Cambridge University in 1773 at the age of fourteen. After 'graduating', he studied law and was called to the Bar in 1780, the same year he lost in his first attempt to become the MP for Cambridge University. The next year at 21 he was returned as MP for Appleby in Cumbria, and he proved to be a talented parliamentary speaker.

In 1782 he became Chancellor of the Exchequer under Lord Shelburne, whose government was quickly replaced by a coalition under the Duke of Portland, which was dismissed in 1783. Pitt became the youngest Prime Minister at the age of 24, and against early predictions, his ministry survived for 17 years. He stood for parliamentary reform to reduce the direct influence of the monarchy and the capacity for bribery; union with Ireland; Catholic emancipation; reorganization of the East India Company; reduce the National Debt; and free trade.

In the 1790's, the French Revolution caused Pitt to worry about its effect on Britain, and he declared war on France. War lead to increased taxes and duties, and he was forced to introduce Britain's first ever income tax. Ireland was formally united into a single realm with Great Britain in 1801, but Pitt's attempts to abolish restrictions on Roman Catholics, who formed a majority in Ireland, were thwarted by King George III, and Pitt resigned, to be replaced by Addington.

"Necessity is the argument of tyrants, it is the creed of slaves"

Three years later, the King asked Pitt to form a second government, and after victory against the French at Trafalgar, Pitt was hailed as Europe's saviour, although Napoleon's subsequent victories were profound personal blows to him. He had been a keen gardener and loved riding and shooting. Pitt never married, and died at the age of 46 in debt to the tune of £40,000: Parliament agreed to pay the sum on his behalf.

Charles KEMPE
Artist

37 Nottingham Place Map Ref 21

CHARLES EAMER KEMPE 1837-1907 Stained glass artist lived and worked here

Charles Eamer Kempe was born at Ovingdean Hall, near Brighton in East Sussex. His maternal grandfather was Sir John Eamer, who served as Lord Mayor of London in 1801. He studied for the priesthood at Pembroke College, Oxford, but it was obvious that his severe stammer would curtail his ability to preach, and decided he could not be a priest.

He determined that his future lay in decorating churches and designing beautiful windows, wall paintings and embroideries. Kempe sketched old windows in England and on the continent before studying church decoration with G.F.Bodley, the leading Gothic-revival architects of the 19th century. He also studied stained glass production with one of the most prolific manufacturers, Clayton & Bell, who employed over 300 people at their premises in Regent Street, London, and who were often used by the noted architect George Gilbert Scott.

Kempe opened his own studio in London in 1868, but even before this Bodley had asked him to help with wall paintings at All Saints, Cambridge and Bodley was to become one of his major customers, for whom he supplied stained glass, furnishings and vestments. The style then in vogue reflected a resurgence of interest in high-church practices. Although he was not a trained artist, he was nevertheless artistic, and able to suggest ideas which could be developed by his artists and cartoonists. Kempe's greatest stylistic influence was the stained glass of Northern Germany and Flanders from the 16th century: he took many trips to Europe, often taking Kempe Company artists with him. He insisted that only the firm's name take credit for the standard of work produced, and individual members of his studio remain anonymous.

Amongst his first commissions were wall paintings in Bodley's new church of St John at Tuebrook in Liverpool, and Clayton & Bell asked him to design a memorial window in Gloucester Cathedral. Kempe's output was enormous, with designs for windows in India, including Bombay Cathedral, and he created over 200 windows for the USA, hundreds in Australia, Canada, Africa, Ireland, and his windows can be seen in churches all over Britain. His later windows are far more elaborate than the earlier ones, with elaborately patterned brocades and pearls. He was a shy person and never married.

Leonard STOKOWKSI
Conductor

63 Marylebone High Street **Map Ref 22**

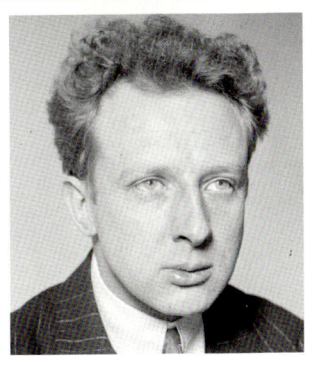

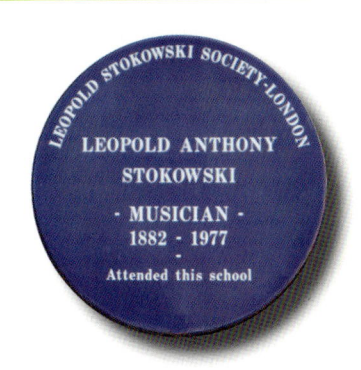

LEOPOLD STOKOWSKI SOCIETY·LONDON
LEOPOLD ANTHONY STOKOWSKI
- MUSICIAN -
1882 - 1977
Attended this school

Leopold Anthony Stokowski was born in Upper Marylebone Street (now New Cavendish Street), the first of three children to Kopernik Joseph Stokowski, a cabinet maker, and Anne Marion (nee Moore). His father was of Polish extraction, and his mother hailed from Ireland.

He was a precocious young musician, and learned to play the violin, piano and organ. His formal schooling was limited, but at the age of 13 he became the youngest person to be admitted to the Royal College of Music. At 16 he was elected to the Royal College of Organists, by 18 had been appointed organist and choirmaster at St James's Church, Piccadilly, and at 20 formed the choir of St Mary's Church, Charing Cross Road. He attended Queen's College, Oxford, where he obtained a Bachelor of Music in 1903.

In 1905 Stokowski moved to the USA as organist and choirmaster of St Bartholomew's in New York City. He returned to Europe every summer for further musical studies, and when the conductor of the Colonne Orchestra fell ill in Paris in 1908, he made his debut. The impact he made lead to a position with the Cincinnati Symphony Orchestra, and in 1912 he was invited to take over the Philadelphia Orchestra, giving them what became known as the 'Philadelphia sound'. He was a relentless innovator, pioneering the use of 'free' bowing, and abandoning the baton, preferring to shape the music with his hands.

Influenced by his wife, the pianist Olga Samarth, whom he had married in 1911, he gave himself an air of mystery and social acceptability by developing a 'foreign accent', and claimed to have been born in Poland. He divorced in 1923, and three years later married Evangaline Johnson (daughter of the founder of Johnson & Johnson). He saw film as way to disseminate music to the masses, making his first movie appearance in The Big Broadcast in 1937, featuring Benny Goodman and Jack Benny. In the same year he began a spectacular affair with Greta Garbo, which led to his divorce from Evangeline.

He was the first conductor to become a superstar, appearing most famously as the orchestra leader in Walt Disney's animated classic Fantasia in 1940. In 1955 Stokowski was appointed music director of Houston Symphony Orchestra, the year in which his third wife, Gloria Vanderbilt, began divorce proceedings against him. Stokowski was a major figure in the history of conducting, combining a serious interest in art and a passion for technology and public relations.

Octavia HILL
Social Reformer

2 Garbutt Place **Map Ref 23**

Octavia Hill was born in Wisbech, Cambridgeshire, the eighth daughter of James Hill, a prosperous corn merchant and former banker. James built an infant school, run by Octavia's mother, Caroline Southwood (nee Smith), the daughter of Dr Thomas Smith, the pioneer of sanitary reform. According to Octavia, she was the first Englishwoman to teach using the Pestalozzi method. She became particularly interested in the welfare of the inhabitants of cities.

In 1840, James Hill became bankrupt, and Caroline left Wisbech and brought up her children alone in Finchley, north London. Octavia learned her lifelong love of the countryside from these childhood days, and her reform work can be seen as a continuation of her parents' efforts. She was influenced by her maternal grandfather, Dr Thomas Smith, a friend of the legal and social reformer Jeremy Bentham, and tireless campaigner for decent living conditions for poor people.

The family moved from the outskirts into London in 1851, where the grim urban poverty horrified Octavia. Other early influences on her life were F D Maurice, the leader of the Christian Socialists, who inspired her confirmation into the Anglican Church, and the influential art critic, John Ruskin, who was disenchanted with the existing social order. As a teenager she began working with slum children, and became aware of the terrible conditions and lack of interest from landlords.

Octavia worked with her sister, Miranda, who founded the Kyrle Society, whose aim was to enhance the quality of life in poor communities by providing art, books and open spaces. At the age of 21, in 1859, she created the Southwark unit of the Army Cadet Force, which was a youth organization providing military and adventure training for boys and girls between the ages of 12 and 18. It had been created to prepare youths to enlist in the army in anticipation of a possible French invasion.

She developed the idea of a model-housing scheme, providing acceptable living conditions, with the profit from the moderate rents going towards improvements, which lead to the Artisans Dwelling Act of 1875. She campaigned for Hampstead Heath not to be built on, and was determined to improve people's lives by allowing them access to green spaces. She was the first to use the expression "Green Belt" and co-founded the National Trust.

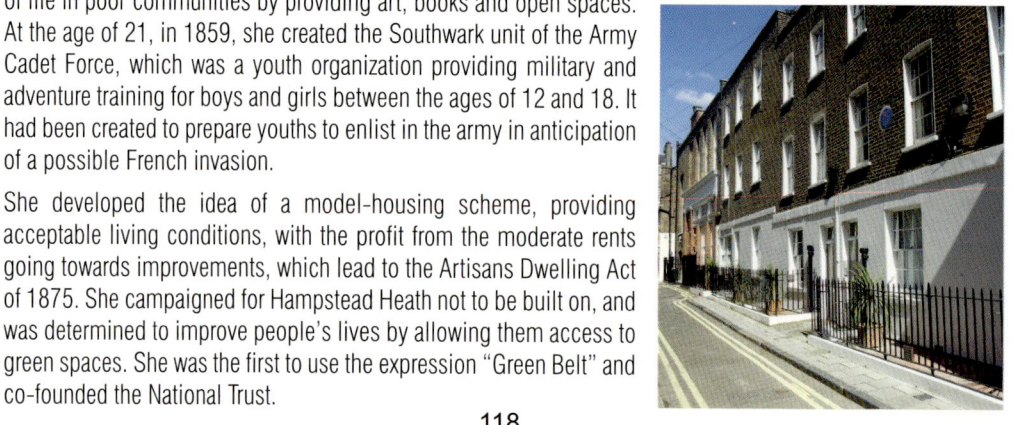

Charles BABBAGE
Computer Pioneer

1a Dorset Street　　　　　　　　　　　　　　　　　　　**Map Ref 24**

Charles Babbage was born in south London to Benjamin Babbage, a banker, and Betsy Plumleigh (nee Teape). He was a mathematician and inventor of the calculating machine and may well be described as the founding father of the modern digital computer. He was often unwell and consequently much of his education was at home, but as his father was a rich man, it was possible for him to receive his early education from a number of elite schools and tutors. He spent time at a local country school, a grammar school, and an academy, where he learned to love mathematics.

In 1810 he went up to Trinity College, Cambridge, but was disappointed with the mathematics teaching, and transferred to Peterhouse College. After graduation in 1814, he was hired by the Royal Institution to lecture on calculus. Within two years he was elected as a member of the Royal Society, and between 1820 and 1839 he was Lucasian Professor of Mathematics at Cambridge.

In Babbage's times there was a high error rate in the calculation of maths tables, and as early as 1812 he planned to find a new method that could be used to remove the human error factor. Babbage worked for nearly fifty years and anticipated many of the features incorporated in electronic computers. These included the feeding-in of information by punched cards, the printing out of results and the creation of a large information store or memory.

In 1824, Babbage won the Gold Medal of the Astronomical Society – which he had helped to found – "for his invention of an engine for calculating mathematical and astronomical tables". He contributed to several scientific periodicals, helped to found the Statistical Society, and worked in the fields of philosophy and cryptology, where he achieved notable success in code-breaking. Babbage also invented the 'pilot', the cow-catcher attached to the front of locomotives that cleared the tracks of obstacles.

Babbage married Georgina Whitmore, with whom he had eight children, although only three survived to adulthood. He was an eccentric in many ways, and although he had a strong distaste for 'commoners', he tried to enter public life, but failed in his two attempts to become a Member of Parliament for Finsbury. Sir Clive Sinclair, the inventor and creator of the first ever-true pocket calculator, unveiled the plaque.

Sir Henry SEGRAVE
Racing Pioneer
St Andrews Mansions, Chiltern Street — Map Ref 25

Henry O'Neil de Hane Segrave was a British national born in Baltimore, Maryland, USA to an Irish father and an American mother. Segrave was famous for his exploits in achieving land and water speed records. He was raised in Ireland, and then schooled at Bilton Grange near Rugby, in Warwickshire, before going to Eton College.

Segrave spent a brief time at Sandhurst, where all officers in the British army are trained, but was commissioned in the Royal Warwickshire regiment, and saw action in France in the 1st World War. In 1915 he transferred to the Royal Flying Corps, where he was promoted to Flight Commander, and was twice shot down and wounded.

After the war, he pursued his interest in cars and motorcycles, and started motor racing. After winning several races in 1923 at Brooklands, the world's first purpose-built motor racing circuit in Surrey, he became the first Briton for twenty-one years to win a Grand Prix in a British car at the French Grand Prix, and in the following year, the San Sebastian Grand Prix in a Sunbeam-Talbot. After another victory in France, he began to concentrate on speed records, and in 1926 set his first land-speed record of 152.33mph on the sands at Southport, in Lancashire.

Despite his successes, Segrave retired from Grand Prix racing in 1927 and took a job as sales director with Portland Cement, as he was concerned that "his luck might run out". Nevertheless, he continued to make world record attempts, achieving over 200mph at Daytona Beach, Florida, that same year, and two years later 231.36mph in the British-built Golden Arrow. Upon returning home, he received a knighthood.

In 1927, Segrave began racing boats, and reached 98.76 mph in 1930 piloting Miss England on Lake Windermere in Cumbria, beating the previous record by 6 mph. However, disaster struck when his boat capsized on a further run, and he died from his injuries at the age of thirty-three. Segrave also re-ignited his love of flying in the late 1920's, when he designed a twin-engined aircraft, but he will be remembered for winning four Grands Prix, breaking the world land speed record three times and the world water speed record once, and being the first person to hold both records concurrently. His autobiography entitled *The Lure of Speed* epitomises the essence of the man

Michael FARADAY
Chemist and Physicist

48 Blandford Street **Map Ref 26**

Michael Faraday was born in Southwark in south London, the third of four children His father, James had been an apprentice to the village blacksmith in Westmoreland (now part of Cumbria), before bringing the family down to London. The family was not well off, and he finished his basic education at the age of fourteen, when he became apprenticed to a local bookbinder. During the next seven years he educated himself by reading books on a wide range of scientific subjects, and became one of the most influential scientists in history.

In 1812, at the age of 21, Faraday attended lectures given by the chemist Humphry Davy at the Royal Institution, and he subsequently wrote to Davy asking for a job as his assistant. He was turned down, but the following year, Davy appointed him to the job of chemical assistant at the Royal Institution. In 1814, Davy invited Faraday to join him and his wife on an 18 month European tour. She treated him as little more than a valet, but the trip did give him the opportunity to meet many influential scientists. Upon their return, Faraday continued to work at the Royal Institution, helping with experiments.

Faraday published his work on electromagnetism in 1821, the principle behind the electric motor, and by 1826, he was organizing meetings and lectures at the Royal Institution, establishing himself as the outstanding scientific lecturer of his time. In 1831, he discovered electromagnetic induction, which allowed electricity to be transformed from a curiosity into a powerful new technology. He invented an early form of Bunsen burner, which is used in all laboratories as a source of heat, and he discovered chemical substances such as benzene and chlorine. During the 1830's he worked on developing his ideas about electricity, and was responsible for coining such familiar words as 'electrode', 'cathode', and 'ion'.

Faraday's scientific knowledge was harnessed for practical use through the roles he performed as Scientific Advisor between 1836 and 1865 to Trinity House —established to ensure the safety of shipping and the well-being of seafarers — and Professor of Chemistry at the Royal Military Academy in Woolwich between 1830 and 1851. He was a devout Christian and a member of the Sandemanian Church, a sect that demanded total faith and commitment. He married Sarah (nee Barnard) in 1821 after meeting her at their church in the Barbican in London.

Sir Francis BEAUFORT
Inventor

51 Manchester Street **Map Ref 27**

Francis Beaufort was born in Navan, County Neath, Ireland, the son of the Protestant clergyman, Rev. Daniel Augustus Beaufort. The Beauforts were descended from the French Huguenots who fled from France and settled in Ireland. He joined the British Navy at the age of 13 and was to become renowned for his work with nautical maps: it is significant that his father created and published a new map of Ireland when Francis was 18.

Beaufort became aware of the risks of faulty maps after being shipwrecked at the age of fifteen due to a faulty chart. His first voyage was on a British East India Company ship, and he was promoted through the ranks, making Commander in 1800. Whilst on manoeuvres on HMS Phaeton he received 19 wounds, and during his recuperation, he devised a semaphore telegraph system with his brother-in-law, which could quickly transmit messages across the country.

In 1805 he was given command of HMS Woolwich, which was to have far-reaching effects on Beaufort's career. The ship was part of an expedition, which in 1806 seized Buenos Aires, then a possession of Spain, which was allied to Britain's enemy, France, that lead to the establishment of the Republic of Argentina. The expedition was able to give Beaufort the opportunity to show his excellence as a hydrographer, and upon his return he impressed Alexander Dalrymple, head of the British Admiralty's Hydrographic Office.

The tendency of all people is to undervalue what they do not understand.

Beaufort had studied Dalrymple's Treatise on Navigation, which included a table on the 'Velocity and force of wind', prepared by John Smeaton. Beaufort's famous Scale, first draw-up in 1806, is an adaption and modification for maritime needs of Smeaton's table. His scale culminates in a Force 12 hurricane, 'which no canvas can withstand', when the speed of the wind is above 63 knots. In 1829, at the age of 55, Beaufort became Hydrographer of the British Navy a position he occupied for 26 years, and the British Admiralty Chart became what even today is the most trusted navigational document available.

He was also an expert cryptographer, and devised a wholly original message-code system, and promoted the development of reliable tide tables. He was a member of the Royal Society and helped found the Royal Geographic Society in 1830.

Lord Alfred MILNER
Statesman

14 Manchester Square **Map Ref 28**

Alfred Milner was born in Giessen, Germany, the only son to Charles Milner, a physician, and of Major General John Ready's daughter. His parents were English, and although he lived part of his youth in Germany, his mother insisted that he was educated in England, where he attended King's College School, London, and then Balliol College, Oxford. He played a key role in determining British foreign and domestic policy from the mid-1890's to the 1920's.

Milner started out on a legal career, but then turned to journalism, spending four years with the *Pall Mall Gazette*. He was interested in many facets of economics and politics, but in 1885 lost in his attempt to become an MP for Harrow. He was private secretary to G J Goschen, who became an MP, and his official private secretary, when he became Chancellor of the Exchequer. Goschen secured him a financial position in Egypt under Sir Evelyn Baring, and in 1892 brought him back to England as Chairman of the Inland Revenue.

Anglo-Boer trouble in South Africa was approaching deadlock when Milner was chosen to go there as High Commissioner in 1897. He believed in British imperialism and the necessity of protecting British interests, and became convinced that war was unavoidable. He could not believe the Boers were acting in good faith when they sought a peaceful compromise, and the result was the Boer War, which came to dominate the entire British political scene. He is remembered for his part in the British victory, and for his work in building up South Africa's physical and economic base, although his support for concentration camps during the war and importation of Chinese labour at its conclusion led to widespread condemnation.

Upon his return to England in 1905, he occupied himself with business matters, becoming Chairman of Rio Tinto Zinc, and sat in the House of Lords, where he opposed much of the legislation sponsored by the Liberals. When the 1st World War started, Milner was called-upon, first to increase food production, and then to be a member of PM Lloyd George's War Cabinet. In 1918, he was appointed War Secretary, and then Colonial Secretary, before retiring in 1921 at a time when his views on imperialism were waning in popularity. In the same year, at the grand age of 67, he married Lady Violet Gascoyne-Cecil, widow of Lord Edward Cecil.

Simon BOLIVAR
Statesman

4 Duke Street **Map Ref 29**

Simon Bolivar was born in Caracas, Venezuela to Colonel Juan Vicente Bolivar y Ponte and Concepcion Palacios Blanco, a distinguished and wealthy family of Basque origin, who had lived in Venezuela since the end of the sixteenth century. He had two sisters and a brother, and their father died when he was three, which led to their mother supervising their education and managing the family's estates.

In addition to his paternal heritage, he received a substantial inheritance from his cousin, a priest, when he was just a year old. His mother died when he was nine, and with his two sisters now married, he and his brother lived with them and their maternal grandfather, who became their tutor. When his grandfather died, after living with an uncle for a short time, he developed a friendship with a teacher Don Simon Rodriguez, which led to a lifelong friendship.

At 14, Bolivar joined the Battalion in the White Militia, which had been headed by his father, where he continued his education, and within a year he was promoted to 2nd Lieutenant. Two years later he travelled to Madrid, and pursued his studies assiduously, before meeting Maria Teresa Rodriguez. They married in 1802 and travelled to Venezuela, where his bride died within a year, and he returned to Europe to live in Paris and travel Europe.

He returned to Venezuela in 1810 and joined the group of patriots that had seized Caracas, and proclaimed independence from Spain. He went to England in search of aid, but could only get a promise of British neutrality. When he returned to Venezuela, he took command of a patriot army, and recaptured Caracas from the spanish. The Spaniards forced Bolivar to retreat to what is now Columbia, where he took command of the forces, but new defeats led him to retreat to Jamaica. He gathered a force in Haiti that landed in Venezuela in 1816 and appointed himself as its dictator.

Over the next six years, Bolivar crushed the Spanish armies across South America, winning independence for Panama, Columbia, Ecuador, Peru and Venezuela. In 1825 Upper Peru became a separate state, named Bolivia in his honour. He drew up a constitution for the new state, in which his ideas for the consolidation of order and the independence of the recently emancipated nations are expressed.

John JACKSON
Neurologist

3 Manchester Square **Map Ref 30**

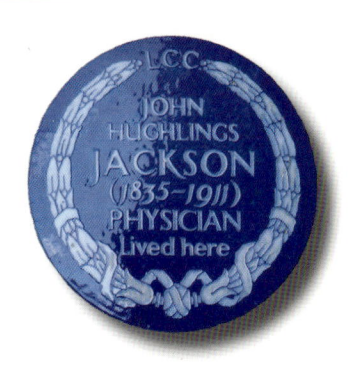

John Hughlings Jackson was born in Harrogate, Yorkshire, the son of Samuel Jackson, a farmer, and Sarah (nee Hughling), the daughter of a Welsh revenue collector. The youngest of five children, and his mother died when he was just over year old: he attended local schools at Green Hammerton and Tadcaster. At the age of 15 he was apprenticed to a Dr Anderson, a lecturer at York Hospital Medical School, and completed his medical education at St Bartholomew's Hospital in London between 1855 and 1856.

Now a member of the Royal College of Surgeons, he returned to York as Resident Medical Officer at the York Dispensary, where he worked for Thomas Laycock, who specialised in the brain and was the first person who considered the brain as subject to the laws of reflex action. The biologist and social philosopher Herbert Spencer, who coined the phrase "survival of the fittest" influenced Laycock, and Jackson gave serious consideration to the thought of pursuing the study of philosophy.

In 1859, he returned to London, where Sir Jonathan Hutchinson, the noted surgeon, encouraged him to continue with medicine, and with his help Jackson became a medical journalist. In the same year he was made a lecturer in pathology at the London Hospital, and in 1861 was admitted to the Royal College of Physicians. From 1863, and for the next fifty-eight years, Jackson worked at the London Hospital as a physician. During the same period, he was also a neurological physician at the National Hospital for the Paralysed and Epileptic, and worked at Moorfields Eye Hospital, where he became familiar with the ophthalmoscope, which he popularised in English neurology.

In 1865, Jackson married his cousin Elizabeth Dade, who suffered from epilepsy and died childless. He studied her, and concluded that the epileptic seizures were electrical discharges within the brain, and it was his work more than anybody else's that established the present concept of epilepsy. Jackson established a private practice, wrote many papers dealing with opthalmological problems, and was elected as a Fellow of the Royal College of Physicians in 1868, and of the Royal Society in 1878. In the same year he was one of the founders and editor of the important Brain magazine, which is still published today, in 1885 he became the first President of the Neurological Society, and in 1892 was one of the founding members of the National Society for Epilepsy.

Sir Julius BENEDICT
Musical Composer

2 Manchester Square   **Map Ref 31**

Julius Benedict was born in Stuttgart, Germany, the son of a Jewish banker. He was a composer and orchestra conductor, whose early musical career was spent in Germany but who lived most of his life in England. He learned composition from Johann Hummel, the piano virtuoso and a pupil of Mozart, who made Weimar into a European musical capital, and Carl Mann von Weber, one of the first significant composers of the Romantic School at Dresden, home of important orchestras such as the Staatskapelle.

Weber introduced Benedict to Beethoven in Vienna when he was 19, and in 1823 he was appointed Kapellmeister at the Karnthnerthor Theatre in Vienna, and two years later at the San Carlo Theatre in Naples. Benedict's first opera, *Giacinta ed Ernesto*, was performed in Naples in 1829, followed by *I Portoghesi* in Goa the following year, neither of which were great successes. In 1834 he went to Paris, and the following year Maria Malibran, the very first diva - the original female superstar of the music world - who was herself a Parisian, suggested Benedict should go to London, where he spent the rest of his life.

In 1836 he became a conductor in London, initially at the Lyceum Theatre, and two years later conductor of the English opera at the Theatre Royal, Drury Lane, during the time when Michael Balfe, the Irish composer and singer, was extremely popular. He conducted Mendelssohn's Elijah for the first appearance of Jenny Lind, the Swedish opera singer in 1848, and two years later he went as her accompanist on her tour to America. He returned to London in 1852 and became the conductor at Her Majesty's Theatre, and over the following years continued to produce his operas across the country, including his best-known work *The Lily of Killarney* at Covent Garden in London.

In 1875, Benedict contacted W S Gilbert about working together on a comic opera, but Gilbert was too busy and the idea was dropped. He conducted every Norwich Festival from 1845 and 1878, and the Liverpool Philharmonic Society's concerts from 1876 and 1880. He was knighted in 1871 by Queen Victoria.

George GROSSMITH
Actor-Manager

3 Spanish Place **Map Ref 32**

George Grossmith was born in Islington, London, the eldest of three children to George Grossmith, who was the chief reporter for *The Times* newspaper at Bow Street Magistrates' Court, a lecturer and entertainer: his mother was Louisa Emmerline (nee Weedon). At 8 he went to boarding school in Hampstead, and when 12 moved to North London Collegiate School in Camden Town. The Grossmith family had many friends involved in the theatre, including Ellen Terry and Henry Irving.

Our George's first venture into 'show business' was as an entertainer at the piano for private patrons, in the days when 'nice' people didn't go to the theatre. He made his first professional appearance in 1870 in *Human Oddities*, a sketch written by his father, which included a co-written song, *The Gay Photographer*. Over the next seven years, Grossmith toured the country with a series of partners, and amongst this number was Florence Marryat, daughter of Captain Frederick Marryat. During this time he became friendly with many in the entertainment business, including the impresario, Richard D'Oyle Carte. This led to him appearing in a benefit performance of *Trial by Jury*, at the Haymarket Theatre, London, in 1877, where he met Arthur Sullivan. Soon afterwards he played the major role of the Judge, and was noticed by W.S. Gilbert and these occasions led to Sullivan offering him a part in his new comic opera, *The Sorcerer*.

All the directors of the Comedy Opera Company, who then ran the operas, objected to Grossmith, except Gilbert, Sullivan and Carte. Grossmith got the part and was an instantaneous success. From this point he became a regular member of the D'Oyle Carte Company, and created all of the lead comic baritone roles in Savoy Operas from 1877 to 1889, including *HMS Pinafore, The Pirates of Penzance, The Mikado,* and *Iolanthe*. After *Yeoman of the Guard*, Grossmith quit the stage and returned to his former piano entertaining, and with his now-established reputation was highly successful. His comic song *See Me Dance The Polka* was extremely popular and has been used in a number of films, and he achieved great success as part-author, with his brother, of *The Diary of a Nobody*.

In 1873, Grossmith had married Emmeline Rosa Noyce, the daughter of a neighbourhood physician, with whom he had four children, and George Jnr. became very famous in his own right as an actor.

The Idler magazine - 1897 (Top)
Sheet Music - 1870 (Above)

Captain Frederick MARRYAT
Novelist

3 Spanish Place **Map Ref 32**

CAPTAIN FREDERICK MARRYAT 1792-1848 NOVELIST lived here

Frederick Marryat was born into a large middle-class family in London to Joseph, a Member of Parliament, and Charlotte (nee von Geyer), who was of German descent. He was educated privately, but he disliked his teachers, and the 'rebel' ran away from home several times. At the age of 14 in 1806, he joined the Royal Navy, which ultimately led him to be an early pioneer of the sea story.

He first sailed as a midshipman on HMS Imperieuse under Captain Lord Cochrane, whose character left marks on Marryat's heroes, and who was also the model for C S Forester's *Horatio Hornblower*. Marryat saw active service in the Mediterranean, and participated in many campaigns throughout the world, including the West Indies and North America. By 1815 he had been appointed as Commander, and cruised off St Helena to guard against the escape of Napoleon. Marryat was involved in the suppression of Channel smuggling between 1820 and 1822, and served in the First Burmese War, retiring in 1830 with a Captain's rank.

From 1832 to 1835 Marryat edited the *Metropolitan Magazine*, although he had written his first novel, *The Naval Officer*, in 1829. One of his best-known works, the semi-biographical *Mr Midshipman Easy* was written in 1836, the same year that he lived in Brussels. Between 1837 and 1839 he lived in North America, where he recorded his impressions in *A Diary in America*. From 1839 he lived in London, in the circle of writers such as Charles Dickens, and in the 1840's he turned to write children's books, mainly because they usually sold well. *Masterman Ready* was written in 1841, and other children's books included *The Children of the New Forest*, an historical novel set in the times of Cromwell and the Civil War.

Marryat's last novel was *The Little Savages* which was completed in 1849 by his son, Frank, after his death. His tales of battles, storms, and shipwrecks drew on his own experiences at sea, and although Marryat has been criticised for writing too much and too rapidly, his style has been praised for its lucidity and effectiveness. He married Catherine (nee Shairp) of Linlithgow in Scotland, with whom he had four sons and seven daughters. He was named a Fellow of the Royal Society, particularly in recognition of his inventing a new system of maritime flag signalling.

Dame Rose MACAULAY
Author

11 Hinde Street   **Map Ref 33**

Emilie Rose Macaulay was born in Rugby, the second of seven children to George Campbell Macaulay, assistant master at Rugby School, and Grace Mary (nee Conybeare). For seven years she lived with her family in Genoa, Italy, and received her early education from her parents. When she was thirteen, the family returned to England, she attended Oxford High School, and then went to Somerville College, Oxford, to read modern history. After graduating, she published poems in the *Westminster Gazette* and her first novel, *Abbots Verney*, and by her late twenties she had written six more novels, all sombre and concerned with a woman's life. She did not reach public notice as a novelist until The Lee Shore, which won a competition in 1912, and its success enabled her to buy a flat in London, and she began to move in literary circles.

In 1914 she published *The Making of a Bigot*, a comic novel, which was followed by two collections of poems. During the 1st World War she worked as a land girl and a nurse, and then became a civil servant in the War Office. After the war, Macaulay worked as a publisher's reader, and in the 1920's her talent as a novelist with wit and lightness of touch won her a large following. In 1920 *Potterism* became her first best-seller, and she entered the Bloomsbury set, forming a friendship with Virginia Wolfe. In the 1930's Macaulay published a biography of Milton, and she became increasingly absorbed in the 17th century, resulting in her only historical novel, *They Were Defeated* in 1932. In this period, her writing had an academic emphasis, and she published her best volume of essays *Personal Pleasures*.

During the 2nd World War she served as an ambulance driver, and the 40's and 50's saw her writing travel books. In 1956 she wrote a worldwide best-seller, *The Towers of Trebizond*, bringing her celebrity status. In her later years she wrote prolifically for high profile periodicals such as *The Spectator*. She met Gerald O'Donovan in 1918, a novelist ten years her senior, with whom she formed a close liaison. He was married and they became lovers: he never left his family, but Macaulay's relationship lasted until his death in 1942.

"It is a common delusion that you make things better by talking about them"

"Love's a disease. But curable"

Sir Paolo TOSTI
Musician

12 Mandeville Place　　　　　　　　　　　　　　**Map Ref 34**

Francesco Paolo Tosti was born in Abruzzi, on the east coast of Italy. At the age of 12 he went to Naples to study at the Conservatorio di San Majellam, the successor to the earlier Neapolitan conservatoires, and from where many famous musicians graduated. The accomplished violinist Pinto was his violin tutor, and he had two teachers for composition. Initially Saverio Mercadante, the director of the Collegio di San Sebastian, the leading conservatory in Naples, who wrote 60 operas, 21 masses, ballets and chamber music. Listz believed Mercandante to be Italy's best composer. Tosti was also taught by Carlo Conti, professor and later director of composition at San Pietro a Majella, regarded by Rossini as the most remarkable contrapuntal composer of the time.

Tosti was an exceptional student and he was appointed as 'maestrino' – pupil teacher – but the strain of overwork caused his health to suffer badly, and in 1869 he returned to his hometown to convalesce. During his period of recuperation he wrote two songs, *Non m'ama piu* and *Lamento d'amore*, which later became popular tunes. The next year Tosti went to Rome, where the pianist Giovanni Sgambati, who had been a pupil of Listz and was a key figure of musical life in Rome, recognized his talent and encouraged him.

Princess Margherita of Savoy, who became Queen of Italy between 1878 and 1900 during the reign of her husband Humbert I, attended a concert at the Sala Dante in Rome at which Tosti sang. She appointed him as her singing teacher, and later keeper of the musical archives of the Italian Court. In 1875 he made his first trip to London, where he became popular in fashionable circles, and five years later at the age of 34, he decided to live in London permanently, after Queen Victoria appointed him as the singing teacher for the Royal Family. Tosti gave lessons to Princess Louise of Wales and sang duets with the Queen.

In 1894 Tosti became a teacher of singing at the Royal Academy of Music, Britain's oldest degree-granting musical school. Tosti continued to gain a reputation for his songwriting, and his most popular songs were ballads, of which *Goodbye*, with lyrics by George Whyte-Melville was the most famous, and his songs had lyrics written in English, Italian and French. Tosti lived in London until he was 67, when he returned to Rome for the final three years of his life.

MARYLEBONE EAST W1
CITY OF WESTMINSTER

Hector BERLIOZ 1803-1869 COMPOSER stayed here in 1851

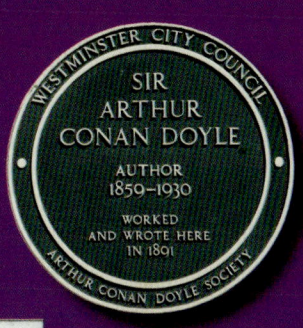

SIR ARTHUR CONAN DOYLE AUTHOR 1850-1930 WORKED AND WROTE HERE IN 1891

EARL ROBERTS (1832-1914) FIELD-MARSHAL LIVED HERE

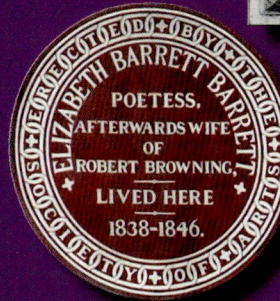

ELIZABETH BARRETT BARRETT POETESS, AFTERWARDS WIFE OF ROBERT BROWNING, LIVED HERE 1838-1846

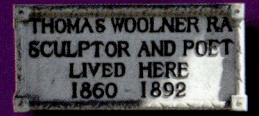

THOMAS WOOLNER RA SCULPTOR AND POET LIVED HERE 1860-1892

MARYLEBONE EAST W1
CITY OF WESTMINSTER

A large part of the Walk was built by the de Walden Estate, which owns, leases, and manages the majority of the 92 acres of real estate in Marylebone from Marylebone High Street in the west to Portland Place in the east, and from Wigmore Street in the south to Marylebone Road in the north. Members of the family own the properties directly or indirectly and the de Walden estate probably contains the greatest concentration of plaques in London.

The area consists of some of London's most beautiful Georgian architecture, but Marylebone is unknown territory, not just for tourists, but also for many Londoners. Yet, this part of Marylebone is an exciting and cosmopolitan mix of the old and the new. The area has its own distinctive style, which attracted the prosperous middle-classes who wanted to be close to the capital's bustling centre. London grew in the late 18th century, and by the time of Richard Horwood's map of 1792-99, the whole area from Oxford Street to the New Road (now Marylebone Road) was covered with houses.

From the outset Cavendish Square set the tone and attracted the wealthy and fashionable. The Scottish architects, the Adams Brothers, were commissioned to design Chandos Street, Mansfield Street and the overall layout and design of Portland Place, which John Nash (1752-1835) - himself responsible for the layout of much of Regency London - called "the most magnificent street in London". The area has attracted people who understand attractive buildings, including many artists and architects, and there are plaques commemorating six of them in this walk, it contains a number of the most famous streets in the capital, and large and stylish houses were built in Harley Street and Wimpole Street.

St Peters Church tower in Vere Street

A florists in Crawford Street

In addition to the people who lived on this Walk who are remembered with a plaque, there are a number of others who are not so commemorated. Edward Gibbon wrote much of The Decline and Fall of the Roman Empire when living at number 7 Bentinck Street in the 1770's, and Charles Dickens lived at number 18 whilst working as a court reporter in the 1830's. The Cambridge spies, Guy Burgess and Anthony Blunt shared a flat in the street.

During the latter part of the nineteenth century doctors began to move into Harley Street, a trend given additional impetus when The Medical Society of London moved to Chandos Street in 1872 and the Royal Society of Medicine to Wimpole Street in 1912. Since then, the number of doctors in and around Harley Street has spiralled – from about 20 in 1860, to almost 200 by 1914, and by the time the national Health Service was established in 1948 there were around 1500, and contrary to expectation the figure has never fallen.

Schools and educational institutions have become another particular feature of the area. The Regent Polytechnic Institute, now part of the University of Westminster, was founded in Regent Street in 1839. Queen's College, Harley Street, was the first college in the country for the higher education of women in 1848. More recently two schools have opened in Portland Place.

To mark the birth of Lord Byron in 1788, the Royal Society of Arts erected London's first commemorative plaque in 1867 south of Cavendish Square at 24 Holles Street, which was sadly demolished. Cavendish Square was one of several to be laid out during the 18th century: planted with forest trees and shrubs, it was the first development on the 2nd Earl of Oxford's estate and named for his wife, Henrietta Cavendish-Hollace. The square became one of the most fashionable in London, made famous from references by Charles Dickens in his books *Nicholas Nickleby, Little Dorrit* and *Barnaby Rudge*. Today the garden is enjoyed by the public throughout the year.

Quintin Hogg Statue in Cavendish Square

West of Cavendish Square down Henrietta Place is St Peter's Church, which today is the base for The London Institute for Contemporary Christianity. It was built by the Portland Estate from a design by James Gibbs, and was originally known as the Oxford Chapel. It was built in what has been described as the 'mock-heroic classical revival style'. At the east end of Hinde Street is the James Weir designed Hinde Street Methodist Church, which dates from 1887, and has the same two-storeyed portico as St Paul's Cathedral.

Wigmore Hall

Wigmore Hall in Wigmore Street was originally called the Bechstein Hall, situated as it is next door to where the German piano manufacturer had a showroom. It was designed by Thomas Collcutt, who was also the architect of the Savoy Hotel in the Strand. The Hall is a leading international recital venue, and holds over 400 events a year, including classic song, early music, chamber music and jazz.

Hinde Street Church

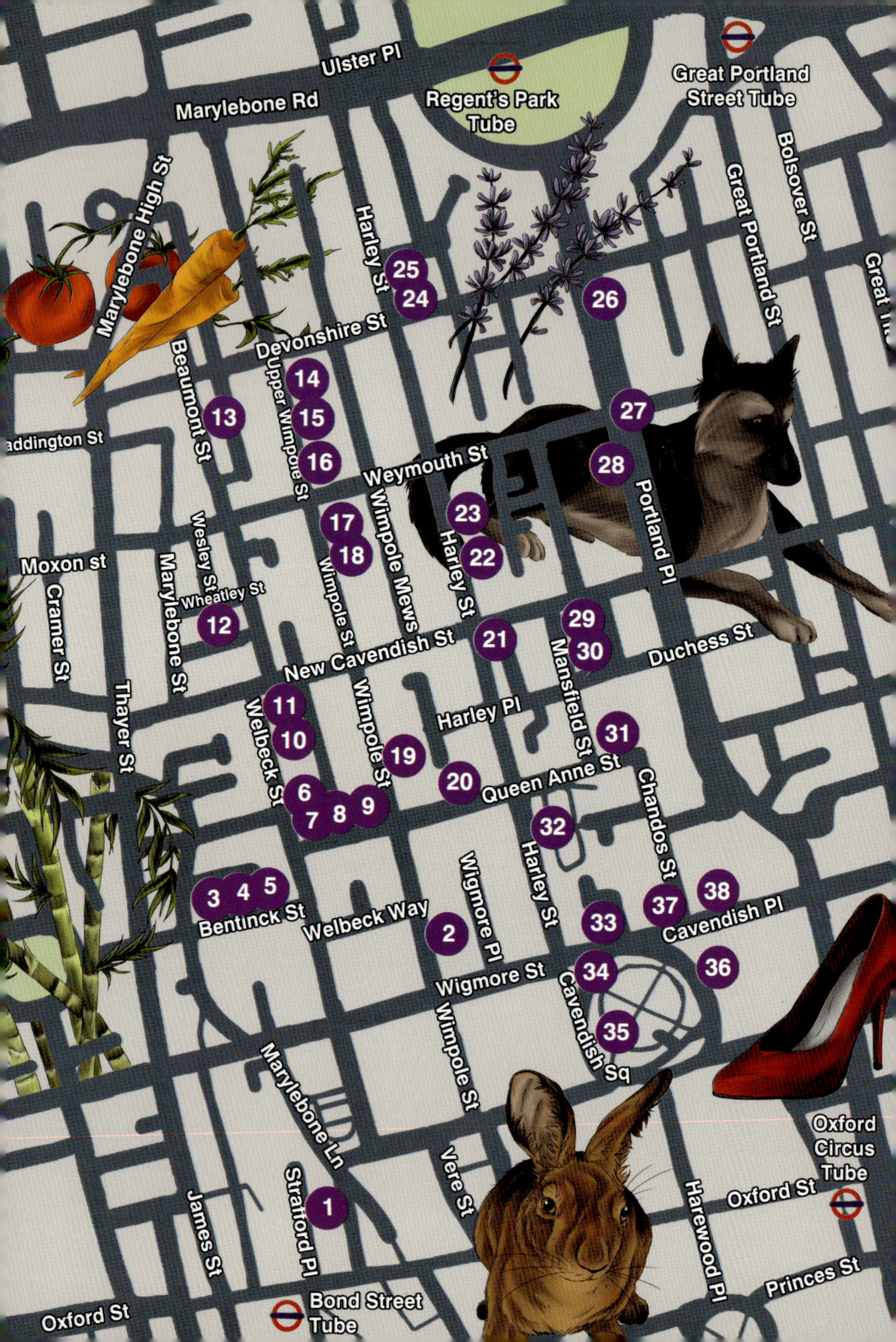

Ulster Pl
Marylebone Rd
Regent's Park Tube
Great Portland Street Tube
Bolsover St
Great Portland St
Marylebone High St
Harley St
Devonshire St
Beaumont St
Upper Wimpole St
addington St
Weymouth St
Portland Pl
Wimpole Mews
Harley St
Moxon st
Cramer St
Wesley St
Wheatley St
Marylebone St
Wimpole St
New Cavendish St
Duchess St
Mansfield St
Thayer St
Welbeck St
Harley Pl
Wimpole St
Queen Anne St
Chandos St
Harley St
Wigmore Pl
Bentinck St
Welbeck Way
Cavendish Pl
Wigmore St
Cavendish Sq
Wimpole St
Marylebone Ln
Oxford Circus Tube
Vere St
Stratford Pl
James St
Harewood Pl
Oxford St
Princes St
Oxford St
Bond Street Tube
1
2
3
4
5
6
7
8
9
10
11
12
13
14
15
16
17
18
19
20
21
22
23
24
25
26
27
28
29
30
31
32
33
34
35
36
37
38

MARYLEBONE EAST WALK GUIDE

Page	Ref	Person	Place
136	1	Martin VAN BUREN	7 Stratford Place
137	2	Sir Frederick TREVES	6 Wimpole Street
138	3	James SMITHSON	9 Bentinck Street
139	4	Sir James MACKENZIE	17 Bentinck Street
140	5	Edward GIBBON	7 Bentinck Street
141	6	Thomas YOUNG	48 Welbeck Street
142	7	Sir Patrick MANSON	50 Welbeck Street
143	8	Hector BERLIOZ	58 Queen Anne Street
144	9	Stephen PEARCE	54 Queen Anne Street
145	10	Thomas WOOLNER	29 Welbeck Street
146	11	Victor WEISZ	35 Welbeck Street
147	12	Charles WESLEY	1 Wheatley Street
148	13	John GREEN	5 Beaumont Street
149	14	Sir John MILSOM REES	18 Upper Wimpole Street
150	15	Ethel BEDFORD-FENWICK	20 Upper Wimpole Street
151	16	Sir Arthur Conan DOYLE	2 Upper Wimpole Street
152	17	Elizabeth BARRETT BROWNING	50 Wimpole Street
153	18	Evelyn BARING (1st Earl of Cromer)	36 Wimpole Street
154	19	Henry HALLAM	67 Wimpole Street
155	20	Sir George STILL	28 Queen Anne Street
156	21	Sir Stewart DUKE-ELDER	63 Harley Street
157	22	Sir Charles LYELL	73 Harley Street
157	22	William Ewart GLADSTONE	73 Harley Street
158	23	George BODLEY	109 Harley Street
159	24	Sir Arthur PINERO	115a Harley Street
160	25	Lionel LOGUE	146 Harley Street
161	26	Frances BURNETT	63 Portland Place
162	27	Field Marshall Earl ROBERTS	47 Portland Place
163	28	General Thomas GAGE	41 Portland Place
164	29	General Charles STANHOPE	20 Mansfield Street
165	30	John PEARSON	13 Mansfield Street
166	30	Sir Edwin LUTYENS	13 Mansfield Street
167	31	Sir Robert MAYER	2 Mansfield Street
168	32	Dr Grantly DICK-READ	25 Harley Street
169	33	Sir Jonathan HUTCHINSON	15 Cavendish Square
170	34	Ronald ROSS	18 Cavendish Square
171	35	H H ASQUITH	20 Cavendish Square
172	36	Quintin HOGG	5 Cavendish Square
173	37	G.E. STREET	14 Cavendish Place
174	38	Dr Joseph CLOVER	3 Cavendish Place

Distance : 2.2 miles (3.5 Km)
Starting Point: Bond Street
Finish Point: Oxford Circus
                  Underground Stations

Jubilee	Central
Victoria	Central
	Bakerloo

Martin VAN BUREN
President of the United States of America

7 Stratford Place   **Map Ref 1**

MARTIN VAN BUREN
1782 – 1862
Eighth U.S. President lived here
GREATER LONDON COUNCIL

Martin Van Buren was born in the village of Kinderhook, New York, to Abraham Van Buren a farmer and tavern-keeper, and Maria Hoes Van Alen, who was of Dutch ancestry. He had two brothers and a sister, and two half-brothers and a half-sister from his mother's first marriage. He became the first President born a citizen of the United States of America, and the only President who spoke English as a second language. Van Buren received a very basic education, and at 14 studied law at a local practice, moved to New York City for a year, and was called to the bar at 21. As a young lawyer, he became involved in New York politics and as a leader of the 'Albany Regency', he shrewdly dispensed public offices in a way that was calculated to bring votes. In 1821 he was elected a U.S. Senator.

He was a principal supporter of Andrew Jackson, and in 1827 after just two months as Governor of New York, President Jackson rewarded Van Buren by appointing him as Secretary of State. The Cabinet Members appointed by Vice-President John C Calhoun began to demonstrate only secondary loyalty to Jackson, and Van Buren emerged as the President's most trusted adviser. The rift in the Cabinet became serious because of Jackson's differences with Calhoun, Van Buren suggested a way out of the impasse – he and Secretary of War resigned, so that Calhoun would also resign. Jackson appointed a new Cabinet in 1831 and rewarded Van Buren by appointing him Minister to Great Britain. After five months in post in London, he learned that his nomination had been rejected, with Vice President Calhoun, as President of the Senate, casting the deciding vote, thus making a martyr of Van Buren. After a brief tour of Europe, he was elected as Vice President at the Democrat's Convention in 1832, and won the Presidency in 1836.

In 1837 panic began in the economy, with hundreds of banks and businesses failing, and for the duration of Van Buren's Presidency, the United States was wracked with the worst depression in its history. His remedy was to continue Jackson's deflationary policies, which only deepened and prolonged the depression. The opposition Whig party defeated him in 1840 for re-election, and William Henry Harrison became the ninth President. Van Buren had married his childhood sweetheart cousin, Hannah Hoes, in 1807, with whom he had four children, and although she died at 35, he never remarried.

Sir Frederick TREVES
Surgeon

6 Wimpole Street　　　　　　　　　　　　　　　　　　　　**Map Ref   2**

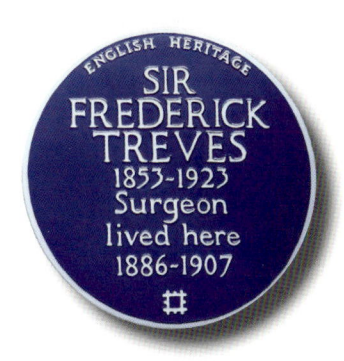

Frederick Treves was born in Dorchester, Dorset, the son of William, an upholsterer, and Jane (nee Knight). He attended school run by the Dorset dialect poet, William Barnes, followed by Merchant Taylors and then Suffolk Street, London. He left in 1871 and attended University College London before receiving medical education at the London School of Medicine. In 1879 he became a surgical registrar and assistant surgeon at the London Hospital, and for a period was a lecturer of practical anatomy and demonstrator in anatomy, before becoming surgeon and head of the school of anatomy in 1883. In 1885 Treves was appointed Professor of Anatomy at the Royal College of Surgeons, and three years later performed the first appendectomy in England. He was myopic and generally wore glasses, but when operating he would remove them and operate with his head close to the wound.

Treves' fame rests upon his association with Joseph Merrick, who is better known as the 'Elephant Man'. He was apparently normal until the age of five, when he began to show signs of a strange disorder that caused overgrowths over much of his skin and bone surfaces. His head became enormous, the 3 feet circumference was that of a man's waist. Treves first saw Merrick being exhibited as a sideshow freak in 1884, with a sign in front of him stating 'The Deadly Fruit of Original Sin'. He was appalled at the degradation of this poor deformed creature, and led Treves to befriend Merrick and took him to the London Hospital, where he lived until his death in 1890.

During the Second Boer War that began in 1899, Treves volunteered to work at a field hospital in South Africa treating the wounded: he related his experiences in The Tale of a Field Hospital, a series of articles written for the British Medical Journal. Upon his return, King Edward VII appointed him as Serjeant Surgeon, a medical officer in the Royal Household, and before he performed an appendectomy on the King in 1902 - still a radical operation – he was honoured with a baronetcy.

He married Ann Elizabeth Mason in 1877, with whom he had two daughters. Treves retired from medical practice to become an author, and in addition to medical works he wrote several travel books, including a highly popular guide to his native Dorset. He was the first President of the Society of Dorset Men, and was a founder of the British Red Cross, part of the worldwide impartial humanitarian organization. In 1918 he moved to Switzerland, where he continued to write and pursued his love of photography.

James SMITHSON
Scientist

9 Bentinck Street   Map Ref 3

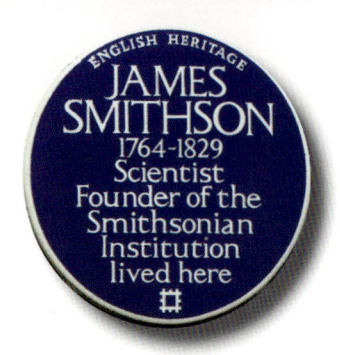

James Smithson was born in Paris, France, the illegitimate son of Sir Hugh Smithson, 4th Baronet of Stanwick, North Yorkshire, and his mistress, Elizabeth Hungerford Keate. She was the widow of John Macie, and young James was originally known as Jacques Louis Macie. He is best known for the bequest in his will, that led to the creation of the Smithsonian Institution in America, which is now world's largest museum complex and research organization.

He was educated in England, and attended university at Pembroke College, Oxford. After graduating in 1782, under the name of James Lewis Macie, he was elected the youngest Fellow of the Royal Society. Smithson became a mineralogist and chemist, and dedicated his life to investigating the natural world, seeking crystals and minerals across Europe, on which he could perform experiments to discover and classify their elemental properties. Wherever he went he made minute observations on the climate, physical features and geographical structure of the localities he visited, the characteristics of their minerals and the methods employed in mining and smelting ores.

Smithson presented his first paper to the Royal Society in 1791 entitled *An Account of some Chemical Experiments on Tabasheer,* (an ingredient used in traditional Chinese medicines), and over the next sixteen years presented a further eight papers on minerals. He wrote articles for scientific journals, and his studies covered a range of subjects as diverse as the chemical content of a teardrop and an improved method of making coffee.

During his life, Smithson was a shrewd investor and amassed a fortune. He died in 1829, and in his will he left all of his wealth to his brother's son, Henry Dickinson, whom he had 'encouraged' to change his surname to Hungerford, one of his mother's names. The will determined that if his nephew died without children, the money would go to "the United States of America, to found at Washington an establishment for the increase and diffusion of knowledge among men". Henry died in 1835 without issue, and the United States Congress accepted Smithson's bequest in 1836. Smithson had never been to the United States, and the motives behind his gift of $500,000 remain mysterious. Some have suggested that it was motivated in part by revenge against the rigidity of British society, which had denied Smithson the right to use his father's name.

Sir James MACKENZIE
Cardiologist

17 Bentinck Street **Map Ref 4**

SIR JAMES MACKENZIE F.R.S. 1853–1925 PHYSICIAN lived and worked here 1907–1911

James Mackenzie was born in Scone, Scotland, the third child and second son of a tenant farmer. He attended the local primary school, and at 12 went to Perth Academy, but left after three years to serve an apprenticeship as a dispensing chemist for four years. After working as an assistant chemist in Glasgow for a year, he decided to study medicine. He was a pioneer in the study of arrhythmias, which determines how effectively the heart pumps blood.

After completing his degree at Edinburgh University in 1878 he worked as a locum in County Durham, took a year's resident post at Edinburgh Royal Infirmary, before joining a general practice in Burnley, Lancashire. Whilst there, he had over fifty papers published, and although many were on cardiology, he also wrote on neurology and pain mechanisms. He managed to find the time to do an immense amount of research, and he was driven to advance his understanding of disease. At the age of 49, *The Study of the Pulse* was published, after twenty-three years in general practice. By this time he had become the world clinical authority on heart disease.

He left Burnley for London in 1907 and set-up as a consulting physician, and joined the West End Hospital for nervous disease, and was appointed to the staff of Mount Vernon Hospital. His second book, *Diseases of the Heart* was published in 1908, and the following year he rented consulting rooms in Harley Street and became very busy with private patients. He was elected a fellow of the Royal College of Physicians in 1909, and was appointed lecturer in cardiac research in 1911. His third book, *Symptoms and Their Interpretation*, was published in 1909, and in 1913 he was appointed Physician-in-Charge of the new cardiac department and involved in setting-up a military cardiac department at Mount Vernon Hospital. In 1916 he was elected a Fellow of the Royal Society.

To all intents he had made it, being made a consultant at the London Hospital, and doing well financially. It was a surprise when, at 64, he moved to St Andrews in Scotland to establish an institute for research in general practice. He had married Frances Jackson in 1883, with whom he had two daughters, and in his spare time, he studied Greek and German, played golf and started to write a novel.

Edward GIBBON
Historian

7 Bentinck Street Map Ref 5

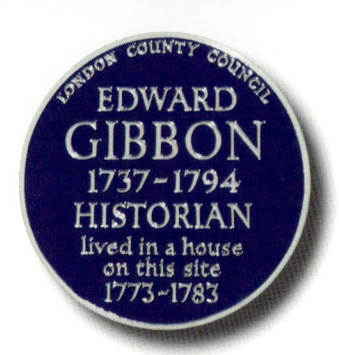

Blue plaque: London County Council — EDWARD GIBBON 1737–1794 HISTORIAN lived in a house on this site 1773–1783

Edward Gibbon was born in Putney, now a suburb to the west of London into a prosperous family. His father was a wealthy Tory Member of Parliament, who inherited a substantial estate from Edward's grandfather. He had six siblings, all of whom died in infancy, and he was left in the care of an aunt. At the age of nine he went to Dr Woddeson's school in Kingston-on-Thames, before boarding at Westminster School, and then going up to Magdalen College, Oxford.

In 1753 Gibbon was sent to Lausanne in Switzerland after being expelled from university for converting to Roman Catholicism. He boarded with a Calvinist pastor and scholar, who convinced Gibbon to rejoin the Anglican faith. In Lausanne he fell in love, but his father ended the relationship, and he remained unmarried for the rest of his life. After five years, he returned to England and from 1759 to 1762 held a commission in the Hampshire militia, reaching the rank of Colonel.

In 1761 he published his first book, Essai sur L'etude de la Literature, and in 1763 he set-off on the Grand Tour of continental Europe, visiting Rome, which inspired him to write the history of the city from the death of Marcus Aurelius, a Roman Emperor from the second century, to the year 1453. Gibbons father died in 1770, and left him financially well provided, and he was able to settle in London to proceed with his great work.

Between 1774 and 1783 Gibbon sat in the House of Commons as the MP for Liskeard in Cornwall, and became a Lord Commissioner of Trade and Plantations, partly because he was considered a nuisance as a politician! Over the twelve years from 1776 to 1788, Gibbon published in six volumes, what would become his life's major achievement, *The History of the Decline and Fall of the Roman Empire*. The book was a bestseller, and offered the reading public a vivid narrative of the past, instead of an antiquarian picture. Gibbon had finished the last two volumes in Lausanne, and returned to London to celebrate its publication. He divided his later years between Switzerland and England, spending considerable time with his lifelong friend, Lord Sheffield. Gibbon's work influenced many writers including Churchill and Evelyn Waugh.

> "I devoured Gibbon....I rode triumphantly through it from end to end".   **Winston Churchill**

Thomas YOUNG
Physician

48 Welbeck Street Map Ref 6

THOMAS YOUNG 1773 - 1829 MAN OF SCIENCE lived here — London County Council plaque

Thomas Young was born into a Quaker family in Milverton, Somerset, the youngest of ten children. He was a boy prodigy, and showed an amazing capacity for learning from an early age – he had read the Bible through, twice, by the age of four, and was fluent in Greek and Latin by the age of fourteen. He has been described as Britain's greatest ever polymath, and his recent biography by Robinson describes him as "the last man who knew everything".

Young began to study medicine at St Bartholomew's Hospital in London in 1792, but left in 1794 to continue his studies in Edinburgh, and from there travelled to Gottingen in Germany, where he was awarded a Doctor of Physics degree in 1796. He produced a paper in 1793 on the mechanism of accommodation of focus in the human eye, which resulted in his uncle, the prominent physician Dr Brocklesby, proposing him for a fellowship of the Royal Society at the age of twenty-one.

In 1797 Young moved to Emmanuel College, Cambridge, where he added a medical degree, and taught and began to research scientific matters outside the scope of medicine. Having received a substantial inheritance on the death of his uncle, he moved to London in 1799 and established himself as a physician at 48 Welbeck Street. His medical practice was not particularly successful, but Young maintained that medicine was his primary occupation, and published papers anonymously to avoid damaging his reputation as a physician. He was appointed Professor of Natural Philosophy at the Royal Institution in 1801, and besides his 91 lectures that were later published, he researched a wide variety of topics in both theoretical and applied science.

In 1802, he was appointed foreign secretary of the Royal Society, in 1811 became physician to St George's Hospital, and in 1814 he served on the committee to examine the introduction of gas into London. Despite the impact of his work on medical scholarship, he is perhaps best known for his groundbreaking work in a wide-ranging variety of other fields: - his Wave Theory of Light (in which he disproved Newton's light particle theory); Young's Modulus relating to the characterisation of elasticity; his Vision and Colour Theory; his translations and the mastery of numerous languages; a new way of tuning musical instruments; and he was one of the first to try and decipher Egyptian hieroglyphics.

"A man eminent in almost every department of human learning."
Inscribed on Young's monument in Westminster Abbey

Sir Patrick MANSON
Physician

50 Welbeck Street   **Map Ref 7**

Blue plaque: GREATER LONDON COUNCIL — SIR PATRICK MANSON 1844-1922 Father of Modern Tropical Medicine lived here

Patrick Manson was the second son of John Manson and Elizabeth (nee Blakie) in Oldmeldrum, Aberdeenshire, Scotland. He studied medicine at Aberdeen University, where he obtained a Master of Surgery and Medical Doctorate. His interest in tropical parasites made him a pioneer in the founding of the specialty of tropical medicine. His first medical appointment was as assistant medical officer at Durham County Mental Asylum.

Manson's older brother worked in Shanghai and persuaded him to travel to China, and in 1866 he was appointed as medical officer for the Chinese Customs in Formosa (Taiwan). It was Manson's responsibility to inspect ships and treat crews, which allowed him the opportunity to observe tropical diseases. At the end of 1870 he was caught in the political dispute between China and Japan, and on the British Consul's advice he left Formosa to settle in Xiamen, on China's south coast. Here he worked at the Baptist Missionary Hospital and ran a private practice, which enabled him to continue his observation of elephantiasis, leprosy and beriberi.

Manson returned to England for a year in 1874 and after extensive research he developed his own theories of mosquito transmission. Back in China, he continued his research and discovered that mosquitoes spread the agent that causes malaria, that they carry filariasis, and that the embryonic filariae only appear in the patient's blood stream at night when mosquitoes feed. Manson moved to Hong Kong in 1883, and founded the first western-style medical school. He continued his research and clinical work, until the depreciation of the Chinese dollar in 1890 and the subsequent failure of his Chinese investments, and returned to work at the Seamen's Hospital, London. Here there were many examples of tropical diseases and from 1894 along with his colleague, Ronald Ross, Manson further examined the mosquito-malaria theory.

He advocated specialized training for doctors planning to work in the tropics, and helped to set-up the world's first school of tropical medicine in Liverpool. After being appointed Medical Advisor to the Colonial Office, he persuaded the Colonial Secretary, Joseph Chamberlain, to support a London School of Tropical Medicine, which opened in 1899, where he taught for fifteen years. Manson published his *Manual of Tropical Diseases* in 1898, and he helped found the Royal Society of Tropical Medicine in 1907, serving as its first president. He had married Henrietta Isabella Thurbun in 1876, with whom he had four children. He retired in 1912 to fish in Ireland but returned to London at the beginning of the 1st World War.

Hector BERLIOZ
Composer

58 Queen Anne Street **Map Ref 8**

Louis-Hector Berlioz was born near Lyon in France, one of six children to Louis, a doctor, and Marie-Antoinette-Josephine. He was a French Romantic composer, best known for his composition *Symphonie Fantastique*. After the closure of a local seminary, his father took charge of his education, and he began studying music at the age of 12. His father discouraged his learning the piano, preferring instead to push him in the direction of the guitar, flageolet and flute.

At the age of 18, Berlioz went to Paris to read medicine, but preferred to pursue his interest in music. He was introduced to Le Sueur, a Professor at the Paris Conservatoire, who encouraged his composing. After receiving a Bachelor in Physical Sciences, he abandoned his medical studies, and devoted himself to learning more about music and writing.

Berlioz attended the Conservatoire in 1826 to study composition, and in order to fund his studies, he became a chorus singer in the theatre. He set himself the target of winning the 'Prix de Rome' for composition, which he achieved in 1830 after a number of disappointments. The next year he moved to Rome, where he continued his studies for two years, following which he spent the years from 1832 to 1842 back in Paris, writing many of his most popular compositions, including *Romeo et Juliette*.

From 1842 to 1848, Berlioz followed his musical career abroad, playing in cities across Belgium and Germany, culminating in a seven-month visit to London, where he became the musical director at the Theatre Royal, Drury Lane. He returned to Paris, where he became head librarian at the Conservatoire, but in 1851 he was in London again, when he was sent by the French Government as part of an international commission, examining musical instruments at the Great Exhibition.

Berlioz took England seriously as one of the major musical centres of Europe, where he was able to develop his love of Shakespeare. He continued to return to London from 1852 to 1854 to conduct, and he also regularly toured Italy and Germany, where he had be-friended Listz. He married twice, firstly to the actress Harriet Smithson, and then to Marie Recio, with whom he lived for 14 years before marrying her in 1854. He was made an *Officier de la Legion d'honneur*, and left a legacy of orchestral works and over 50 songs.

Stephen PEARCE
Artist

54 Queen Anne Street   **Map Ref   9**

STEPHEN PEARCE
1819 - 1904
Portrait and Equestrian Painter
Lived Here
1856 - 1884

Stephen Pearce was born in Charing Cross, London to Stephen Pearce, and his wife Ann (nee Whittington). Pearce Senior was an official in the Department of the Master of the Horse, which was the third most important office at the Royal Court, responsible for everything to do with the Monarch's stables, races, and breeding of horses. The family lived at the Royal Mews, and it was perhaps no wonder that Pearce Junior took an interest in horses, and was to become an equestrian painter.

In 1840 Pearce attended the School of Drawing and Painting run by Henry Sass, the London-born son of a Russian father, which gave him sufficient competence to be admitted to the Royal Academy Schools the same year. There he became a pupil of Sir Martin Shee, who was born in Dublin of an old Catholic family, and who was a prominent portrait painter and sometime President of the Royal Academy. From 1842 he acted as a secretary to the Irish novelist Charles Lever, who had originally taken a degree in medicine from Trinity College, Dublin. To continue his artistic training, he left Lever in 1846 and travelled to Italy.

Pearce exhibited his first work at the Royal Academy in 1839, a portrait of *Tartar,* one of his favourite horses in Queen Victoria's stables. This painting established the theme of much of his future work, and he became known for his equestrian portraits, including many paintings of the Queen's horses. Sir John Franklin was a British Royal Navy officer and Arctic explorer, who had mapped two thirds of the North American coastline and became Governor of Tasmania: Colonel John Barrow, keeper of the Admiralty records, commissioned his friend Pearce to paint *The Arctic Council Discussing a Plan of Search for Sir John Franklin.* The work was seen and admired by Queen Victoria and Prince Albert, which helped to enhance his reputation as a portrait painter. Lady Franklin commissioned Pearce to paint the portraits of other Arctic explorers, all of which are now at the National Portrait Gallery in London.

Pearce married Matilda Jane Cheswright in 1858, and they had five sons. Throughout his career he regularly exhibited at the Royal Academy, the British Institution and the Grosvenor Gallery. A year before he died, Pearce published his autobiography *Memories of the Past.*

Thomas WOOLNER
Sculptor and Poet

29 Welbeck Street **Map Ref 10**

THOMAS WOOLNER RA
SCULPTOR AND POET
LIVED HERE
1860 - 1892

Thomas Woolner (1825 – 1892) was born in Hadleigh in Suffolk. At the age of 13 he left for London and studied sculpture with William Behnes, the British-born son of a Hanoverian piano-maker, who later became 'Sculptor in Ordinary' to Queen Victoria. In 1842 he joined the Royal Academy Schools, and by the age of 18 was exhibiting work at the Academy.

In 1848 he was one of the founders of the Pre-Raphaelite Brotherhood, seven artists whose goal was to develop a 'natural' style of art, and throw away the rules drummed into students' heads. Woolner made his name with forceful portrait busts and medallions, but was unable to make a living, and left for Australia in 1854 to seek a wealthier life. He was very popular in Australia, where he spent three years, specialising in portrait medallions. He was able to return to England in 1857 with an enhanced reputation, and he became an art-dealer and the portrait-sculptor-of-choice to the great and good. Amongst others, he did poets Tennyson and Wordsworth, politicians Palmerston and Gladstone, authors Dickens and Kingsley, and heroes Captain Cook and Sir Stamford Raffles.

Cornhill Magazine, a literary journal edited by William Thackeray, commented "Woolner's busts…are what may be called a new style, they purport to represent the actual man, without any smoothing over or idealising. We have no objection to the style – the more realistic the better. But we object to Mr Woolner's rendering of it…" A potentially more damaging criticism was of his bust of Gladstone, where Mrs Gladstone thought he had given the portrait " a high forehead, instead of his actual wide but rather low one".

In London, Woolner has a wealth of pieces, including St Paul's Cathedral (Edwin Landseer, the animal painter), Westminster Abbey (Tennyson), Victoria Embankment Gardens (John Stuart Mill), and Parliament Square (Palmerston). His work can be seen in Edinburgh (Carlyle), Birmingham (Queen Victoria), Manchester (Bacon), and further afield in Singapore (Sir Stamford Raffles) and Sydney, Australia (Captain Cook).

He counted amongst his friends A L Tennyson, and he was a poet of some note himself, with his early poem *My Beautiful Lady* being much admired. His speculation about the human anatomy impressed Charles Darwin, and he was elected in 1875 a member of the Royal Academy, and appointed Professor of Sculpture in 1877.

Victor WEISZ
Cartoonist

35 Welbeck Street Map Ref 11

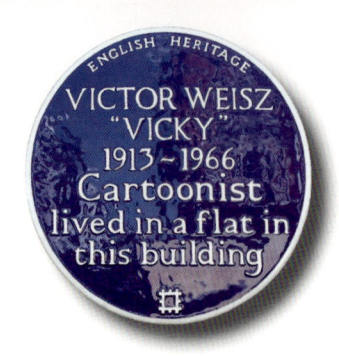

Victor Weisz was born in Berlin, East Germany to Hungarian-Jewish parents. He studied with the painter Tennstedt from the age of eleven, and when his father, who had been a jeweller and goldsmith, committed suicide when he was fifteen, he began drawing caricatures freelance.

He joined the graphics department of the radical anti-Hitler magazine 12 Uhr Blatt, and by the age of sixteen was its sports and theatre cartoonist. He produced his first anti-Nazi cartoon in 1929, but four years later the paper was taken over by the Nazis, in the same year that Hitler was sworn in as Chancellor. Weisz became a marked man, and fled to London with the Gestapo at his heels in 1935, and it is believed that if he had not had an Hungarian passport he would not have got away.

Weisz arrived in London unable to speak a word of English, but he fortunately met and made friends with Gerald Barry, who was the Editor of the *News Chronicle* from 1936. He helped him to learn English, and told Weisz that if he were to become a successful cartoonist, he would need to take a crash-course in English humour. The reading list was extensive (exhaustive?) and included Shakespeare, Edward Lear, Alice in Wonderland, Just William, Jeeves, Punch magazines…and he listened to Tommy Handley's ITMA, watched George Formby and Will Hay films, Gilbert and Sullivan operas..

His first work in London was drawing caricatures and cartoons for many of the leading newspapers including the *Daily Mail*, the *Daily Telegraph* and the *Daily Express*. In 1939 he began working for the pro-Liberal *News Chronicle*, and joined as their political cartoonist two years later, using the pseudonym 'Vicky'. In 1947 he became a British citizen. He fell out with the new editor, and in 1954 joined the *Daily Mirror*, but regretted the move complaining "nobody reads the Daily Mirror". In 1958 he joined the *Evening Standard*, where his most memorable character was 'Supermac', a parody of Prime Minister Macmillan.

"He'd have been horrified to meet a cloth-capped worker"
James Cameron

Weisz was a passionate socialist, but James Cameron, the respected journalist, realised that Weisz's socialism was largely theoretical – "he'd have been horrified to meet a cloth-capped worker". He angered a lot of people, but didn't influence people. In 1965 he admitted to being desperate about his "ideas drying up", which caused him to suffer from depression, and in 1966 he committed suicide.

Charles WESLEY
Clergyman and Composer

1 Wheatley Street **Map Ref 12**

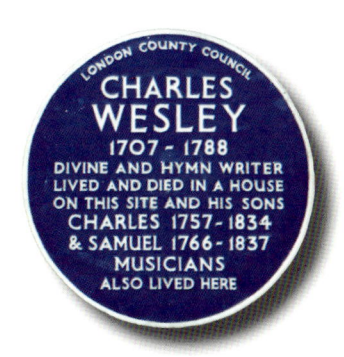

Charles Wesley was born in Epworth, Lincolnshire to Anglican clergyman and poet, Rev. Samuel Wesley, and Susanna, (nee Annesley). He was the youngest of nineteen children, of whom ten survived their infancy. Wesley is known as the founder of the Methodist arm of the Christian Church, and for being a prolific writer of hymns.

For the first eight years of his life he was under the tuition of his mother, and then obtained a scholarship to attend Westminster School, London, where his eldest brother John was one of the teachers. He went up to Christ Church College, Oxford, where he achieved a Master's degree in classical languages and literature, and it was during this time that he began to observe the method of study, which ultimately lead to his creating the Methodist religious denomination.

After university he was ordained as a priest in the Church of England, and at the age of 28 he accompanied brother John as a missionary to the State of Georgia in America. Upon his return, he toured the United Kingdom extensively as an evangelical preacher, until he settled in London where he continued to preach for the rest of his life.

Wesley began to write hymns in his twenties, and his first volume was published in 1739. He continued to write hymns for the rest of his life, and many of the 6000 he composed are still sung today, including Love Divine, All Loves Excelling, often sung at weddings, Christ the Lord is Risen Today at Easter, and Hark! the Herald Angels Sing, a favourite Christmas Carol. Many of his compositions were often suggested by incidents in his personal history, and "See How Great A Flame aspires" was written after preaching to Newcastle colliers, and was suggested by the coal furnaces and burning pit-heaps.

It was not until he was 42 that Wesley married, when he met Sarah whilst on his travels, the daughter of Marmaduke Gwynne, a wealthy Welsh magistrate. The couple had eight children, and Sarah proved to be a constant support throughout his ministry, as she accompanied him on his evangelical journeys.

John GREEN
Historian

5 Beaumont Street **Map Ref 13**

Plaque text: LONDON COUNTY COUNCIL / JOHN RICHARD GREEN / 1837-1883 / HISTORIAN / lived in a house on this site 1869-1876

John Richard Green was born in Oxford, the son of a tradesman, and he had all his education in Oxford, first at Magdalen College School and then at Jesus College, where he obtained an open scholarship. On leaving university, he took holy orders in 1860, and after several years working in a string of London parishes, he became the vicar at St Philip's in Stepney, east London. He was an eloquent preacher and he worked conscientiously with his poor parishioners. At the same time he began to write for the *Saturday Review*, a weekly London newspaper that included articles covering politics, literature, science and the arts.

He began to disagree with the teaching of the Church of England, and with his health deteriorating, he abandoned clerical life and devoted himself to the study of history. In 1868 he took the post of librarian at Lambeth in London, and began to write, which resulted in the publication of his *Short History of the English People* in 1874. This virtually unknown former clergyman sold the rights of this school textbook to Macmillan for £350, a generous sum for a work that was expected to sell a few thousand copies. To everyone's amazement it sold 32,000 in the first year, and half a million copies thereafter.

This publishing phenomenon was a breakthrough in histiography, and whereas earlier histories had focused on kings and statutes, Green's work revolved round the common people, and his chief aim was to depict the progressive life of the English people rather than write a political history of the English state. He changed the writing of history from elites, to a broader history of society and cultural change. He was one of the last great amateurs, at a time when academic specialists were dominating the field.

His style was described as 'bright', and thousands of readers were able to enjoy reading about the history of their own people. His later histories, *The Making of England* (1882) and *The Conquest of England* (1883) were more soberly written than his earlier books, and are valuable contributions to historical knowledge. In 1877 he had married Alice Stopford, and she helped him to complete his books as his health began to deteriorate, as well as writing her own history books.

Sir John MILSOM REES
Laryngologist
18 Upper Wimpole Street   Map Ref 14

John Milsom Rees was born in Neath, South Wales, the son of John Rees. He was a Welsh surgeon and specialist in laryngology. Following schooling in Wales, he studied medicine at St Bartholomew's Hospital in London, and after qualifying as a Fellow of the Royal College of Surgeons at Edinburgh University, he was appointed as an Ear, Nose and Throat surgeon at Mount Vernon Hospital, in Tottenham, north London.

He was appointed to the Royal Household as consultant laryngologist in 1911, and to the Royal Family in 1915, holding the post throughout King George V's reign until 1936. Milsom Rees was also laryngologist to Queen Alexandra and the Queen of Norway, and began his private practice from Upper Wimpole Street in 1914 through to 1939.

The Guildhall School of Music, and the Royal Opera House, Covent Garden employed Milsom Rees as a consultant. He treated many famous opera singers, including Joan Sutherland and invented the 'Melba Spray', named after Nellie Melba, the Australian soprano. He wrote numerous books, including *Care of the Vocal Chords in Singers and Speakers* in 1937. He was associated with many of the leading London teaching hospitals as a Vice President or Governor, and he was a member of the Court of the University of Wales.

Apart from his remarkable success in professional spheres, Milsom Rees also achieved great distinction in many other fields. As a student, he was an excellent cricketer, boxer and – naturally for a Welshman – rugby player. He was a first-class golfer of international standard, and he founded the Medical Golfing Society.

He was very fond of big game hunting, and accounts of his visits to Africa reveal his multifarious interests. His expert surgical craftsmanship was much in demand from local celebrities and native chieftains. He acquired extensive business interests in Africa, including coffee estates in Tanganyika and salt mines in Mozambique.

He married Eleanor, the daughter of William Jones of Finchley in north London, with whom he had a son and a daughter. Milsom Rees left Upper Wimpole Street at the beginning of the 2nd World War, and retired to Broadstairs in Kent.

Ethel BEDFORD-FENWICK
Nursing Reformer
20 Upper Wimpole Street — Map Ref 15

Ethel Gordon Manson was born in Elgin, Morayshire, Scotland, the daughter of a wealthy doctor. When her father died, her mother married George Stoner, a Member of Parliament. She was educated privately at Middlethorpe Hall, in Yorkshire, before beginning nursing training at the age of 21 at the Children's Hospital in Nottingham. She was gifted, rich and articulate and became a pioneer for professional nursing.

She continued her probation period as a nurse at Manchester Royal Infirmary, before moving to London, where she quickly became a Sister at the London Hospital. In 1881, at the age of twenty-four, Ethel began her six years as Matron at St Bartholomew's Hospital, London. It was at 'St Bart's' that she met and married Dr Bedford-Fenwick.

In 1887 Dr and Mrs Bedford-Fenwick invited a number of medical men and matrons to discuss the possibility of founding an organization of nurses, similar to the British Medical Association. HRH Princess Christian, Queen Victoria's third daughter, agreed to become its first President. Many of the nursing leaders of the day suggested that attempts to organize the profession would destroy the 'vocational spirit'. Amongst those opposed to the organization was Florence Nightingale and many of the larger hospitals, but it was granted its Charter in 1893. In the same year, Ethel founded the *Nursing Record* – it was renamed *The British Journal of Nursing* – and remained its editor until 1946, using it as a vehicle for her views on the professional status of nurses. She advocated the idea of a General Council to regulate the profession, and argued for three components for training nurses: - a three-year training; a standard national curriculum; a final examination.

Ethel founded the Florence Nightingale International Foundation in 1899, which became the International Council of Nurses, now a federation of more than 120 national nurses associations. Eventually in 1919 the British Government set-up the General Nursing Council, with Mrs Bedford-Fenwick the first name on the world's first Nursing Register. She was instrumental in forming what became the Royal British Nurses Association, and this was followed in 1926 by the foundation of the British College of Nurses. Her commemorative plaque is just a few steps from the plaque marking Florence Nightingale's departure with her team of 38 nurses for the Crimean battlefields in 1854.

Sir Arthur Conan DOYLE
Author

2 Upper Wimpole Street   **Map Ref 16**

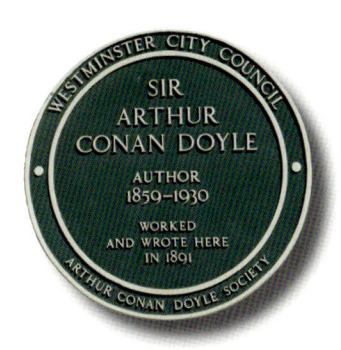

Arthur Ignatius Conan Doyle was born in Edinburgh, Scotland, to a prosperous Irish-Catholic family. His father Charles Altamont Doyle was twenty-two when he married Mary, a vivacious and highly educated woman of seventeen. Conan Doyle qualified in medicine and – as the Westminster Green Plaques citation confirms -is best known for writing fiction. At the age of nine, wealthy members of the Doyle family paid for him to attend a Jesuit boarding school in Lancashire, where he amused his fellow students with his talent for storytelling.

Doyle went up to Edinburgh University at seventeen to study medicine, where he began to write stories for magazines including Chamber's Edinburgh Journal and London Society. During his 3rd year, he took-up the post of ship's surgeon on an Arctic whaling boat, and after graduating, his first gainful employment was as a medical officer on SS Mayumba, a battered old vessel navigating between Liverpool and Africa. After a short stint at a medical practice in Plymouth with an unscrupulous partner, he left for Portsmouth to open his first practice. Initially it was not successful, and whilst waiting for patients he wrote stories: he divided his time between being a good doctor and struggling to become a recognized author.

In 1887 his A Study in Scarlet appeared in Beeton's Christmas Annual and featured the first appearance of Sherlock Holmes and Dr Watson. Future Holmes stories appeared in the Strand magazine, and in 1890 The Sign of Four firmly established Holmes once and for all in the annals of literature. In the same year he headed for Vienna to study ophthalmology, and returned the following year to practice in London. Doyle was already popular in America, and in 1894 he sailed to New York and gave talks in more than 30 cities. In the late 1890's he wrote a play starring Holmes, panned by the critics but a great box-office success. He served as a physician in the Boer War between 1899and 1902, and upon his return The Hound of the Baskervilles was published.

Doyle had married Louisa (nee Hawkins) in 1885, with whom he had two children, and following her death he married Jean Elizabeth (nee Leckie) in 1907, with whom he had three children. He was an accomplished sportsman, playing association football, cricket (10 appearances for the MCC), and golf. During his later years he turned to spiritualism.

Elizabeth BARRETT BROWNING
Poet

50 Wimpole Street — Map Ref 17

Elizabeth Barrett Browning 1806-1861, is one of the few individuals who has more than one plaque commemorating their life. Her biography can be found in the Marylebone West walk (Map Ref 13.) Here are some of her verses.

In the pleasant orchard closes,
'God bless all our gains' say we;
But 'May God bless all our losses'
Better suits with our degree.

The Lost Bower

Life treads on life, and heart on heart!
We press too close in church and mart
To keep a dream or grave apart

A Vision of Poets

"God's gifts put man's best gifts to shame"

"How do I love thee? Let me count the ways,
I love thee to the depth and breadth and height
My soul can reach, when feeling out of sight
For the ends of Being and ideal Grace"

"I tell you, hopeless grief's passionless"

"If thou must love me, let it be for naught
Except for love's sake only"

"I love thee with a love I seemed to lose
With my lost saints – I love thee with the breath,
Smiles, tears, of all my life! – and if God choose,
I shall but love thee better after death"

"Since when was genius found respectable?"
Aurura Leigh

O earth, so full of dreary noises!
O men with wailing in your voices!
O delivered gold, the waiters keep!
O strife, O curse, that o'er it fall!
God strikes a silence through you all,
And giveth his beloved, sleep.

The Sleep

Evelyn BARING (1st Earl of Cromer)
Statesman

36 Wimpole Street   **Map Ref 18**

Evelyn Baring was born at Cromer Hall, Norfolk, the ninth son of Henry Baring, the grandson of the founder of Baring's Bank, and his second wife, Cecilia Anne (nee Windham). When he was seven, Evelyn was sent to boarding school, and at fourteen he entered the Royal Military Academy in Woolwich, and graduated at seventeen as a Lieutenant in the Royal Artillery. His first military posting in 1858 was to the island of Corfu, and in 1862 he was aide-de-camp to Sir Henry Storks, the High Commissioner to the Ionian Islands, a role that ended in 1864 when Greece acquired Corfu. After service in Malta and Jamaica, he entered the Army's Staff College in 1867, later moving into intelligence work for the War Office.

In 1872 he was appointed private secretary to his cousin, Lord Northbrook, the Viceroy of India, until the latter's resignation in 1876, when Baring returned to England. The next year he was sent as Commissioner to Egypt to represent British financial interests. Ismail Pasha was the Khedive of Egypt, who had borrowed millions of pounds, and Baring directed investigations into the bankrupt administration, leading to Baring becoming British Controller-General in Egypt in 1879.

He was appointed Finance Minister in India between 1880 and 1883, and returned to Egypt after Arabi Pasha's nationalist revolt, and he became British Consul-General. He instituted a form of government known as Veiled Protectorate, whereby Baring ruled the Egyptian khedives. Egypt was made financially solvent by 1887, and during his twenty-four years in post he reformed Egyptian education, justice and administration, abolished forced labour, improved the railroads, and increased its prosperity.

Baring opposed the growing Egyptian nationalist movement, which demanded that Britain withdraw. Several Egyptian peasants were executed in 1906, which incensed the nationalists, and gained them sympathy in Britain. PM Campbell-Bannerman insisted on progress towards self-government in Egypt, but Baring could not adjust to these new policies and resigned in 1907.

He had married Ethel Barrington in 1876, with whom he had three children. Upon his return to England at the age of 66, he became active in politics, and as Lord Cromer he took his seat in the House of Lords. He was a leader of the anti-suffragette cause, leading the Leagues for Opposing Woman Suffrage, and devoted a considerable amount of his time writing.

Henry HALLAM
Historian

67 Wimpole Street **Map Ref 19**

Henry Hallam's son Arthur Henry

Henry Hallam was the only son of John Hallam, the Canon of Windsor and Dean of Bristol, and Eleanor, sister of the provost of Eton College, where he was educated before going up to Christ Church, Oxford. His first choice of career was law, and he was admitted to Lincoln's Inn in 1798, and called to the bar in 1802. He practised for many years on the Oxford circuit, but when his father died in 1812 he inherited his family's estate in Lincolnshire, and devoted his time to academic study and writing.

In 1806 he was appointed Commissioner of Stamps, a sinecure with light duties, thanks to the influence of his Whig friends, a role that he retained until 1826. Although he never sat in Parliament, he took a keen interest in political questions, and supported many of the policies pursued by the Whigs. Hallam distrusted democracy and feared that the Reform Act of 1832 would eliminate the aristocratic influence that he valued as a stabilizing force in the House of Commons.

Amongst his early literary pieces were the articles he wrote for the Whig-supporting publication, *The Edinburgh Review*, and his first substantial historical work was *The View of the State of Europe during the Middle Ages* in 1818. In 1827 he wrote the *Constitutional History of England*, which was followed eleven years later by *Introduction to the Literature of Europe in the 15th, 16th and 17th Centuries*. Hallam has been described as a "philosophical historian", and he made great play of the relative importance of men and things, looking at history as it related to the whole of society, and not simply concentrating on dates of battles and the fate of kings and queens

In 1807 Hallam married Julia Maria Elton, the daughter of a baronet, and they had eleven children, all but four of whom died prematurely. His eldest and favourite son, Arthur Henry, was a poet and essayist, and Hallam Snr was devastated when he died at the age of 22. He was encouraged to publish a selection of his son's work, which he did in 1834 under the nomenclature of *The Remains in Prose and Verse of Arthur Henry Hallam*, in which he wrote an accompanying memoir. In 1852 he published *Literature Essays and Characters from the Literature of Europe,* and although Hallam's reputation rests on his work as an historian, he made other contributions to Victorian intellectual life, including being a trustee of the British Museum. He became a Fellow of the Society of Antiquaries in 1805, and a member of the Royal Society in 1821 and King George IV presented him with the Gold Medal for History in 1830.

Sir George STILL
Paediatrician

28 Queen Anne Street　　　　　　　　　　　　　　**Map Ref 20**

George Frederick Still was born in the north London suburb of Islington, to a Customs Inspector at the Port of London, and Emma, who hailed from Cornwall. They had met in Dublin, but all their twelve children were born in London. He went to Merchant Taylors School and then Caius College, Cambridge, where he pursued his love of reading works in their original language, including Greek, Latin, Hebrew and Arabic.

After Cambridge he attended Guy's Hospital, from where he graduated in 1893 and worked as House Physician with James Goodhart, who encouraged Still to take an interest in paediatrics. He gained experience at Shadwell's Children's Hospital and at the Waterloo Hospital for Women and Children, before becoming a clinical assistant at the renowned Great Ormond Street Children's Hospital. In 1894 Still won a scholarship at the College of Physicians, and published his first two papers. The following year he became medical registrar and pathologist for four years at the Cambridge Children's Hospital.

In 1899 he was made a permanent staff member at Great Ormond Street, and was appointed physician of the diseases of children to King's College Hospital, London, the first hospital with a medical school to establish a section for children. In 1906 he became their first Professor of Diseases for Children, the first chair of paediatrics in England. He spent thirty-four years at King's College, and built-up a thriving private practice in Queen Anne Street, where his waiting room was full of toys to amuse the children waiting to see him. He was reputed to be the most popular paediatrician in London, so that almost every sick child of well-off parents had seen him at one time or another, which made him a rich man, and which allowed him to treat families for free who couldn't afford to pay.

Still wrote a number of books, including the textbooks *Common Diseases of Children* and *The System of Medicine*, and after giving a series of lectures on medical history, he wrote *A History of Paediatrics*. He was knighted on his retirement in 1937 for having been the personal physician to the Princesses Elizabeth and Margaret. Still was a bachelor who lived for little else but his work, and even in his younger days showed no interest in sport or the social side of life: he dedicated himself to improving the life chances of sick children, although in his later years he compensated with the pursuit of fly-fishing.

Sir Stewart DUKE-ELDER
Ophthalmic Surgeon

63 Harley Street **Map Ref 21**

Sir STEWART DUKE-ELDER 1898-1978 Ophthalmologist lived and worked here 1934-1976

William Stewart Elder was born in Dundee, Scotland, the second of three sons to Neil Stewart Elder, a Minister in the United Free Church of Scotland, and Isabella (nee Duke), daughter of John Duke, a Minister at the same church in Campsie, Stirlingshire. He went to the Morgan Academy, Dundee, where he was an exemplary student, before studying at St Andrew's University, where he became President of the Student's Union, read Natural Science and also obtained a degree in Physiology. He became the pre-eminent ophthalmologist of his time.

He completed his medical training at the Royal Infirmaries at Dundee and Edinburgh in 1923. After graduating, he held junior appointments at St George's Hospital, before being appointed at the age of 27 as honorary consulting surgeon there, and at Moorfields Eye Hospital. His main interest was in the physiology of the eye, and he was made a Fellow of the Royal College of Surgery. In 1932 he operated on the Prime Minister, Ramsay MacDonald for glaucoma, and during the 2nd World War he was Consultant Ophthalmic Surgeon, for which he obtained the rank of Brigadier in the Royal Army Medical Corps.

Elder made four important contributions in his field of study: - his publication in seven volumes of what became the definitive work, The Textbook of Ophthalmology, which was a distillation of all the world's ophthalmic literature; he created the Institute of Ophthalmology in London, which was closely linked with Moorfields, the pre-eminent eye hospital, where he was Director of Research until 1965; the inauguration in 1945 of the faculty of ophthalmologists at the Royal College of Surgeons, where Elder was its first President; and the creation of the 80-bed St John of Jerusalem Hospital in 1960.

He served for many years as the Editor of the British Journal of Ophthalmology and Ophthalmic Literature, and was the Surgeon Oculist to King Edward VII, George VI and Queen Elizabeth II. Despite his worldwide reputation, he never lost interest in and concern for young ophthalmologists, who became known as Duke-Elderberries! He received countless plaudits for his work, including the honorary membership of twenty-seven national ophthalmic societies. He changed his name by deed poll shortly before his marriage to Phyllis Mary Edgar, from plain 'Elder' to 'Duke'-Elder to incorporate his mother's maiden name. She was also an ophthalmologist, and played an active part in the production of his great work. They had no children.

Sir Charles LYELL
Geologist

73 Harley Street　　　　　　　　　　　　　　　　　　　　　**Map Ref 22**

Charles Lyell was born on the family estate in Kinnordy, Forfar, in Scotland, the eldest son of Charles Lyell, a lawyer and minor botanist. During his early childhood the family moved to Lyndhurst in Hampshire, where he had his early education. At the age of 15 he read *Introduction to Geology* by Robert Bakewell, which generated his interest in geology. He went up to Exeter College, Oxford in 1816, where he studied classics, and also attended geology lectures with William Buckland, who is remembered as the first man to identify a dinosaur.

After graduating, Lyell entered Lincoln's Inn in London to study law, but an eye complaint interrupted his studies, and he developed an even greater affinity for geological study. He joined the Geological Society and became its secretary in 1823, making several geological tours of England and Scotland and Europe. He returned to the law in 1825 and practiced intermittently for three years, whilst at the same time publishing papers on geological subjects. Lyell's geographical interests ranged from volcanoes and geographical dynamics to prehistoric archaeology and paleonthropology. However, he is best known for his part in popularising the principle of uniformitarianism, and in *Principles of Geology* Lyell tried to explain "the former changes of the earth's surface by reference to causes now in operation". He continuously revised and expanded the book over forty years. His central argument was that "the present is the key to the past". The book was an important influence on Charles Darwin, as was Lyell himself, and they were good friends throughout Darwin's later life.

Lyell was elected as a fellow of the Royal Society in 1826, and was appointed as the first Professor of Geology at King's College in London from 1831 to 1833. He continued to write, including *Manual of Elementary Geology* published in 1838, two books based on his North American travels in 1845 and 1849, and *Geological Evidence of the Antiquity of Man* between 1863 and 1873, which explored the implications of Darwinian evolution for humans. Lyell had married Mary Horner, the daughter of Leonard Horner in 1832, another Scottish geologist, who was an early member in 1808 of the Geographical Society, and a radical educational reformer. It is perhaps no surprise that the couple spent their honeymoon in Switzerland and Italy – on a geological tour.

W E Gladstone shares this plaque. His biography can be found in St.James's Walk Map Reference 11

George BODLEY
Architect
109 Harley Street — Map Ref 23

GEORGE FREDERICK BODLEY
1827-1907
Architect
lived here
1862-1873

George Frederick Bodley was born in Hull, in what was then South Yorkshire, the sixth child and youngest son of Dr William Hulme Bodley, a physician, and Mary Ann (nee Hamilton), the daughter of a Brighton church minister. At the age of 18 he became articled to the famous architect George Gilbert Scott, whose brother Samuel was married to Bodley's sister, Georgina. Bodley became known for his work in the Gothic revival style, and was the most influential architect working in the Anglican Church in the last third of the 19th century.

Following five years as Scott's first pupil, Bodley set up his own practice in 1850 at the age of 23 in Brighton, where he worked for five years before moving to London. Gothic architecture was experiencing a creative renewal, led by G E Street and William White, two of Bodley's ex-colleagues from Scott's office. His first church was at Longgrove in Herefordshire in 1856 and family contacts helped him obtain the commission for his first major town church at St Michaels in Brighton in 1858. As his style developed, it strongly influenced the Queen Anne revival in the 1870's. An increasing workload led Bodley to collaborate with another of Scott's pupils, Thomas Garner, who left his own practice in 1869 to begin a twenty-eight year partnership. The majority of their work was ecclesiastical design, but they also designed and restored country houses, and he worked with his lifelong friend, Charles Kempe, the stained glass designer. He worked with William Morris in the 1850's, the most influential designer of the 19th century, but in 1874 he eschewed this 'bohemian' talent to establish his own business to design and produce wallpaper, textiles and furniture.

In 1882, Bodley was appointed architect to York Minster, and consultant architect to a number of cathedrals. He continued to design with unflagging energy, even after Garner converted to Roman Catholicism in 1896, and they dissolved the partnership. In 1902 Bodley was one of the assessors for the competition to design the new Liverpool Anglican Cathedral. He had married Minna Frances Henrietta Reavely in 1872, with whom he had a son. Bodley was notoriously un-businesslike, and relied on the support of his staff. He had a lifelong love of music and entertained dinner guests with his piano playing. In 1899 he published a modest volume of poetry.

Sir Arthur PINERO
Playwright
115a Harley Street
Map Ref 24

Arthur Wing Pinero was born in London to Jewish-Portuguese parents. His father, John Daniel Pinero, and his grandfather, were both solicitors, and it was expected that he would become a lawyer. After a private education, this is what he did, but it was a job he grew to dislike. At the age of 15 he attended Birkbeck Institute in London to study elocution, but remained in his father's law office until he was nineteen, when he decided to pursue a career as an actor. He joined the impresarios Mr and Mrs Wyndham playing minor roles for a year at the Theatre Royal in Edinburgh, and followed this as a 'utility actor' with the Royal Alexander Theatre in Liverpool. In 1876 he moved to London and played the Globe Theatre, before serving a five-year apprenticeship with Sir Henry Irving's company at the Lyceum Theatre.

He had taken up writing plays, the first of which, *£200 a Year*, was produced at The Globe in 1877. *Bygones* and *Daisy's Escape* were produced a short time later at the Lyceum, and the success of the latter persuaded him to abandon acting and concentrate on writing plays. *The Squire* (1881) was the first of his plays to show promise, and his first major success, *The Magistrate* (1885), was a farce about a woman who had lied about her age in order to marry her second husband. It was followed by *The Schoolmistress* and *Dandy Dick* in 1886 and 1887, and the sentimental comedy, *Sweet Lavender*, in 1888.

"A financier is a pawn-broker with imagination"
"Where there's tea there's hope"

Pinero was not happy writing only comedy, and one of his early attempts at tragedy was *The Profligate* (1887), but the public was not ready for such a gloomy play. In the years that followed, however, English audiences were exposed to social dramatists such as Ibsen and Shaw, and feeling that the public was now ready to receive his tragic offerings, Pinero composed *The Second Mrs Tanqueray* (1893), the story of a "woman with a past". Although the play raised protests, it was a box-office hit and brought Pinero recognition as a serious social dramatist, and he became the most successful playwright of his time. It was Pinero's custom to direct all rehearsals for his plays and extensively train each actor in the interpretation of their part. He continued to write plays for the rest of his life, and although his popularity began to decline, his 1923 romance *The Enchanted Cottage* was successfully filmed, and *The Magistrate* and *Dandy Dick* were made into films starring Will Hay.

Lionel LOGUE
Speech Therapist

146 Harley Street　　　　　　　　　　　　　　　　　　　**Map Ref 25**

Plaque: CITY OF WESTMINSTER — LIONEL LOGUE C.V.O. 1880-1953 SPEECH THERAPIST TO KING GEORGE VI PRACTISED HERE 1926-1952

Lionel George Logue was born in Adelaide, Australia, the eldest of three children to George Edward Logue, an accountant in the family brewery, and Lavinia (nee Rankin). He was educated at Prince Alfred College, a private school in Adelaide, and studied elocution with Edward Reeves, who "purged his voice of much of his Australian accent".

As a Christian Scientist, Logue wanted to train as a doctor, but soon realized that he did not like the sight of blood. He worked for Reeves as a secretary and assistant teacher, and also studied at the local Conservatorium of Music. In order to build up capital, he moved to Kalgoolie, in Western Australia, to work with an electrical engineering firm at a goldmine. He set up a school for elocution in Perth, where he taught elocution, public speaking and acting, and in 1907, Logue married Myrtle (nee Gruenart), a clerk, and they had three sons.

Logue came to speech therapy during the First World War, when he treated soldiers returned from fighting, who were afflicted a speech disorders as a result of shell-shock. He found he had a special talent for the treatment of stammering, and was said to have effected 'dramatic cures' on these soldiers. He used exercises to relax muscle tension, taught correct breathing and slowed the patient's rate of speech.

In 1924 Logue and his family visited London for what was intended as a holiday. However, while staying in London he saw the possibilities of establishing a speech therapy practice, and rented rooms at 146 Harley Street. Logue had no medical qualifications and little capital, but quickly began making a good living, charging wealthy patrons substantial fees, while providing a free service to poorer people.

The story of how Logue helped the Duke of York, who was to become King George VI, developed into the story of the Academy Award winning film, *The Kings Speech*, in 2011. This is one of the few examples of a commemorative plaque being erected as the result of the person's success only being recognised after a major media activity. Encouraged by his wife, Elizabeth, the then Duchess of York, in 1926 the Duke of York consulted Logue about his dread for public speaking because of his severe stammer.

The Duchess became thoroughly familiar with Logue's programme of breathing exercises so she could help her husband to practice at home. Logue continued to work with the Duke through the 1930's and 1940's, and helped him with his major speeches, his coronation in 1937 and his radio broadcasts during the Second World War. Logue was appointed a Commander of the Royal Victorian Order (CVO) in 1944.

Frances BURNETT
Playwright and Author

63 Portland Place Map Ref 26

Blue plaque: FRANCES HODGSON BURNETT 1849-1924 Writer lived here

Frances Hodgson Burnett was born in Manchester, the third child of five to Edwin Hodgson, who owned an interior decorating business, and Eliza (nee Bond). Her father died when she was three, and over the next twelve years her mother tried unsuccessfully to run the company, and in 1865 she was encouraged by her uncle to move the family to Knoxville, Tennessee, in America. In order to help the family finances Frances began to write childrens' stories, for which she is best known, and in 1867, following the death of her mother, she became the family breadwinner and began to earn a regular income from her writing. Her first story was published in *Godey's Lady's Book* in 1868, followed by regular commissions from *Scriber's Weekly* and *Harper's Bazaar*.

The secret of her stories was how she combined realistic working-class anecdotes with a romantic plot, and her first novel *That Lass o' Lowries*, published in 1877, was a story of Lancashire life. Frances married Dr Swann Burnett in 1873, with whom she had two sons, and after travelling in Europe they returned to America, first to Washington DC and then New York. In 1879 Frances had the first of many stories published in *St. Nicholas Magazine*, and she continued to write novels and *Esmeralda*, a play co-authored with William Gillette. Positive reviews of her work emerged, but it was not until her best-selling novel *Little Lord Fauntleroy* was published in 1886 that her reputation was set. It created a fashion of long curls for boys, and velvet suits with lace collars, and became a stereotypical look for 'rich kids'. The book sold over half a million copies, and in 1888 she won a lawsuit over its dramatic rights, which became part of British copyright law.

Her marriage was not a happy one, and after they divorced in 1898, Frances returned to England and in 1900 married her business manager, Stephen Townsend. She continued to write, including the play *A Little Princess* in 1905, and six years later her best known children's novel, *The Secret Garden*, inspired by the gardens at her country home, the Lutyen's designed Great Maytham Hall, in Rolvenden, Kent. In 1909 she returned to New York – having become a US citizen in 1905 – and continued to write, and studied Spiritualism following the death of her first son, Lionel.

"Where, you tend a rose, my lad,
A thistle cannot grow"   **The Secret Garden**

Field Marshall Earl ROBERTS
Soldier

47 Portland Place   **Map Ref 27**

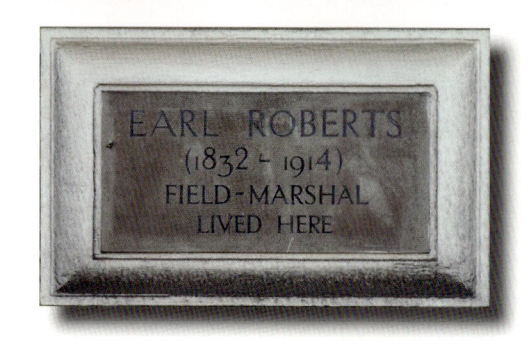

EARL ROBERTS
(1832 – 1914)
FIELD-MARSHAL
LIVED HERE

Frederick Sleigh Roberts was born in Cawnpore, India, the second son of General Sir Abraham Roberts, and his second wife, Isabella (nee Bunbury), both of whom were of Anglo-Irish extraction. At the time, Sir Abraham was commanding the 1st Bengal European regiment, and 'Frederick' was named Sleigh after the garrison commander, Major-General William Sleigh. Abraham returned to England in1834, and settled them at the family home in Clifton, Bristol before he returned to India. Frederick went to Eton College in 1845, but stayed for only a year before going to the Royal Military College, Sandhurst. He wanted to join the army, but his father preferred him to join the East India Company's service, and after two years at Sandhurst he entered the company's military college in Croydon. In 1851 he was commissioned into the Bengal Artillery, and was posted to a battery at Peshawar, where his father was the commander, and for whom he acted as his aide-de-camp.

Roberts fought in the Indian rebellion of 1857, and was awarded the Victoria Cross. Between 1863 and 1872 he served with the British Army in campaigns in India and Abyssinia, and in 1880 was promoted to Major-General in the Second Anglo-Afghan War, before being appointed Commander in Afghanistan. He was Commander-in-Chief (C-in-C) of Madras, and in 1885 C-in-C for the whole of India and was promoted to General in 1890. After relinquishing his Indian command in 1893, he returned as C-in-C of British forces in Ireland, becoming Field Marshal in 1895. In1899 Roberts commanded troops in the Second Boer War, and upon his return to England he was succeeded by Lord Kitchener, and was appointed as the honorary Colonel of the Irish Guards. The now ennobled Lord Roberts served as the last C-in-C of the Forces, before the post was abolished in 1904. He was a strong advocate of introducing conscription, as he saw the threat from Germany, and at the outbreak of war in 1914, Roberts was appointed Colonel-in-Chief of the overseas troops in France, and died of pneumonia while visiting Indian troops there.

He married Nora Henrietta Bews in 1859, with whom he had six children. She was a forceful woman, and in India it was believed that officers could gain advancement through her. Even Queen Victoria was moved to write that Roberts was 'ruled by his wife', and there was talk of 'petticoat government'. Nevertheless, Roberts has been extolled as the ablest field commander since Wellington, quick to grasp a situation, bold and decisive in his solutions, and calm and confident in the face of difficulties.

General Thomas GAGE
Soldier

41 Portland Place **Map Ref 28**

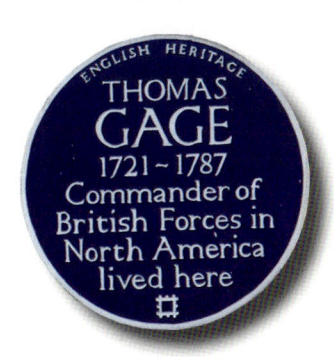

Thomas Gage was born at the family's estate, High Meadow in Firle, Sussex. He was the second son of three children to Benedicta (nee Hall) and the 1st Viscount Thomas Gage of Castle Island and Baron Gage of Castlebar. His father's titles were attached to property in Ireland. At the age of eight he went to Westminster School with his brother, and after leaving school he joined the British Army, where his early duties consisted of recruiting.

In 1741 he bought a Lieutenant's commission, and in 1743 was promoted to Captain, seeing action in the War of Austrian Succession in Flanders, whilst serving as aide-de-camp to Lord Albemarle. He fought in the Second Jacobite Rising, which culminated in 1746 at the Battle of Culloden. In 1748 he purchased a Major's commission with the 44th Regiment, and in 1751 was promoted to Lieutenant Colonel. This was one of two regiments sent to America under General Braddock in 1754, and he took part in the ill-fated expedition against Fort Duquesne.

Gage fought in the last of the North American wars between France and Britain (known as the French and Indian Wars), and in 1760 he was appointed Governor of Montreal before being appointed as Commander-in-Chief of the British forces in North America in 1763. In 1773, Gage visited England on leave, and in 1774 he returned with the additional title of Governor of Massachusetts. His first task was to keep the port of Boston closed in punishment for the Boston Tea party. Gage had been told by his superiors in England to make the colonists see reason, and if they would not, to put them down. He kept the peace for as long as he could, finally in 1775 giving the orders that led to the confrontations at Lexington and Concord, Massachusetts, and the start of the American Revolution.

He resigned later that year and returned to England, being succeeded by General Howe as Commander-in-Chief in the colonies and by General Carleton as Commander in Canada. Gage was briefly reactivated in 1781, when he was given responsibility for mobilizing troops in preparation for a possible French invasion, and was promoted to General in 1782. A common-law marriage had earlier come to an abrupt end with his wife's death, and a failed political foray had been attempted shortly before he was ordered to America.

General Charles STANHOPE (3rd Earl of Harrington)
Soldier

20 Mansfield Street   **Map Ref 29**

Charles Stanhope was born the eldest son of William, the 2nd Earl of Harrington, and Lady Caroline Fitzroy, daughter of the 2nd Duke Grafton. Part of his education was conducted at Eton College, and in 1769 at the age of 16, following his father and grandfather, he joined the Coldstream Guards. He was promoted to the rank of Captain four years later.

In 1774, he made a short foray into the world of politics, briefly becoming MP for Thetford, and two years later for Westminster. In the same year he set sail for North America, to join battle in the American War of Independence, against the thirteen former colonies. The war was the culmination of the American Revolution, as the colonists rejected the rights of the British Parliament to govern them without representation. He commanded the 29th Regiment of Foot's Grenadier Company, and acted as an Aide-de-Camp to General John Burgoyne, the commander of British forces in the north.

Stanhope returned to England in 1779, and defended his Commanding Officer, when giving evidence to a House of Commons Select Committee of Enquiry. In the same year he took his seat in the House of Lords, and in the following year he was in Jamaica defending the local populace from a possible French invasion. He remained in the army, and was rewarded with promotion to General, and Commander-in-Chief in Ireland.

He inherited family estates in Derby and London, and in 1779 he married Jane, daughter of Sir John Fleming, 1st Baronet of Brompton Park, and Jane Coleman. She was a Lady of the Bedchamber for Queen Charlotte, King George III's wife, and was a known society hostess. The couple had 8 sons and 3 daughters.

Stanhope was responsible for introducing a sword that became standard army issue in the early 19th century. He undertook diplomatic missions to Berlin and Vienna in 1805 and 1806, and in 1812 he was appointed Governor of Windsor Castle, a position he held until his death. In 1817 James Wyatt built Elvaston Castle for him, which belonged to the Stanhope family until the middle of the 20th century.

John PEARSON
Architect

13 Mansfield Street **Map Ref 30**

John Loughborough Pearson was born in Brussels in Belgium, the youngest of eleven children to William Pearson, an artist from Durham, in the North East of England, and his wife Nancy, who hailed from the Isle of Man. At the age of 14 he was articled to the architect Ignatius Bonomi, an Italian based in Durham, where an interest in church building, furniture and fittings was fostered and developed in him. Bonomi was also known as the "railway architect".

He moved to London to the offices of Anthony Salvin and then Philip Hardwick (architect of Lincoln's Inn in London), but at the age of 26 he established his own practice, specialising in the design and restoration of churches across the country. The influential Tractarians, who distributed argumentative pieces (tracts) arguing for the recovery of traditional aspects of the Christian faith, commissioned Pearson to design churches, schools, and houses in the Gothic style. They were a High Church Anglican movement, which developed into Anglo-Catholics.

Whilst continuing to design new churches, he was increasingly involved in controversy surrounding his restorations – which accounted for half of his output - and he was branded a 'destroyer'. His masterpiece is arguably Truro Cathedral; he extended Bristol and Wakefield Cathedrals; and designed the churches of St Agnes & St Pancras, in Liverpool and St Margaret's in Westminster. He also added and restored colleges at Oxford and Cambridge Universities.

Pearson had no reputation for innovation or for promoting his own architectural principles. His work was based on a conservative tradition, and above all saw in Gothic architecture its potential for picturesque sublimity. His style was at first influenced by Pugin, who designed the Houses of Parliament, and many of his churches feature the vertical, with tall towers.

He didn't marry until 1862, when he was in his mid-forties, and his wife Jemima Christian was the cousin of Manxman and fellow-architect Ewan Christian. She died when she was only 36, and their only son, Frank, followed in his father's footsteps as an architect. He was awarded the Royal Institute of Architects' Royal Gold Medal in 1880, and although he was sociable, Pearson was always modest and never made his views public.

Sir Edwin LUTYENS
Architect

13 Mansfield Street **Map Ref 30**

Here lived and died JOHN LOUGHBOROUGH PEARSON 1817–1897 and later SIR EDWIN LANDSEER LUTYENS 1869–1944 Architects

Edwin Landseer Lutyens was born in London the 10th child, and 9th boy of thirteen children to Charles and Mary Lutyens. Edwin was always called Ned, and as a delicate child, he was the only boy who didn't go to school or university, but shared his sister's governess. He had a flair for drawing and mathematics, and it became apparent that he was cut-out to be an architect.

At the age of 16, Lutyens attended South Kensington School of Art in London, and after two years joined Ernest George's architectural practice. Within a year, in 1888, he had opened his own practice, and was inspired early on by the Arts and Crafts movement, and later by the disciplines of the classic. Lutyen's initial houses were designed in the informal manner of the 'English Free School', utilizing historical references within a local context in terms of materials and building traditions.

He met Gertrude Jekyll, the garden designer, and through her social connections she helped Lutyens accumulate many commissions. He designed her house, Munstead Wood, and together they created over 100 gardens. He designed over forty major large country houses, and altered and added to many more.

Much of Lutyens' work was featured in the lifestyle magazine, Country Life, and from this exposure he was commissioned for many designs, including the remodelling of Lindisfarne Castle. His range of work was extremely varied, from the British Embassy in Washington, to Castle Drigo in Devon, and from the Viceroy's House in Delhi, India, to the monument to commemorate the dead of the 1st World War at the Cenotaph in Whitehall, London. He also indulged in light-hearted projects such as Queen Mary's Dolls' House at Windsor House.

Lutyens has been described as the "greatest British architect". He was knighted in 1918, and created a Knight Commander of the Order of the Indian Empire in 1930. He had married Lady Emily Lytton, the daughter of a former Viceroy of India, in 1897. They had five children but they had no interests in common, and the marriage was a failure.

Lutyens' Cenotaph in Whitehall constructed between 1919 and 1920

Sir Robert MAYER
Philanthropist and Patron of Music

2 Mansfield Street **Map Ref 31**

Robert Mayer was born in Mannheim, Germany, and immigrated to England when he was 17. His early life was steeped in music and he later became a major champion and sponsor of music and young musicians. From the age of five he attended the Mannheim Conservatoire, where he learned to play the piano, and studied under Felix Weingartner, the Croatian conductor and composer.

Despite his early musical training, he was "encouraged" by his family to go into business, and he began working in the lace trade. He moved to England in 1896 and began training to become a banker, but continued his musical interests. One of his piano tutors was Guernsey-born Fanny Davies, who was an early performer of Debussy, and who was the first person to give a piano recital at Westminster Abbey.

Mayer became a British citizen in 1902, and joined the British Army at the start of the 1st World War. Through his musical connections he met the soprano, Dorothy Moulton, whom he married in 1919, and she encouraged him to develop his music interests further. They lived in America in the early 1920's and he came across children's concerts run by Walter Damrosch, the American-German composer, who went on to conduct the New York Symphony Orchestra.

Back in England in 1923, Damrosch's success stimulated him to create the Robert Mayer Concerts for Children, for which the leading conductors Adrian Boult and Malcolm Sargent conducted early performances. In 1932, with Sir Thomas Beecham, he founded the London Philharmonic Orchestra, one of the major orchestras in the UK, which is based at the Royal Festival Hall and is the main resident orchestra of the Glyndebourne Festival Opera.

Mayer helped to create the London Schools Symphony Orchestra, which offers young people the opportunity to study and perform major symphonic repertoire under the guidance of some of the finest professional musicians in the world. The Times Educational Supplement describes it as "one of the capital's most valuable assets". He was also involved in the creation of the International School for Contemporary Music with Egon Wellesz, the Austrian-born pupil of Schoenberg.

On his 100th birthday he became the oldest person to be knighted, and three years later Queen Elizabeth II dubbed him a Knight of the Royal Victorian Order (KCVO).

Dr Grantly DICK-READ
Obstetrician

25 Harley Street **Map Ref 32**

Grantly Dick-Read was born in Suffolk, the son of a Norfolk miller, and the sixth of seven children. He is regarded by many as the father of the natural childbirth movement. He was educated at Cambridge University, and was an excellent athlete and horseman. After university, he received his medical training at the London Hospital, Whitechapel, where he qualified in 1914 as a doctor at the age of twenty-four. He was badly wounded at Gallipoli during the 1st World War, but later served in France as a medical officer.

In the early 1920's he worked at a clinic in Woking, Surrey, where he specialised in childbirth and care, observing and writing-up case histories and notes. He dedicated his life to educating expectant parents about the benefits of giving birth naturally, with as little interference from the 'professionals' as possible. He believed that much of the pain in childbirth emanated from society's attitude, which often emphasised the pain.

He published his first book, *Natural Childbirth* in 1933 in his quest to make natural childbirth available to all women who did not have medical conditions that necessitated intervention. Dick-Read established his own clinic in Harley Street in 1934, but his attempts to educate the medical community about the unnecessary risks involved to women in labour and their babies, from the common practice of using anaesthetics during childbirth, met with considerable resistance.

Dick-Read's second book, *Childbirth without Fear*, was aimed at a more general readership, and after the 2nd World War he was invited to lecture on childbirth in the USA and France. He was practising unorthodox methods outside the National Health Service in the UK, and had to struggle against the entrenched attitudes of leading obstetricians and gynaecologists of the day.

In 1948 he moved to South Africa, where he observed traditional African births, which reinforced his faith in these methods. In 1953 he returned to England and continued to lecture and write. In 1956 the Natural Childbirth Association, now the National Childbirth Trust (who sponsored the plaque) was founded, with Dick-Read its first president, becoming the foremost charity concerned with birth and early parenthood. During the years when the professionals ridiculed his philosophy his second wife, Jessica, convinced him that he owed it to women to persevere.

Sir Jonathan HUTCHINSON
Surgeon

15 Cavendish Square Map Ref 33

SIR JONATHAN HUTCHINSON 1828-1913 Surgeon, Scientist and Teacher lived here

Jonathan Hutchinson was born in Selby, Yorkshire, to Quaker parents, where his father owned a prosperous flax business. He shared his parents' religious convictions, and initially planned a career as a medical missionary. Instead he became an apprentice to an apothecary and surgeon in York, before moving in 1850 to St Bartholomew's Hospital in London.

During his time as a student, Hutchinson gained the friendship of his mentor, Sir James Paget, who influenced his decision to become a surgeon. After a brief return to York for his House Surgeon's post he came back to London and in 1851 studied ophthalmology at Moorfields and practised at the London Ophthalmic Hospital. He strove to learn "all he could from all branches of medicine", although for a while medical journalism was his only income, and in 1855 he was writing for the *Medical Times and Gazette*, the main competitor to *The Lancet*.

The work of Hutchinson is remarkable in both quantity and diversity, and he had an encyclopaedic mind, was conversant with virtually every area of medicine and was able to communicate effectively. He presented an austere, seemingly humourless figure, but his amazingly retentive memory, coupled with his genius for teaching, enabled him to fascinate large audiences on a wide-range of subjects.

From 1859 to 1883 he was surgeon to the London Hospital, and he also worked at the Blackfriars Hospital for Diseaeases of the Skin. He made numerous observations, most notably in the area of skin diseases, and congenital syphilis, which was common in London at the time, and it is said that he saw more than one million patients with syphilis.

Much of his work is preserved in his eleven volume *Archives of Surgery*, a quarterly journal, and he published his observations in more than 1200 medical articles. He was a fellow of the Royal College of Surgeons from 1862 and Professor of Surgery there from 1879 to 1883, and a founder of the London School of Medicine. During his student days, Hutchinson had become involved with Quaker Missions, with the aim of alleviating misery and uplifting the impoverished, but he pursued his medical calling. In his personal life, he had 31 years of happy marriage with his wife, Jane, and their numerous offspring.

Ronald ROSS
Scientist

18 Cavendish Square   **Map Ref 34**

SIR RONALD ROSS 1857–1932 Nobel Laureate Discoverer of the mosquito transmission of malaria lived here

Ronald Ross was born in an Himalayan hill station in the North-Western Provinces of India. He was the eldest of ten children to General Sir Campbell Claye Grant Ross, a captain in the Ghurkhas, and Matilda Charlotte (nee Ederton), the daughter of a London solicitor. He was sent to school in England when he was 8, where he lived with his great-uncle in Ryde, Isle of Wight, and at 12 he was sent to Springhill Boarding School, near Southampton.

He would have preferred a career in the army or as an artist, but his father insisted that he become a doctor in the Indian Medical Service. In 1874 he studied at St Bartholomew's in London, and after gaining membership of the Royal College of Surgeons, became a ship's surgeon. He continued his medical career in India, where he focused his attention on malaria, and on a visit to England he met the tropical disease specialist Patrick Manson, who urged him to concentrate on the quest for the mechanism of mosquito transmission of malaria. Ross worked around Madras, where malaria was highly endemic and often fatal. After much painstaking work, he discovered that only the small inconspicuous female anopheline mosquitoes carried the malaria parasite. During later work in Sierra Leone and Egypt, Ross created models showing the life-cycles of the malaria parasite in humans and mosquitoes, publishing his findings in a series of papers.

He returned to England in 1899 as a lecturer at the Liverpool School of Tropical Medicines, newly established by Liverpool philanthropists including Sir Alfred Jones. London, however, always attracted him as a more suitable arena for his talents and he returned permanently in 1912, becoming consultant physician at King's College Hospital. In the 1st World War, Ross was made consultant in malaria at the War Office, and travelled to Macedonia, Italy and Egypt, where he also advised on the prevention and treatment of dysentery. After the war, he was appointed as a consultant to the Ministry of Pensions.

It has been said that he was easier man to admire than to like. He didn't suffer fools gladly, but at the same time, he was capable of self-parody and his memoirs record instances of jokes at his own expense. Unusually, he looked at the cost of sanitary reform as an investment, not a current expenditure.

H H ASQUITH
Prime Minister

20 Cavendish Square **Map Ref 35**

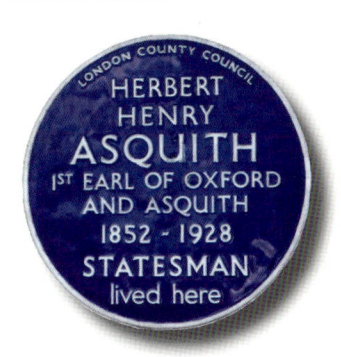

Herbert Henry Asquith was born in Morley, Yorkshire, the second son of five children to a wool merchant. He was educated at Huddersfield College and the Moravian School, Leeds, and went up to Balliol College, Oxford, where he was President of the Union. He became a lawyer and was called to the bar in 1876. In 1886 he was elected as the Liberal MP for East Fife, in Scotland, and quickly made his mark with his intellect and oratory skills, and PM Gladstone appointed him as Home Secretary in 1892.

The Liberals were out of office for ten years from 1895, and Asquith returned to his barrister's practice. In 1906 the Liberals were returned to power under Campbell-Bannerman, and he was appointed Chancellor of the Exchequer, introducing higher taxes on unearned income, which helped to pay for pensions for everybody over 70 years old.

In 1908, Campbell-Bannerman resigned, and Asquith became Prime Minister, where he took on the House of Lords, who often blocked Liberal proposals. In order to finance welfare legislation, and building up the Royal Navy to counter the threat from Germany, the Chancellor of the Exchequer, David Lloyd-George introduced a radical budget in 1909. The Lords rejected it, and the 1910 election was billed as a referendum on this Lords v Commons issue. Asquith did not get an overall majority, but it gave him public support, and the Parliament Act of 1911 ended the Lords ability to veto financial legislation.

"Youth would be an ideal state if it came a little later in life"

In 1912, Asquith's renewed attempts to introduce home rule in Ireland provoked fierce opposition, and civil war was only averted by the outbreak of the 1st World War in 1914. To maximise support he formed a coalition in 1915, but it was unsuccessful and 1916 was even worse, with the Easter Rising in Ireland and the Battle of the Somme with its massive casualties. Asquith was blamed for military failures and he resigned and was replaced by Lloyd-George: the success of Lloyd-George's government consigned Asquith to the political wilderness, but despite losing his seat, he remained leader of the Liberal Party.

Asquith married Helen Kelsall (nee Mellard), with whom he had five children. She died of typhoid, and his second marriage was to Emma Tennant, with whom he had two children. One of Asquith's descendents is British-born Hollywood actress, Helena Bonham-Carter.

Quintin HOGG
Educationalist and Philanthropist

5 Cavendish Square **Map Ref 36**

Quintin Hogg was born in London, the seventh son of Sir James Hogg, 1st Baronet, who was a Member of Parliament. He was educated at Eton College, and his strong religious beliefs and love for sport, greatly influenced his future educational beliefs. He is remembered as the founder of the educational establishment now known as the University of Westminster.

After school, he entered the tea and sugar businesses. Hogg's job in the tea trade was based in a poor part of London, and he was moved to sympathy for the waifs playing in the nearby streets. In an effort to obtain firsthand experience with the problems of lower-class children, he disguised himself as a shoeblack and worked nights alongside the boys. He was motivated by his Christian beliefs and began to turn his energies to educational reforms.

His attempts to teach reading with the Bible as a textbook led to the opening of his Ragged School in Charing Cross, London in 1864, which attempted to get young and destitute children off the street and provide a very basic education. In 1878 he set-up his Working Lads Institute at Long Acre, which offered trade classes, along with a combination of education and religious work. Three years later he opened the Young Men's Christian Institute, which offered a number of trade subjects for youths aged 16 to 22, and reflecting Hogg's interests, the Institute was also a social and athletic club. It was renamed the Regent Street Polytechnic, and now as the University of Westminster, it is still the largest provider of adult education in London.

His role in trade took him frequently to the West Indies, where he joined his brother-in-law in the sugar business. He modernized sugar production in Demerara, in what is now Guyana, and he played cricket twice for the colony (unfortunately, his record shows he scored only 18 runs in four innings!). Hogg was an accomplished sportsman, and along with many old Etonians, he was a pioneer of Association Football. He made appearances for Wanderers FC (winners of the first FA Cup), and despite being English, he played for Scotland in two football internationals against England! He married Alice Anna Graham in 1871, and they had four children: Hogg was the grandfather of Quintin Hogg, Lord Hailsham, a Tory grandee of the post-2nd World War period.

G.E. STREET
Architect

14 Cavendish Place   **Map Ref 37**

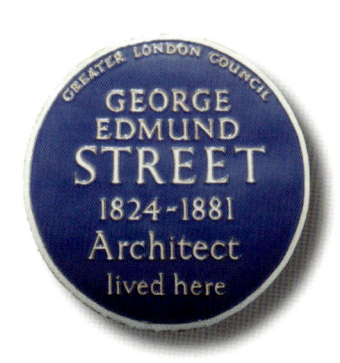

George Edmund Street was born in Woodford, Essex, the third son of Thomas Street, a leading solicitor, by his second wife, Mary Anne, (nee Millington). He went to school in Mitcham and then Camberwell in South London, and left when he was 15. He was prolific and innovative, and became a leader of the High Victorian generation of British architects.

He took painting lessons as a teenager, and showed an interest in architecture, but his first job was in the family law office in London. Upon his father's death, he went to live with his mother and sister, who had moved to Exeter. At 17 he seriously began a career in architecture, when he was articled to Owen Carter in Winchester. Three years later he moved to London, where he obtained a place at the offices of George Gilbert Scott, the architect responsible for such iconic buildings as St.Pancras Station and Battersea Power Station.

His first commission was for the design of Biscoray Church in Cornwall. and at the age of 25 he established his own office. From an early age, he was deeply interested in the principles of Gothic architecture, and he moved to London in 1856 with a national reputation. He published books on Italian architecture in the Middle Ages, and the Gothic Architecture of Spain, richly illustrated with his own drawings.

Street's philosophy was that an architect's personal style was synonymous with his moral dignity. He was highly religious, and the majority of his buildings were for ecclesiastical use, notably the convent of East Grinstead, with the largest being the nave of Bristol Cathedral, and the choir of the Cathedral in Dublin. By the late 1860's, High Victorian architecture was losing its appeal and Street's work reflected some of the ideas of the new Queen Anne taste, led by his working with leading designers of the new generation, including William Morris. Their influence shows in his greatest commission, the Royal Courts Of Justice in London.

He was elected as associate of the Royal Academy in 1866, president of the Royal Institute of British Architects, and at the time of his death was Professor of Architecture to the Royal Academy. Street was married twice, first in 1852 to Mariquita Proctor, and following her death, to Jessie Holland.

Dr Joseph CLOVER
Anaesthetist and Surgeon
3 Cavendish Place — Map Ref 38

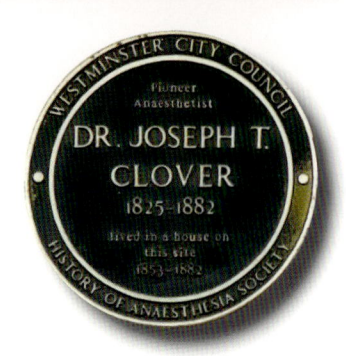

Joseph Clover was born in Aylsham, Norfolk, and went to school in Norwich. He became a pioneer anaesthetist, and the first prominent member of his family was his great-grandfather, also Joseph Clover, who was one of the founders of Veterinary Science. His grandfather moved to Aylsham and set-up a drapery business, which his father inherited, before he became a farmer and landowner.

Clover's early education was in Norwich and he started his medical studies at the age of 16 as an apprentice to a local surgeon as a surgical dresser at Norfolk and Norwich Hospital. After his training was interrupted due to ill-health, he completed his education at University College London (UCL) in 1844, where he qualified in medicine. He became house surgeon to James Syme, who had been the leading consultant surgeon in Scotland before moving to UCL, and where Clover became Resident Medical Officer in 1848.

Clover was admitted as a Fellow at the Royal College of Surgeons in 1850, and after developing an interest in the field of urology he practiced as a surgeon, inventing two instruments for the crushing and removal of bladder stones. Ill-health caused him to give up in 1853, and he turned to general practice, residing and carrying out his experiments at 3 Cavendish Place. He soon began to specialise in anaesthetics and became the leading anaesthetist and scientific investigator in anaesthetics in London.

In England the practice of anaesthesia was established on a firm foundation of basis science by John Snow, who devised inhalers, which allowed him to know and control the strength of the vapour that the patient was breathing. Snow introduced quantitative methods into anaesthesia, and he recorded the amount used in each case and established that the potency of an anaesthetic agent is inversely related to the solubility in the blood. At his death his mantle fell on Clover, who devoted his life to making anaesthesia safer.

He attended many famous people, amongst whom were Princess (later Queen) Alexandra, the exiled Emperor Napoleon III, Sir Robert Peel and Florence Nightingale. Clover invented apparatus for the administration of anaesthetic ether, and chloroform, and was recognised by his colleagues as having done more than anyone else at the time to render the administration of anaesthetics safer for his patients.

ST.JAMES'S
SW1
CITY OF WESTMINSTER

IN A HOUSE ON THIS SITE LIVED
NELL GWYNNE
FROM
1671 ~ 1687

WESTMINSTER CITY COUNCIL
SIR WINSTON CHURCHILL
spoke here at the former
CAXTON HALL
1937 – 1942
STAKIS PLC

L.C.C.
WILLIAM EWART GLADSTONE
(1809-1898)
Statesman
Lived here

WESTMINSTER CITY COUNCIL
Pioneer Aviator, Sailor and Author
SIR FRANCIS CHICHESTER KBE
1901–1972
single-handed circumnavigator of the World 1966-67
lived here 1944–1972
THE ROYAL INSTITUTE OF NAVIGATION

GREATER LONDON COUNCIL
GENERAL CHARLES DE GAULLE
President of the French National Committee
set up the Headquarters of the Free French Forces here in 1940

ST. JAMES'S SW1
CITY OF WESTMINSTER

St James's is even more exclusive than Mayfair. The area's historic streets have remained virtually unchanged for centuries. In this walk, we have taken in the official St James's area bounded by Piccadilly, Haymarket, The Mall and Green Park, plus the area to the south of St James's Park. It provides – if it were necessary! – an excuse to feed the ducks and watch the pelicans as you meander across St James's Park.

Horse Guards Parade from St James's Park

The Park, which covers 58 acres, is open every day and was originally a marsh. It was drained by Henry VIII in 1531 to create a deer park when he established the Court of St James's. In 1603 the park was laid out for James I, and then re-landscaped in 1660 for Charles II in the formal French style by Andre Le Notre. He built an aviary to the south, hence Birdcage Walk. In 1827 John Nash was appointed by George IV to create the landscape we see today.

Queen Anne's Gate features a number of pre-Georgian (literally Queen Anne) houses, with a marble statue of Queen Anne from 1705. A left-turn into Birdcage Walk leads to the Guard's Museum, which is open every day from 10.00am to 4.00pm. It tells the history of the five regiments of Foot Guards – Grenadier, Coldstream, Scots, Irish and Welsh. They, along with the two Household Cavalry regiments, have the responsibility of protecting the Monarch.

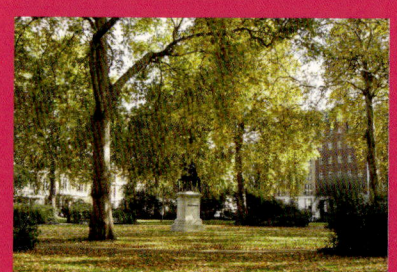

St James's Square Garden

Carlton House Terrace

In The Mall, beneath Nash's Carlton House Terrace, is the Institute of Contemporary Art (ICA), conceived in 1947 by poet and art critic Herbert Read, with a group of artists. It is the home of new art and culture from around the world. Contributing to its history have been luminaries as varied as T S Eliot, Ronnie Scott and Vivienne Westwood. The arts centre and exhibition galleries are open every day from noon to 10.30pm. Adjacent to the ICA is the Mall galleries, which is open every day from 9.00am to 5pm, and shows new work by established artists and new emerging talent.

The main thoroughfare through St James's is Pall Mall, which leads the Wren-designed Marlborough House, and to St James's Palace, built by Henry VIII in 1532, and is still the official Royal Court. In Stable Yard Road, are the 1827 Nash-designed Clarence House (open in August and September) and Lancaster House, designed in 1825 by Benjamin Wyatt. In St James's Place is the Palladian Palace, Spencer House, which is open most of the year, and the Queen's Chapel in Marlborough Street, open in the spring and early summer. The name of the street emanates from the game Palle-Maille, a cross between croquet and golf, and was played in front of the Palace in the 18th century.

Pall Mall has impressive examples of Georgian England, with the Houses of Parliament architect Charles Barry's 1836 Reform Club at number 104, and the Travellers' Club at number 106. At number 116 was the United Services Club, a favourite haunt of the Duke of Wellington, built by Nash in 1827, and which now houses the Institute of Directors. The Royal Automobile Club (RAC) was founded in 1897 at number 89, which is next to the building that has the plaque to Frederick Winser.

Queen Anne Statue

These and other 'gentlemen's clubs' evolved from the coffee houses of the 17th century as meeting places for rich young aristocrats to talk, drink and gamble. There are a number still active in St James's Street, including Whites, which opened in 1693, Brooks, and The Carlton Club. At 107 Pall Mall stands the Athenaeum, established in 1823 and described as "the power house of the British establishment".

In the middle of the grand Georgian and neo-Georgian houses in St James's Square is an 1817 Nash-designed garden, which is the only square in St James's. It is open between 10.00 and 4.30pm, Monday to Friday. The square is dominated by the equestrian statue of William III, created by John Bacon and completed by his son in 1808.

St James's Church Tower

Jermyn Street is one of London's most elegant thoroughfares, lined with shops catering for classic gentlemen's fashion. The only church in St James's sits between Jermyn Street and Piccadilly. Originally designed by Sir Christopher Wren in 1684, St James's was severely damaged in the Blitz. The church boasts a rich mixture of religious services, speakers and musical concerts every week. In the church grounds there is an Antiques and Collectables Market every Tuesday, and an Arts and Crafts Markets from Wednesday to Saturday.

The Antheneum Club Waterloo Place

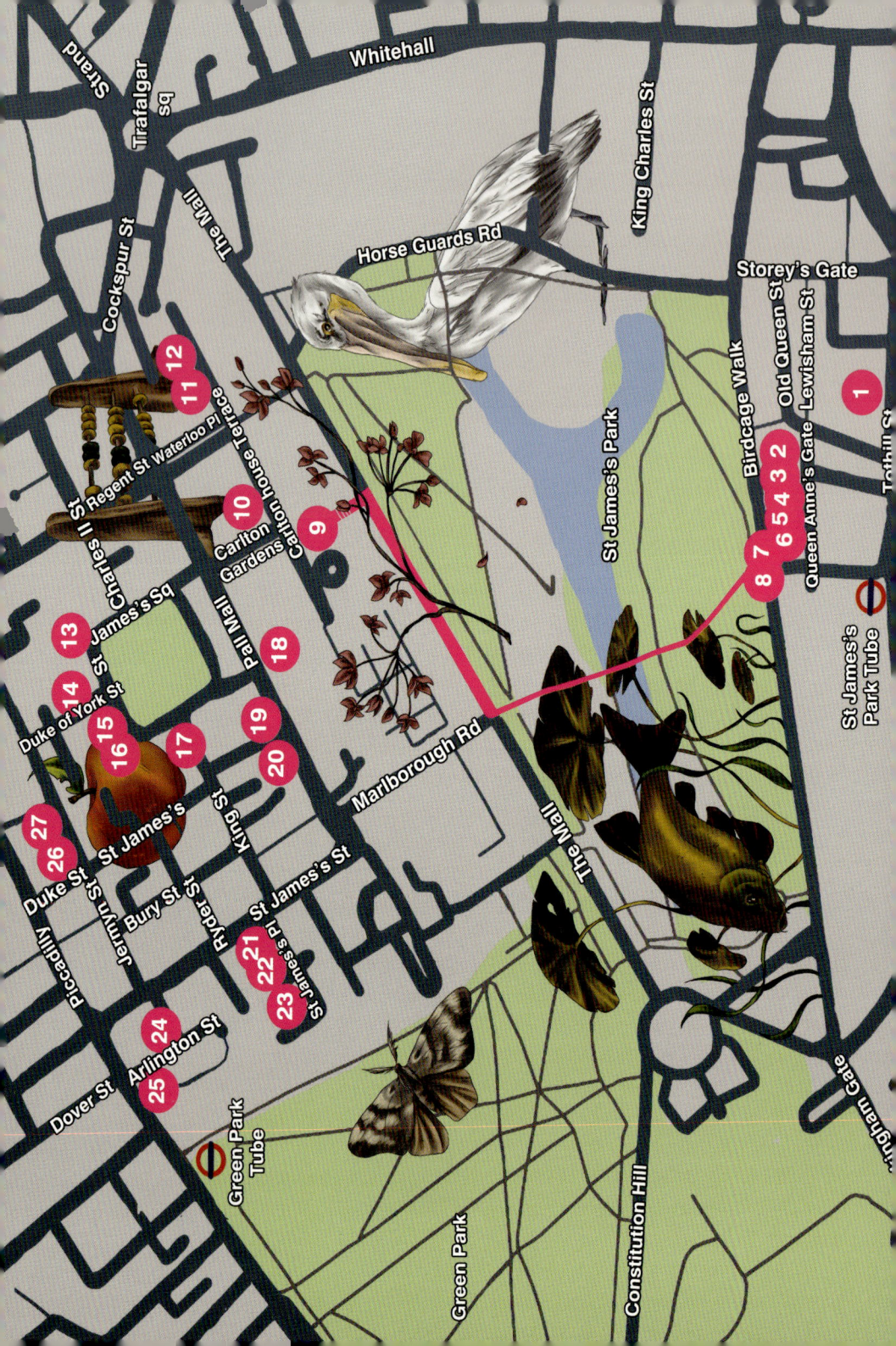

Strand
Whitehall
Trafalgar Sq
Cockspur St
King Charles St
Horse Guards Rd
Storey's Gate
The Mall
Old Queen St
Lewisham St
1
Tothill St
Regent St
Waterloo Pl
12
11
Birdcage Walk
2
3
4
5
6
Carlton House Terrace
Carlton Gardens
10
9
7
Queen Anne's Gate
8
St James's Park
Charles II St
St James's Sq
13
St James's Park Tube
14
Duke of York St
Pall Mall
18
15
17
19
16
King St
20
Ryder St
Marlborough Rd
Jermyn St
Bury St
St James's
21
The Mall
22 St James's Pl
23 St James's St
Piccadilly
Duke St
26
27
24
Arlington St
25
Dover St
Green Park Tube
Green Park
Constitution Hill
Buckingham Gate

St James's Walk Guide

Page	Ref	Person	Place
180	1	Sir Winston CHURCHILL	Caxton Hall, Tothill Street
181	2	Sir Edward GREY	3 Queen Anne's Gate
182	3	Charles TOWNLEY	14 Queen Anne's Gate
183	4	Admiral Jackie FISHER	16 Queen Anne's Gate
184	5	William SMITH	16 Queen Anne's Gate
185	6	Lord PALMERSTON	20 Queen Anne's Gate
186	7	Lord HALDANE	28 Queen Anne's Gate
187	8	Jeremy BENTHAM	50 Queen Anne's Gate
188	9	Lord Horatio KITCHENER	2 Carlton Gardens
189	10	Charles de GAULLE	4 Carlton Gardens
189	10	Lord PALMERSTON	4 Carlton Gardens
190	11	George CURZON	1 Carlton House Terrace
191	12	William GLADSTONE	11 Carlton House Terrace
192	13	Nancy ASTOR	4 St James's Square
193	14	Henry JERMYN (1st Earl of St Albans)	2 Duke Of York Street
194	15	William PITT (The Elder)	10 St James's Square
194	15	William GLADSTONE	10 St James's Square
195	15	Earl Edward STANLEY	10 St James's Square
196	16	Ada, Countess of LOVELACE	12 St James's Square
197	17	NAPOLEON III	1c King Street
198	18	Frederick WINSOR	89 Pall Mall
199	19	Thomas GAINSBOROUGH	80 - 82 Pall Mall
200	20	Nell GWYNNE	79 Pall Mall
201	21	Frederic CHOPIN	4 St James's Place
202	22	Sir Francis CHICHESTER	9 St James Place
203	23	William HUSKISSON	28 St James's Place
204	24	Sir Robert WALPOLE	17 Arlington Street
205	24	Horace WALPOLE	17 Arlington Street
206	25	Henry PELHAM	22 Arlington Street
207	26	Rosa LEWIS	Cavendish Hotel, 82 Jermyn Street
208	27	Sir Isaac NEWTON	87 Jermyn Street

Distance : 2.1 miles (3.4 Km)
Starting Point: St James's Park Underground Station

Finish Point: Green Park Underground Station

Circle
District
Jubilee
Victoria
Piccadilly

Sir Winston CHURCHILL
Prime Minister
Caxton Hall, Tothill Street — Map Ref 1

Winston Leonard Spencer-Churchill (1874 – 1965) was born at Blenheim Palace, Woodstock in Oxfordshire to Lord Randolph Churchill, a politician, and Jennie, nee Jerome, the daughter of a wealthy American. He was the eldest of two sons, and became the 20th century's most famous and celebrated Prime Minister. He was educated at three independent schools, then Harrow and Sandhurst Royal Military College and saw service in India and the Sudan. In order to improve his income, he acted off-duty as a war correspondent for several newspapers. Churchill left the army in 1899 at the age of 25 to take up politics, but first went to South Africa as a journalist covering the Boer War, where he was captured, but made a daring escape.

He became Conservative MP for Oldham in 1900, but his willingness to work with any side that agreed with his views led him to become President of the Board of Trade in Asquith's Liberal Government. He set-up labour exchanges and unemployment insurance, and in 1910, as Home Secretary, he improved safety in the coal mines, and prevented the employment of child miners. In 1911 he was appointed First Lord of the Admiralty, and ensured the Navy was ready for the outbreak of war in 1914. After being demoted in the war-time coalition government, he was made Minister for Munitions under PM Lloyd George. He returned to the Conservative Party in the 1920's, and spent five years as Stanley Baldwin's Chancellor of the Exchequer, before again falling out with his party. His warnings about the threat of the Nazis went unheeded, but Chamberlain's attempts at appeasement failed and Churchill was asked to form a government in 1940.

He represented the spirit of Britain in the 2nd World War with his stirring rhetoric, and was key to raising national morale. After the war, Churchill was defeated, but returned as Conservative PM after the 1951 election. He spent much of his time in developing the 'special relationship' with America, but failed in his efforts to end the Cold war with Russia. Frustrated and in poor health, he resigned in 1955 aged 81.

Churchill had married Clementine Hozier in 1908, with whom he had one son and four daughters. He was a prolific writer of books, most notably his *A History of the English-Speaking Nations*, and he enjoyed painting, polo and board games. His state funeral in 1965 was beamed around the World by the BBC.

Sir Edward GREY
Statesman

3 Queen Anne's Gate   **Map Ref 2**

Viscount Grey of Falloden SIR EDWARD GREY 1862-1933 Foreign Secretary lived here

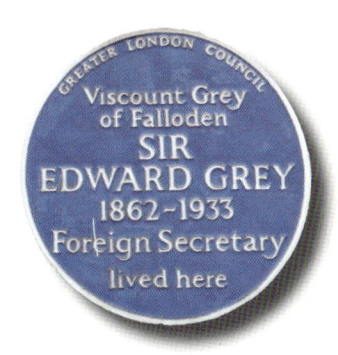

Edward Grey was born in London, the eldest of seven children to Colonel George Henry Grey and Harriet Jane, nee Pearson. He attended Temple Grove School from the age of 11, and when his father died a year later, his grandfather took responsibility for his education and sent him to Winchester College. In 1880 Grey went up to Balliol College, Oxford to read Greats, where he spent more time pursuing sports activities - such as football, where he represented his College, and tennis, where he went on to become British champion - than his academic studies.

After university, he sought career advise from his neighbour, First Lord of the Admiralty, Lord Northbrook, and took-up the role in 1884 of unpaid assistant private secretary to the Chancellor of the Exchequer, Hugh Childers. Grey beat the sitting Conservative MP in Berwick-upon-Tweed at the general election of 1885, which he continued to represent for over thirty years. In 1892 he was appointed Under-Secretary of State for Foreign Affairs under Gladstone, until the Liberals were defeated in 1895 and he remained as a backbencher.

Balfour's Conservative government was defeated in 1906, and Grey was appointed Foreign Secretary under Asquith and then Lloyd-George, a position he held for eleven years. During his tenure of office he worked assiduously to create an entente with Russia, and had to contend with crises in Bosnia and Morocco. As Foreign Secretary, Grey set the course of British policy before and during the early years of the 1st World War. He moved to the House of Lords in 1916, as Viscount Grey of Fallondon.

He was British Ambassador to the United States of America from 1919 to 1920, after which he returned to the Lords, and from 1923 he served there as the Leader of the Liberals. Grey had married Dorothy Widdrington in 1885, and in 1902 he became a member of the 'Coefficients', a dining club for social reformers, established by Sidney and Beatrice Webb. He published a book about his favourite pastime, fishing, and was a keen ornithologist.

"The lamps are going out all over Europe. We shall not see them lit again in our time."

Charles TOWNLEY
Art collector and Antiquarian
14 Queen Anne's Gate
Map Ref 3

CHARLES TOWNLEY 1737-1805 Antiquary and Collector lived here

Charles Townley (or Towneley) was born at Towneley Hall in Burnley, Lancashire, which was the family seat for this landed Catholic family. As Catholics, they were excluded from public office and from attending university. Townley was educated mainly in France: firstly he was sent to Douai College, the catholic seminary in Northern France, which was established after hundreds of Catholics left England at the resumption of Protestantism, on the accession to the throne of Elizabeth I, and later taught by John Turberville Needham, the English scientist and Catholic Priest.

In 1758 he took up residence at Towneley Hall after the death of his father, and he lived the life of a wealthy English country gentleman. At the age of 34, he left England to make the first of three Grand Tours. In an age of avid British collectors of classical works of art, Townley was prominent as an individual responsible for one of the great collections of Graeco-Roman sculpture, and he became a keen collector of all manner of antiquities. He was assisted in the acquisition of his collection, known especially for the 'Towneley Marbles', by the artist and antiquarian Gavin Hamilton and Thomas Jenkins, a dealer in antiquities in Rome.

Joseph Nollekens, one of the foremost portrait sculptors of his age, met Townley in Rome during the latter's first visit to Rome. When both men had returned to London, Nollekens often visited Townley at his London home, and in 1783 sold him a collection of ancient Italian terracottas. They were acquired by the British Museum after Townley's death, along with much of his sculpture collection, a transaction that transformed the museum's collection.

Nollekens made an imposing marble bust of Townley in 1807, and it became a 'cause celebre' in 2008, when the British government placed a temporary ban on its export. The Committee responsible for the overseeing of the export of works of art recommended that the decision to export be deferred, on the grounds that the sculpture was of outstanding aesthetic importance and of outstanding significance. A grant from the National Heritage Memorial Fund was made and the bust remained at the Towneley Hall Museum.

"By knowing ancient things you will have a clear understanding of the new"
Inscription on the bust of Townley by Joseph Nollekens.

Admiral Jackie FISHER
Admiral of the Fleet

16 Queen Anne's Gate **Map Ref 4**

Admiral of the Fleet LORD FISHER 1841-1920 lived here as First Sea Lord 1904-1910

John Arbuthnot Fisher was born in Ceylon (now Sri Lanka), and joined the Royal Navy at the age of 13. He was an outstanding innovator and administrator responsible for wide-ranging reforms, and is regarded as one of Britain's greatest admirals. His first ship was *HMS Victory*, Nelson's flagship at the Battle of Trafalgar, and he spent most of his naval training learning the art of sailing, but he was fascinated by any technical development that he believed would make the Royal Navy stronger. He was a midshipman in the Crimean War and in China between 1859 and 1860, when he took part in the capture of Canton.

From its invention, Fisher was a supporter of the torpedo and submarines, and in 1872 was appointed to the Royal Navy's gunnery school. In 1874 he was promoted to Captain and took a prominent part in the bombardment of Alexandra in 1882, as Commander of the battleship *HMS Inflexible*. In 1887 he held the post of Director of Naval Ordnance, and in the 1890's Fisher masterminded the adoption of the torpedo boat destroyer. On becoming 3rd Sea Lord in 1892, he was responsible for the efficiency of the fleet and in 1899 Fisher was appointed Commander-in-Chief of the Mediterranean Fleet, improving the fleet's reliability, and encouraging independent tactical thinking by junior officers.

He had a great capacity for self-publicity, gaining rapid promotion, and in 1904 he was appointed First Sea Lord. He made changes to the organization of the fleet, the administration of the dockyards, improved ship conditions, scrapped old ships, converted many from coal to oil, masterminded gunnery development, and persuaded the government to construct eight new battleships.

Most notably, Fisher applied the all-big-gun concept to both battleships and battlecruisers, producing the revolutionary *HMS Dreadnought (*pictured right). His main failing was his personality, and made enemies both within the Royal Navy and in politics. Finding himself isolated by the navy's hierarchy he retired in 1910, but his innovative policies helped Britain win the naval race against the German threat. In 1914 Churchill brought him back as First Sea Lord, but their similar temperaments meant a clash was inevitable, and after disagreeing about the increasing use of naval forces in the Dardanelles campaign against Turkey, he resigned in 1915

The essence of war is violence; moderation in war is imbecility.

William SMITH
Politician

16 Queen Anne's Gate **Map Ref 5**

William Smith was born in Clapham, in south London. His parents were part of the Christian sect known as 'Independents', and he was educated at the 'dissenting academy' at Daventry, East Midlands. The dissenters didn't conform to all the beliefs of the Church of England, and from where such luminaries as Joseph Priestly, the clergyman and scientist noted for discovering oxygen, graduated.

He came under the influence of the Unitarians whilst at school, a Christian faction who believed in the single personality of God, in contrast to the perceived doctrine of the Trinity. At the conclusion of his education he joined the family grocery business, and his father made him a partner in 1777, when he was 21.

Smith was one of the leading independent politicians of his day, and became Member of Parliament for Sudbury in Suffolk in 1784. He was prevented from attaining high office of state, both by his own dissenting Christian convictions, but also his desire to remain out of the limelight. Nevertheless, he played a leading role in most of the key contemporary parliamentary issues of the day, including the attempt to repeal the Test and Corporation Acts, which required that non-Christians were excluded from holding public office.

In 1787, Smith was one of the first to support William Wilberforce in his efforts to abolish the slave trade, a cause he pursued for the rest of his political life. Over the next twenty years he sat as MP for three different constituencies, Camelford, Cornwall, Sudbury, and Norwich. Smith initially had sympathies with the revolutionary movement in France, visiting Paris in 1790, and with the contacts he had made in France, this led to him being encouraged to arrange meetings between William Pitt and Maret, Napoleon's Foreign Minister, in an effort to avoid war.

In 1792 he was one of the founding members of the Friends of the People Society, whose actions led to the repeal of the Test Acts and the introduction of the Catholic Relief Act in 1828. He faced financial ruin after the collapse of his business ventures, but he was supported by his friends Charles James Fox and William Wilberforce, and by his wife, Frances, daughter of John and Hannah Coape. She bore him ten children, including Frances, who married William Nightingale, and who was the mother of Florence Nightingale.

Lord PALMERSTON
Prime Minister

20 Queen Anne's Gate　　　　　　　　　　**Map Ref　6**

Henry John Temple 1784 – 1865 is one of the few individuals who has more than one plaque commemorating their life, his biography is detailed at his other address, 94 Piccadilly, in the Mayfair South Walk (Map Ref 5).

Lord Palmerston was England's great renegade in the arena of foreign affairs: he was often the bane of both Prince Albert and Queen Victoria. He was not fashionable and the Whigs looked askance at him.

> "England is strong enough to brave consequences"

The Whigs tolerated him only as an unpleasant necessity thrust on them by fate.

He was in office almost continuously from 1807 until his death in 1865. He started as a Tory and concluded as a Liberal. He directed British foreign policy through a period when Britain was at the height of its power.

A Proportionate Response?

In 1850, Palmerston – as Foreign Secretary – sent the British fleet to blockade Piraeus, the port of Athens. A British citizen was refused compensation by the Greek government after his home was attacked and vandalised by a violent mob.

"As the Roman, in days of old, held himself free from indignity, when he could say 'CIVIS ROMANUS SUM' (I am a Roman citizen) so also a British subject, in whatever land he may be, shall feel confident that the watchful eye and the strong arm of England will protect him against injustice and wrong"

Palmerston was one of the great Irish landed proprietors

"It is true that the peasantry of Ireland do not enjoy all the comforts which are enjoyed by all the peasantry of England. Still, however, the Irish peasant has his own comforts. He is well supplied with fish, and is seldom (Ed- 4 days out of 6) at a loss for food. But this is not all the comfort he has – he has a greater cheerfulness than his English fellow-sufferer."

Florence Nightingale said of Palmerston: -

"Tho' he made a joke when asked to do the right thing, he always did it…he was so much more in earnest than he appeared, he did not do himself justice"

Lord HALDANE
Statesman

28 Queen Anne's Gate   **Map Ref 7**

LORD HALDANE
1856 - 1928
STATESMAN
LAWYER AND
PHILOSOPHER
LIVED HERE

Richard Burdon Sanderson Haldane was born in Edinburgh, Scotland, to Robert and Mary Elizabeth, nee Burdon-Sanderson. He was a politician, philosopher and lawyer, and received his education at the Edinburgh Academy, Gottingen University – in Germany – and the University of Edinburgh, where he took a 1st class honours degree in Philosophy. He moved to London and enjoyed a successful career as a lawyer after being called to the bar in 1879.

Haldane was returned as a Liberal MP in 1885 for the Haddingtonshire constituency, which was a county in Scotland until 1974. He became an ardent campaigner for social reform, and from 1905 held ministerial office as Secretary of State for War for seven years under Prime Minister Bannerman and then Asquith. Haldane was a strong advocate of British commitments on the European continent, and ensured that Britain had an army ready for, what was to be, the 1st World War. He was instrumental in creating the Special Reserve, the Officer Training Corps, the Imperial General Staff, and the Territorial Army, which had 269,000 members by the beginning of the war.

He was actively involved in the creation of the Advisory Committee for Aeronautics in 1909, which ensured the sound development of aircraft for many years to come. In 1912 he was appointed Lord Chancellor under Asquith, but resigned in 1915 after accusations had been made that he had pro-German sympathies. By the general election of 1923 he had switched his allegiance to the Labour Party, and the newly elected Prime Minister, Ramsay McDonald, appointed him as Lord Chancellor, Leader of the House of Commons, and Leader of the Labour Peers.

Led by Sidney and Beatrice Webb, Haldane had helped to create the London School of Economics in 1895, which has become the foremost social science university in the world. He was a President of the Aristotelian Society, which had been formed in 1880 to hear and discuss philosophical papers, which still meets today and is open to the public to attend. He wrote a number of philosophical works, including *The Reign of Relativity* in 1921, which examined the philosophical implications of Albert Einstein's Theory of Relativity. He never married.

Jeremy BENTHAM
Philosopher

50 Queen Anne's Gate **Map Ref 8**

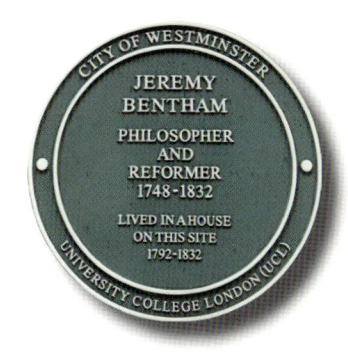

Plaque:
CITY OF WESTMINSTER
JEREMY BENTHAM
PHILOSOPHER AND REFORMER
1748-1832
LIVED IN A HOUSE ON THIS SITE
1792-1832
UNIVERSITY COLLEGE LONDON (UCL)

Jeremy Bentham was one of seven children born in Hounsditch in London to Jeremiah Bentham, an attorney, and Alicia Woodward (nee Whitehorne). She died when Jeremy was only eleven, and his father was very ambitious for his eldest child, beginning to teach him Latin at the age of three. He attended Westminster School at seven, and went up to Queen's College, Oxford when only twelve.

At sixteen Bentham achieved a BA degree, thus becoming the youngest graduate at Oxbridge: in 1763 he was admitted to Lincoln's Inn, and in 1769 was admitted to the bar. He was a shy, unhappy young man, small in stature and physically weak: he felt isolated and under the rule of his father. He decided to leave the law and concentrate on writing: with an allowance from his father, he produced a series of books on philosophy, economics and politics.

Bentham devised the doctrine of utilitarianism, arguing that the greatest happiness of the greatest number is the only right and proper end of government. He was exasperated with the complexity of English law, and was a major thinker in the field of legal philosophy. When the American colonies published their Declaration of Independence in 1776, the British government commissioned John Lind, a lawyer, to publish a rebuttal, which included an attack by Bentham on the American's political philosophy. In 1798 he wrote Principles of International Law where he argued that universal peace could only be achieved by first achieving European unity.

In 1824 Bentham joined James Mill to found the Westminster Review, the journal of philosophical radicals, which included contributions by Lord Byron, Samuel Taylor Coleridge and Thomas Carlyle. His publication Constitutional Code in 1830 argued in favour of universal suffrage, annual parliaments and vote by ballot, but that there should be no king, no House of Lords and no established church. The book also suggested the continual inspection of the work of politicians and government officials, pointing out that they are the "servants, not the masters, of the public".

He supported the idea of equal opportunity in education, and his ideas contributed to the foundation of University College London in 1828, the first institution in England to admit students of any race, class, or religion, and the first to welcome women on equal terms with men. Amongst other subjects upon which Bentham expressed his views, he is one of the earliest champions of animal rights, he focused on monetary expansion as a means of helping to create full employment, and called for the abolition of slavery, the death penalty, and physical punishment.

Lord Horatio KITCHENER
Soldier and Statesman

2 Carlton Gardens **Map Ref 9**

Horatio Herbert Kitchener was born in Listowel, County Kerry in Ireland to English parents, Lieutenant Colonel Henry Horatio Kitchener, and Frances Anne (nee Chevallier-Cole). The family moved to Switzerland when Kitchener was 14, in an attempt to cure his mother's illness, and where he continued his education. He became a British military leader and statesman, and was depicted on the most famous recruitment poster ever produced.

He joined the Royal Engineers at the age of 21 in 1871 after studying at Royal Military Academy, Woolwich, and served in France, Palestine, Egypt and Cyprus. He took part in the unsuccessful operation to relieve General Gordon at Khartoum in 1884, and in 1886 was appointed Governor-General of eastern Sudan. Kitchener became commander-in-chief of the Egyptian army, and in 1896 he began the re-conquest of Sudan, culminating in the Battle of Omdurman and the re-occupation of Khartoum in 1898, which resulted in his being appointed as the Governor of Sudan.

In 1900 Kitchener was appointed Chief-of-Staff during the 2nd Boer War, where he dealt with continuing Boer resistance, but his ruthless measures to imprison civilians, in what have become known as concentration camps, were criticised. He returned to England in 1902, was created Viscount Kitchener, and appointed Commander-in Chief in India. In 1911 he became Pro-Consul in Egypt, serving there and in Sudan until 1914.

He was appointed as Secretary of State for War at the beginning of the 1st World War in 1914 by Prime Minister Asquith, a role he held for two years: he organised armies on an unprecedented scale, and ensured that the country had adequate forces for what he predicted would be a long war.

Kitchener was sent on a diplomatic mission to Russia in 1916, but was drowned when a German mine sank his ship *HMS Hampshire* off the Orkneys. His body was never recovered, which has led rise to various conspiracy theories. He never married and some historians have concluded that he was a homosexual, although it is also known that he was thwarted in his desire to marry at least two members of the opposite sex.

Charles de GAULLE
Statesman and Soldier

4 Carlton Gardens **Map Ref 10**

Plaque text: GREATER LONDON COUNCIL — GENERAL CHARLES DE GAULLE President of the French National Committee set up the Headquarters of the Free French Forces here in 1940

Charles de Gaulle (1890-1970) was born in Lille, France, the third of five children of a clever academic family with minor aristocratic roots and right-wing royalist and Catholic convictions. His father was a professor at a Jesuit College, and Charles was educated in Paris at the College Stanislas, and then at the Special Military School of St. Cyr, in Brittany, which Napoleon Bonaparte had founded. He served with distinction in the 1st World War, but his army career was interrupted by capture at Verdun in 1916. While he was incarcerated he wrote *The Enemy or the True Enemy*. He married Yvonne Vendreux in 1921, with whom he had three children, and during the 1920's he was a member of the Army of Occupation in the Rhineland, returning to France in the 1930's. De Gaulle was recognised as an intellectual soldier and author of significant works on future conflict. His advice was ignored, and at the beginning of the 2nd World War the Germans easily captured France.

He briefly commanded an armoured division in the May 1940 Blitzkrieg, and became a junior defence minister, but refused to accept the French Government's truce with the Germans, and escaped to London. He established the French Government in Exile, and became the leader of the 'Free French', which encouraged his countrymen to resist the German occupation, and to work against the Vichy regime, which had signed the armistice with the Nazis. He was a superb radio performer, and by 1944 when Paris was liberated he had won a vast popular following with his broadcasts, and he returned as a hero and was elected as President of the provisional government. His demands for a 'strong presidency' were rejected, and in 1953 after failing to create a new political party he retired.

Lord Palmerston also has a plaque on this property and his biography is detailed in the Mayfair South Walk Map Ref 5

De Gaulle returned as President in 1958 amid the Algerian war and a threatened military coup. Strongly nationalistic, he sought to strengthen the country financially and militarily, sanctioning the development of nuclear weapons, withdrew France from NATO and vetoed Britain's entry into the Common Market. The country rallied behind de Gaulle's government in 1968 after student demonstrations, and a general strike, but he resigned the presidency the following year after he lost a constitutional referendum.

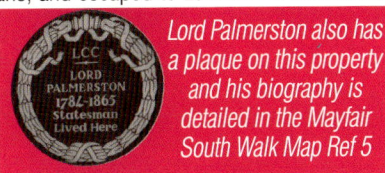

George CURZON (1st Marquess Curzon of Kedleston)
Statesman
1 Carlton House Terrace — Map Ref 11

George Nathaniel Curzon was born in Kedleston in Derbyshire, the eldest son and second of eleven children of Alfred Curzon (4th Baron Scarsdale) and Blanche (nee Senhouse) from Cumberland. He was a Conservative, who became both Viceroy of India and Foreign Secretary.

He was educated initially by a governess, before attending Eton College and Balliol College, Oxford, where he was elected President of the Oxford Union, and took a degree in Greats. Curzon like most aristocrats supported the Conservative Party, and he served as private secretary to Prime Minister, Lord Salisbury in 1885. In 1886 he entered Parliament as MP for Southport, on Merseyside, but neglected his duties as he chose to travel extensively, visiting the Indian sub-continent and China and the Far East.

In 1891, PM Salisbury appointed Curzon as Secretary of State for India, but lost the post when Rosebery formed a Liberal Government in 1894. The following year the Conservatives were returned and he became Under-Secretary for Foreign Affairs, and in 1898 was appointed Viceroy of India. Once in India, he introduced a series of reforms that upset the local civil servants and Lord Kitchener, who had become the Commander of the Indian Army. Curzon understood Indian problems and addressed them, with his goal to strengthen the British Empire in India. In 1905, the new leader of the Conservatives, Arthur Balfour, began to question Curzon's judgement and forced him out of office.

> My name is George Nathaniel Curzon,
> I am a most superior person.
> My cheeks are pink, my hair is sleek,
> I dine at Blenheim twice a week.
> *Fellow student at Balliol*

Upon his return, Curzon lead the campaign against women's suffrage in the House of Lords, and in 1908 helped to establish the Anti-Suffrage League. He refused to join Lloyd-George's War cabinet in 1916, but was appointed Foreign Secretary by Prime Minister Bonar Law in 1919. On the latter's retirement in 1923, Curzon was passed over for his job in favour of Stanley Baldwin, but he remained as Foreign Secretary until Baldwin's government fell in 1924.

Curzon married twice. First to Mary Victoria Leiter, with whom he had three daughters, and after her death at the age of 36, eleven years later in 1917, he married Elinor Glyn, the widowed American romance novelist. The same year he bought Bodiam Castle, in East Sussex, which he bequeathed to the National Trust after extensive restoration.

William GLADSTONE
Prime Minister
11 Carlton House Terrace — Map Ref 12

William Ewart Gladstone was born in Liverpool, the fourth son, and fifth of six children to Sir John Gladstone, a merchant, and his second wife, Anne MacKenzie, (nee Robertson). He was Prime Minister four times over a period 12 years. He went to a Liverpool preparatory school, and at the age of 12 followed his elder brothers to Eton College. He went up to Christ Church, Oxford University, was elected as President of the Oxford Union, and obtained a double first.

After graduating, he undertook the 'grand tour' of Europe and upon his return at the age of 23 he was elected as Conservative MP for Newark. He made his maiden speech defending his father's interest in West Indies sugar plantations, speaking out against the abolition of slavery, and opposed the recent democratic electoral reforms. In 1833 he entered Lincoln's Inn with the intention of becoming a barrister, but he did not pursue this route. PM Peel (q.v.) appointed him as a Junior Lord of the Treasury, and then Under-Secretary for War and the Colonies at the age of 25. He followed Peel in resigning the following year, and spent the next six years in opposition. He was re-elected in 1841, and over the next twenty-five years held senior offices in the governments of Peel, Aberdeen, Palmerston, and Russell.

> "A half-mad firebrand" Queen Victoria

In 1867, Gladstone became leader of the Liberal party, and Prime Minister for the first time. His policies were intended to improve individual liberty, while loosening political and economic restraints. In 1874 a heavy defeat at the General Election led to Gladstone's arch-rival Disraeli (q.v.) becoming PM. Three years later Gladstone became PM again, much against Queen Victoria's will, but in 1885 the government's budget was defeated and he resigned. The following year he was PM for just six months, and then devoted the next six years to convincing the British electorate to grant Home Rule to Ireland. The Liberals won the 1892 election and Gladstone returned as PM for the fourth time.

Gladstone had married Catherine Glynne from Flintshire in 1839, and with whom he had four sons and four daughters. She assisted him in his work to rescue and rehabilitate prostitutes, walking the streets of London, encouraging women to change their ways.

Nancy ASTOR
Politician

4 St James Square   **Map Ref 13**

ENGLISH HERITAGE
NANCY ASTOR
1879-1964
First woman to sit in Parliament lived here

Nancy Langhorne was born in Virginia, USA, the daughter of Chiswell Dabney Langhorne, a wealthy businessman, who had made his fortune from railway development. She had four sisters and three brothers. At 18 she married Robert Gould Shaw with whom she had a son, Bobbie. The marriage did not work, and they divorced six years later. She moved to England with her younger sister, Phyllis, in 1904, where she met her fellow American, the immensely wealthy Waldorf Astor, twelve years her senior. He had inherited a fortune from his father, who had made his money from real estate holdings in New York City, which made Waldorf the richest man in America.

She married Astor and they moved to the magnificent Cliveden estate in Buckinghamshire, and bought 4 St James Square, which today is home to the 'Naval & Military Club'. Astor was the Conservative MP for the Sutton constituency in Plymouth, and on the death of his father – Viscount Astor – he joined the House of Lords. This left a vacancy in the constituency, and Nancy won the resulting by-election, and in 1919 became the first woman to take her seat in the House of Commons.

Nancy was a campaigning MP, and her maiden speech in Parliament was in favour of temperance, with the intention of raising the age that alcohol can be bought to 18. She also sought improved women's suffrage, equal rights in the Civil Service and the provision of nursery schools. In the 1930's, she strongly supported PM Neville Chamberlain's desire for appeasement with the Germans, but once war was declared she voted against him, allowing Winston Churchill to become Prime Minister.

She had four sons and one daughter, who encouraged her to retire from politics; at the same time as many in her party believed she had become a liability. In her latter years, her marriage began to suffer, her public image became tarnished with some of her racial views, and her children began to be estranged from her.

"I married beneath me. All women do."
"The only thing I like about rich people is their money"
Astor to Churchill: "If you were my husband, I'd poison your tea"
Churchill to Astor: "If you were my wife, I'd drink it"

Henry JERMYN (1st Earl of St Albans)
Diplomat
2 Duke Of York Street — Map Ref 14

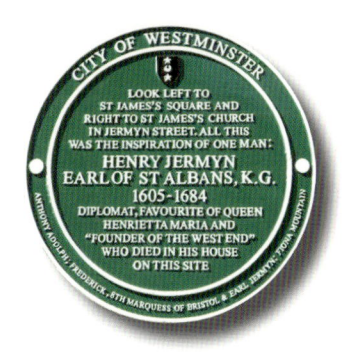

Henry (Germain) Jermyn, the fourth but second surviving son of Sir Thomas Jermyn of Rushbrook in Suffolk, and his wife, Catherine (nee Killigree) of Hanworth, Middlesex. His father was Vice-Chamberlain to King Charles I, and was appointed Governor of Jersey. Jermyn followed his father into royal service, and joined Lord Kensington in his mission to Paris in 1624 to negotiate the marriage of Charles I and Henrietta Maria, the youngest daughter of King Henry IV of France. Jermyn was elected MP for Bodmin in 1625 and 1626 and Liverpool in 1628.

He had joined Henrietta Maria as a gentleman usher in 1627, after she became Queen consort of Charles I, and he quickly became her favourite and confidante. However, in 1633 the King banished him to France over his refusal to marry the pregnant Eleanor Villiers, whom he had seduced. Jermyn returned to Court in 1636 and was appointed Master of Horse to the Queen in 1639. In 1640, he was elected MP for Corfe Castle together with his brother Thomas, and they were both elected MP's for Bury St Edmunds.

In 1641 Jermyn played a prominent part in the plot to bring the King's army from the north to 'frighten' parliament, and was forced to flee to France upon its discovery. In 1642, with civil war about to breakout, he joined Henrietta Maria at The Hague, and assisted her in pawning crown jewels and recruiting troops for the Royalist cause. Jermyn returned to England in 1643, and was appointed Colonel of the Queen's bodyguard, and was raised to the peerage as Baron Jermyn of Edmundsbury. He succeeded his father as Governor of Jersey in 1644, and proposed a plan to cede the Channel Islands to France in exchange for military aid.

He perceived that Charles I's salvation lay in allowing a Presbyterian church settlement in England in order to gain Scottish support, but the King delayed too long. After the defeat of the Royalists in 1649, it fell to Jermyn to break the news of the King's execution to Henrietta Maria. Charles II and his mother took exile in France, and Jermyn sought alliances with foreign powers and made concessions to the Presbyterians, in order to restore the Monarchy. The new King created Jermyn as Earl of St Albans in 1659, and he was richly rewarded with land and property north of St James's Palace. He was appointed Ambassador to France in 1661 and worked to bring closer union between England and France.

Jermyn was a patron of the architect Sir Christopher Wren and was responsible for the development of St James's Square and the surrounding streets, including Jermyn Street, which began the development of London's West End. He was noted for his devotion to gambling and good living.

William PITT (The Elder), Earl of Chatham
Prime Minister
10 St James Square — Map Ref 15

William Pitt was born in London, the second son and fourth of seven children of an Anglo-Irish family, Robert Pitt and Lady Harriet (nee Villiers). His father was an MP who had made a fortune in Ireland. William was Prime Minister for just two years, but he dominated British politics in the middle of the 18th century. He was educated at Eton, Trinity College, Oxford, and then the University of Utrecht, in Holland.

In 1731 he took a commission in the King's Regiment of Horse, but was dismissed in 1736 for a derogatory speech he had made in Parliament. He undertook a short 'grand tour' from 1733 to 1734, and became an MP the following year for Old Sarum, the family's rotten borough. Pitt was an excellent orator, and noted for his commanding figure and clear, dramatic voice. He was an intimidating adversary, and he refused to toe the line in matters of war and commerce. He was very popular, whose influence was so powerful that he effectively served as prime minister in all but name throughout the premierships of Lords Devonshire and Newcastle.

"Where laws end, tyranny begins"
"Unlimited power is apt to corrupt the minds of those who possess it"

Britain suffered military setbacks against the Spanish and the French, and Pitt was highly critical of the government's tactics, and criticised King George III's personal interests. In 1746 PM Newcastle appointed him Paymaster-General, intending to neutralise him, but continuing defeats supported his views, and under PM Devonshire he was appointed War Secretary. He used only British troops, enlarged the Navy, and saw the relationship between war and trading success, conquering India, Canada, the West Indies and West Africa. Pitt was seen as the architect of Britain's success in the 7 Years War against France, as a result of which she became the foremost maritime and commercial nation in the world, and he is credited with the birth of the British Empire.

In 1776 he was given the opportunity of forming his own administration as Prime Minister, but he made errors of judgement with his appointments, tried to 'manage' King George III and after two years he 'retired' to the House of Lords as Earl of Chatham. Lady Hester Grenville had married Pitt late in life for the time – she was 34 and he was 46 – but she soon bore him three sons and two daughters by the time she was 40. Pitt enjoyed cricket, horse riding, military history, and landscape gardening.

Gladstone also shares this plaque, and his biography is detailed in this walk
Map Ref 12

Earl Edward STANLEY
Statesman
10 St James Square **Map Ref 15**

Edward George Geoffrey Smith-Stanley was born in Knowsley, near Liverpool, to wealthy landowners. He was the eldest son, and the first of seven children to Edward Smith-Stanley (13th Earl of Derby) and Charlotte Margaret (nee Hornby). He was unusual in serving in both Whig and Tory administrations, and was Prime Minister on three occasions, none of them lasting more than twelve months. He was educated at Eton College and then Christ Church, Oxford, and being heir to an aristocratic family, he followed the traditional route into politics.

He began his career as a Whig, becoming Member of Parliament from 1822 to 1826 for Stockbridge in Hampshire, then Windsor in 1831, and finally Preston in Lancashire in 1832. He was appointed Chief Secretary in Lord Grey's administration, bringing in the Irish Education Act in 1831, and then Colonial Secretary, introducing measures for the emancipation of slaves.

Derby argued with fellow Whigs, and in 1837 joined Peel's Tory party, where in 1841 he was appointed Colonial Secretary. He had responsibility for issues such as the 'Opium War', the first Anglo-Chinese War, fought to force the Chinese to allow free trade. In 1844 he was called to the House of Lords, and in the following year Derby disagreed with Peel over repealing the Corn Laws, and he became a focus for the protectionists in government.

In 1852 Derby became the PM in a minority government, which collapsed by the end of the year, when Disraeli's budget was defeated. His second administration, 1858-1859, achieved more, notably the India Act, which transferred control of the East India Company to the Crown, and the Jews Relief Act, which ended the exclusion of Jews from sitting in Parliament. His attempts to widen the franchise led to his government's downfall, but his final government in 1867 was responsible for the 2nd Reform Bill, which extended the right to vote further down the class ladder, doubling the electorate.

Derby is considered to be the father of the modern Conservative Party, and his tenure as its leader lasted for a record 22 years. He was married to Emma Caroline Bootle-Wilbranham, with whom he had two sons and a daughter. She was his closest confidante and acted as his personal secretary. His major interests were reading, translating the classics, sport and gambling.

Ada, Countess of LOVELACE
Computer Pioneer

12 St James Square **Map Ref 16**

Augusta 'Ada' King was born in London, the only child of Lord Byron, one of Britain's foremost poets – "mad, bad and dangerous to know" – and his wife, Annabella Milbanke. Ada is widely recognised as being the world's first computer programmer, 150 years before the true power of computers was recognised.

Byron separated from his wife when Ada was a baby, and after giving up his parental rights to his daughter, he left England to settle in Venice. She was raised by her mother at her grandparents' house in Leicestershire, but was a sickly child and at the age of 13 she was paralysed after a bout of measles. She had a slow recovery, and her education was conducted from home by a number of notables, including the renowned mathematician, Augustus de Morgan, who quickly recognised her amazing aptitude to mathematics.

At the age of eighteen, one of her tutors, the scientist Mary Somerville, introduced her to Charles Babbage, a renowned mathematician. He had worked on his *Difference Engine*, a machine that could perform mathematical calculations. The two met and corresponded many times over the ensuing years, and it culminated in Ada completing a mathematical 'programme' for Babbage's more complex *Analytical Engine*.

Ada was a regular at various 'society' events in London, and at the age of nineteen married William King, 8th Baron King, who later became 1st Earl of Lovelace. King was a renowned scientist and a Fellow of the Royal Society. They owned two large estates and the house in London, and had three children, two boys and a girl.

She died at the age of thirty-six, but left a legacy with the recognition that Baggage's engine was an early model for a computer, and the work that Lovelace conducted described what we now know as a computer and software. Significantly, the US Department of Defence's computer language – Ada – was named after her, and the product authenticity hologram on Microsoft's products is her image.

NAPOLEON III
Royalty

1c King Street　　　　　　　　　　　　　　　　　　　　**Map Ref 17**

Napoleon Bonaparte was Napoleon III's uncle. Charles-Louis-Napoleon Bonaparte was born in Paris in 1808, the third son of Napoleon I's brother, Louis Bonaparte (who was King of Holland from 1806 to 1810), and Hortense de Beauharnais Bonaparte, Napoleon I's step-daughter.

After the fall of Napoleon I in 1815, the family were banished from France and fled to Switzerland, where they bought the castle at Arenenberg. After attending grammar school in Augsburg in Germany, he was taught by private tutors. Whilst visiting relatives in Italy and Germany, Louis-Napoleon met other exiled victims and people living in suppression under Austria and Papal rule. He took part in unsuccessful plots against the Papal government in 1830, and the rebellion in central Italy in 1831.

Following the death of his cousin, the Duke of Reichstaadt (Napoleon's only son) in 1832, he considered himself his family's claimant to the French throne. In order to pursue this mission, he began to write treaties on political and military subjects, with the objective of making his name and beliefs more widely understood. King Louis-Phillipe, who reigned France from 1830 to 1848, would have no truck with him, and he was arrested and exiled to Switzerland in 1836.

Between 1838 and 1839, Louis-Napoleon took up residence in England, including a period in Royal Leamington Spa. The following year he was back in France attempting a coup, and this time he was arrested and jailed. In 1846 he escaped, living initially in Southport, near Liverpool, and then moving to 1c King Street. In 1848, after the revolution, King Louis-Philippe was ousted, a Republic was declared, and Louis-Napoleon returned again to France, but was ordered to leave and once more departed for England.

His persistence paid-off and later in 1848 he was elected to the French Assembly. He invoked the legend of Napoleon to win the popular vote as President of the 2nd Republic. Attempting to expand his power, he staged a coup in 1851, declared himself dictator, and became Emperor of the 2nd Republic. He led France into the Crimean War, but overall he was successful in foreign affairs, and his reign saw increased prosperity and political liberalization. Otto von Bismarck encouraged him into the disastrous Franco-Prussian War, which he lost and he was deposed as Emperor.

He settled in England with his Spanish aristocrat wife from Granada, Empress Eugenie, with whom he had a son, Napoleon-Eugene, who was killed fighting for the British army in Zululand.

Frederick WINSOR
Inventor

89 Pall Mall Map Ref 18

Friedrich Albrecht Winsor was born in Brunswick, Germany, and shared his father's name. Little is known of his early years, except for the fact that he was educated in Hamburg, and developed an interest in the technology and the economical use of fuel. He had no technical skills, and essentially he was a persuasive entrepreneur with a flair for promoting extravagant projects. He was one of the pioneers of gas lighting in England and France.

Whilst in Frankfurt in 1802, he learned of the 'Thermo Lampe' (a heat lamp), which had been patented in 1799 by French engineer, Philippe Lebon, who became the first person successfully to use 'artificial' gas as a means of illumination on a large scale. It attracted huge crowds, but unfortunately he had been unable to eliminate the repulsive odour given off by the gas, and the public decided that his invention was not a practical one. Nevertheless, Winsor went to Paris to buy one, and ended up with one to use for demonstrations.

Although gas lighting had been tried outside France, Winsor failed to elicit interest on the continent. Back in England in 1803 circumstances were more favourable, with factory owners looking for safe and more efficient forms of lighting. Between 1804 and 1809 he obtained patents for gas-making equipment, and began his first company in 1804 with a series of lectures in London, explaining how gas could be conveyed to different rooms in the house.

"At every time it shall be light" Zechariah 14:7
Memorial to Winsor in Kensal Green Cemetery

Winsor acquired premises for gas manufacture in Mayfair, and in 1807 staged spectacular demonstrations of gas lighting on the walls of Carlton House Terrace and Pall Mall. In the same year, he issued a prospectus for a central generating gas company, but was ridiculed by such well-known figures as Walter Scott and Humphrey Davy. Nevertheless, hard-headed businessmen could see there could be money in gas.

His application to Parliament for a charter for the Gas Light & Coke Company failed, and he moved to Paris again to found a gas company, but by 1819 it had failed, and he took no further interest in the gas industry. Nevertheless, his pioneering work had lit a spark, and by 1815 thirty miles of gas main had been laid in London, and by 1820 there were over twenty independent provincial companies.

Thomas GAINSBOROUGH
Portrait Painter

80-82 Pall Mall **Map Ref 19**

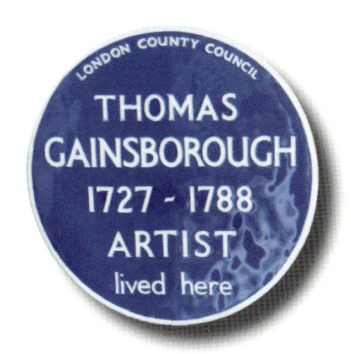

Thomas Gainsborough was born in Sudbury in Suffolk. His father was a clothier and his mother an accomplished flower-painter, who encouraged her son when he showed an early aptitude for drawing. He was to become one of the great English masters of landscape and portrait painting. At the age of 13, he was sent to London to study art, and he spent several years working in the studios of different artists. He trained under the engraver, Hubert Gravelot, and illustrator Francis Hayman, and became associated with William Hogarth and his school.

Gainsborough had married Margaret Burr, an illegitimate daughter of Duke of Beaufort in 1746, and with whom he had two daughters. She had brought an annuity of £200 with her, which had helped him to start his career. He was regarded as a specialist landscape painter in the early period of his life, but his work did not sell well, and in 1748 he returned to Suffolk and concentrated on painting portraits, including his first masterpiece, *Mr and Mrs Robert Andrews*. In 1752 he moved to Ipswich, and again in 1759 to Bath, where Van Dyck and Rubens' work influenced him, and where it was clear there was a ready market for his portraits. By 1761 he was contributing work to the annual Society of Artists exhibitions in London, and showed *The Blue Boy* at the inaugural exhibition in 1769 at the Royal Academy (RA). He continued to submit works to the RA, which helped him acquire a national reputation.

Gainsborough stopped exhibiting at the RA in 1773, and the following year moved to London, where he built a studio in the garden of Schomberg House and continued to attract a wide clientele. Three years later he painted portraits of King George III and began to work for the Royal family, which prompted him to exhibit at the Academy once more. *The Watering Place* was included in the 1777 exhibition, described by one commentator as "by far the finest landscape ever painted in England".

In 1784 he finally broke with the Academy after they refused to hang a Royal Portrait, and instead he began to hold annual exhibitions of his work at Schomberg House. After visiting Antwerp and the Lake District, Gainsborough began to select his sitters more carefully, and often painted relatively simple, ordinary landscapes.

Nell GWYNNE
Actress
79 Pall Mall **Map Ref 20**

IN A HOUSE ON THIS SITE LIVED NELL GWYNNE FROM 1671 ~ 1687

Eleanor Gwynne's (1650 – 1687) birthplace has been claimed by three cities, Oxford, Hereford and London. Her father was Captain Thomas Gwynne, who fought in the Civil War, and her mother was Helena (nee Smith). Thomas appears to have disappeared from the scene by Nell's early childhood, and it is believed that her mother might have run a brothel in Covent Garden. Nell was one of the earliest actresses to receive recognition, and the long-term mistress of King Charles II.

Charles II had been reinstated to the throne in 1660, and after the austere republican rule of Cromwell, which had banned frivolous activities such as the theatre, he granted licences to acting companies. The King's Company formed a new theatre in 1663 in Bridges Street in London, which later became the Theatre Royal, Drury Lane. Nell was employed to sell oranges in the theatre, and at fourteen joined as an actress through the influence of her first lover, the actor Charles Hart. Her first recorded appearance was in 1665 in John Dryden's *Indian Emperor*, and the following year she played in James Howard's comedy *The English Monsieur*. She excelled in the delivery of the risqué, and her success as an actress was largely due to the characters that Dryden wrote for her. She remained a member of the Drury Lane company, playing continuously until 1669 – apart from a short sabbatical when she lived as the mistress of Charles Sackville, Lord Buckhurst.

"Pretty, witty Nell"
- Samuel Pepys
"Let not poor Nelly starve"
- King Charles II

King Charles II had many mistresses, and there was little reason to believe that Gwynn's would endure, but during her first years with the King, there was little competition. She lived either at 79 Pall Mall or in Windsor, in order to be near the King while at his palaces. Her final stage appearance was in 1670 in Dryden's *The Conquest of Granada*, although the production had to be postponed for some months while the theatre awaited her return after the birth of her first son by King Charles, Charles Beauclerk.

King Charles died in 1685, and James II obeyed his brother's deathbed appeal, paying her debts and providing her with other moneys. She had two sons by Charles, the elder was created Earl of Burford, but the younger, James, died while still a boy. Gwynn was the only one of Charles' mistresses to be genuinely popular with the English public, and tradition credits the founding of Chelsea Hospital, home of the Chelsea Pensioners, to her influence over the King.

Frederic CHOPIN
Composer and Musician

4 St.James's Place   **Map Ref 21**

From this house in 1848 FREDERIC CHOPIN 1810-1849 went to Guildhall to give his last public performance

Fryderyk Franciszek Chopin was born in Zelazowa Wola in Poland, to Nicholas a Frenchman, and Justyna Kryzanowska, his Polish mother. He was their second child and only son, and became one of the most famous composers and pianists of the 19th century. The family moved to the capital, Warsaw, when Chopin was seven months old, after his father had been offered a job teaching French at a secondary school.

Music was an important ingredient in the life of the Chopin's: his father played the flute and violin, and his mother played and gave piano lessons. Chopin actually received his first piano lessons from his sister, Ludwika, and he began to receive 'professional' lessons from the age of six. By the age of seven, he began to give public concerts and had composed two Polonaises, and when he was eleven he had played for Czar Alexander I of Russia.

At the age of thirteen, Chopin enrolled in the Warsaw Academy, and three years later in 1826 he began a three-year course at the Warsaw Conservatory. Between 1828 and 1830 he made trips to Germany and Austria, enjoying great success, before leaving Warsaw for good in 1831. He settled in Paris, where he continued to compose and teach the piano. Following an unsuccessful attempt to woo his fellow-Pole, Maria Wodzinskis, in 1837 he began a ten-year relationship with the French authoress known as George Sand.

Chopin's health had never been good, but he continued to compose as he travelled Europe with Sand, who virtually became his nurse. He had never been a prolific performer, but his popularity began to decline, and he made his last performance in Paris in 1848. With the French Revolution in full swing, he escaped to England, where he gave a number of concerts, until his final one at London's Guildhall in November 1848. He returned to Paris, where he died the following year, at the age of 39.

Most of Chopin's compositions were written as solo pieces for the piano, and in all he wrote over 200 works, including sonatas, rondos, scherzos, ballades, polonaises, mazurkas, preludes, impromptus, etudes, nocturnes and waltzes. Many of his compositions have been 'named', including the *Minute Waltz*, the *Military* and the *Heroic*. He influenced many other composers, notably Schumann, Listz, and Brahms.

Sir Francis CHICHESTER
Sailor and aviator

9 St James Place **Map Ref 22**

Francis Charles Chichester was born in Barnstaple, Devon, the second son of the Reverend Charles Chichester, and Emily Annie, nee Page. When asked by the press why he wanted to embark on a single-handed race across the Atlantic at the age of 70 he was unable to give an answer……He was sent to boarding school at the age of 6, and then on to Marlborough College. Chichester immigrated at 18 to New Zealand, where he built-up a successful forestry, mining and property development business, and formed a partnership to run an aviation company between 1927 and 1930.

He returned to England in 1929, where he took flying lessons and qualified as a pilot. In the same year, he bought a Gipsy Moth aircraft, and was the second person to fly solo from England to Australia. In 1931 he made the first solo flight from Australia to New Zealand across the Tasman Sea. In the same year, he made the first long-distance solo seaplane (actually a bi-plane fitted with floats) flight – from New Zealand to Japan.

Chichester decided to circumnavigate the world solo, but only got as far as Japan, where he suffered a severe accident on take-off. He recovered and enlisted in the Royal Air Force at the beginning of the 2nd World War, where he gave distinguished service in air navigation instruction. In 1958 he was diagnosed with lung cancer, fought against the disease, and for convalescence, at the age of 59, he entered and won the first single-handed transatlantic yacht race from Plymouth to New York City in Gypsy Moth III. He went on to break his own record for a single-handed transatlantic crossing in 1962, achieved the fastest voyage around the world by a small vessel, single-handed in 1966-7, and the fastest sustained sailing by a single-handed yacht in 1971.

At the age of 22 he married Murial Blakiston, with whom he had a son George, but she died six years later. His second marriage was to Sheila Craven in 1937, with whom he had a son Giles. In 1945 he started a maps and guide publication business, which is still operating and located in St James Place. In 1963 he wrote a best-selling autobiography The Lonely Sea and the Sky and was knighted by Queen Elizabeth II in 1967.

William HUSKISSON
Statesman

28 St James Place **Map Ref 23**

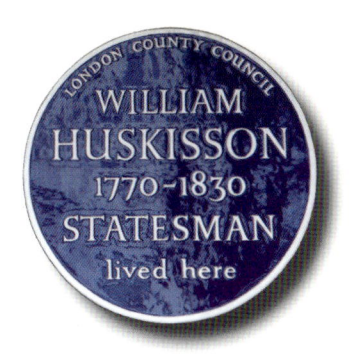

William Huskisson was born in Malvern, Warwickshire to William and Elizabeth, one of four brothers. He was educated privately in England before going to live with his maternal great-uncle, Dr Gem, the physician to the British Embassy in Paris. At the age of 20, the Ambassador, Lord Gower, asked him to become his private secretary. As a result of seeing at first-hand the start of the French Revolution, he developed a life-long interest in politics.

Huskisson returned to England in 1792, and as a result of the contact he had made with William Pitt in France, he was introduced to George Canning who appointed him as Secretary to the Admiralty. He became Tory MP for Morpeth in 1796, and in 1800 when Dr Gem died, he inherited his estates in Worcestershire and Sussex, which made him financially secure for life.

He lost his seat in the 1802 election, but in 1804 was elected as MP for Liskeard, Cornwall. PM William Pitt appointed Huskisson as Secretary to the Treasury, but he returned to the backbenches when Pitt resigned in 1806. In 1810 he published *Depreciation of the Currency*, which gave him a reputation as one of Britain's leading economists. He returned to the House of Commons as MP for Chichester, West Sussex, in 1812, called for changes in the taxation of imports, and ensured the passing of the Corn Law in 1815, which prohibited the importation of corn when the price fell below a certain level.

In 1822, PM Lord Liverpool appointed him as President of the Board of Trade. In the following year, he became MP for Liverpool, and picked up the cudgels for the merchants in the port, and passed several bills that related to trade and the reduction of duties. The Duke of Wellington became Prime Minister in 1828 and Huskisson refused to serve in office under him, which lead to him becoming one of the main reformers of the Tory Party.

He supported the development of railways, and in 1830 was invited to attend the opening of the Liverpool and Manchester Railway, but he was knocked down by the famous 'Stephenson's Rocket' engine, and suffered injuries from which he died. In 1799 he had married Emily Milbanke, the youngest daughter of Admiral Mark Milbanke, the Commander-in-Chief at Portsmouth.

Sir Robert WALPOLE
Prime Minister
17 Arlington Street   Map Ref 24

Robert Walpole was the fifth of 17 children born in Houghton, Norfolk. His father was also Robert, a landowner and MP for Kings Lynn, and his mother, Mary (nee Burwell), the daughter of Sir Jeffrey Burwell, another Suffolk landowner. He was educated at Eton and King's College, Cambridge.

He inherited his family country estate when he was 24, which gave him the financial independence to enter politics. In 1701 he became the Whig MP for Castle Rising, Norfolk, and rose rapidly in parliament as a member of the Admiralty Board, Secretary of War and in 1709, Treasurer of the Navy. Throughout his career, he was accused of bribery and corruption, and he was found guilty of having accepted an illegal payment when he was Secretary of War, and in 1712 was imprisoned for six months in the Tower of London.

Despite this set-back, he returned to government as First Lord of the Treasury and Chancellor of the Exchequer. Whig infighting caused him to resign in 1717, but upon his return in 1720 he was appointed Paymaster-General. This lead to his being selected as Chancellor of the Exchequer for the second time, and he effectively took the powers of the 'Prime Minister', without ever using the 'title'.

Walpole was successful in reducing the national debt and stabilising prices and wages. He often relied on the advice of his brother Horace, a leading diplomat, but his achievements stemmed considerably from his popularity with King George I and the populace at large. George II succeeded his father in 1727, and the new King fell under Walpole's charms, making him a gift of 10 Downing Street in 1735, which has been the Prime Minister's 'base' ever since.

At twenty years, Walpole holds the record of the longest serving Prime Minister, but after a feeble war against Spain in 1739 and a poor general election in 1741, he resigned in 1742. He took his place in the House of Lords and was succeeded as Prime Minister by Spencer Compton, Earl of Wilmington.

He had married Catherine Shorter, a merchant's daughter from Kent, with whom he had five children. Upon her death in 1738, he married his alleged mistress, Maria Skerrett, who was 26 years his junior, but who died in the same year after having a miscarriage. When Walpole first came to London, he lived with his first wife's grandmother, Lady Phillips in Berkeley Street. After his political career progressed, he moved first to Dover Street and in 1715 to Arlington Street, where he lived until his death.

Horace WALPOLE
Author and Politician
17 Arlington Street — Map Ref 24

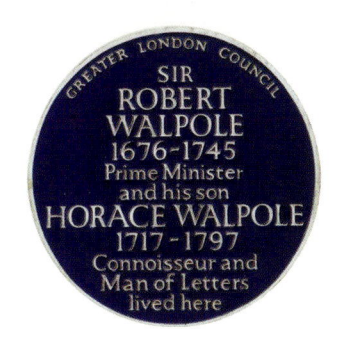

Walpole was born in this house and christened Horatio - he was the 1st Viscount Nelson's cousin. He was the youngest son of Prime Minister, Sir Robert Walpole, the 1st Earl of Orford, and his wife Catherine (nee Shorter). He was tutored at home before continuing his education at Eton College, and King's College, Cambridge. The death of his mother in 1737 was distressing and he left university before finishing his degree a year later.

> "Foolish writers and readers are created for each other"

Walpole's father immediately secured Horace sinecures, and at the age of 20 he was engaged as Inspector of the Imports and Exports in the Custom House, followed by the role of Usher of the Exchequer. He was then appointed Comptroller of the Pipe and Clerk of the Estreats, who ensures that true copies of court proceedings are recorded.

Walpole embarked on the Grand Tour with his friend, the poet Thomas Grey in 1739, but they quarrelled and Walpole returned to England two years later. At the 1741, he was elected Whig MP for Callington in Cornwall, a seat he held for thirteen years. Walpole is better known for the revival of Gothic architecture - with the creation of Strawberry Hill, his home in Twickenham – and as an author, rather than the lack-lustre parliamentarian.

His father, Sir Robert, died in 1745, leaving Horace the house in Arlington Street. In 1754 he became MP for Castle Rising in Norfolk, which he held until 1757, when he was elected as MP for another Norfolk constituency in Kings Lynn, a seat he retained until he retired from the House of Commons in 1768. His retirement enabled him to continue writing, using his own printing press at Strawberry Hill.

He had reconciled with Thomas Gray, and in 1757 published the first edition of his *Pindaris Odes*. Walpole wrote what is considered the first Gothic novel, *Castle of Otranto*, in 1764. Like his father, he had gout and sought a cure in France,

> "I never found that it was necessary to go a thousand miles in search of themes for moralizing"

where he met many social figures, and befriended the intriguing Madame Du Deffad. Walpole published *Historic Doubts on the Life and Reign of Richard III* in 1768, and in 1780 published his essay *On Modern Gardening*.

Upon the death of his elder brother's son in 1791, he succeeded to the title of 4th Earl of Orford, although he never attended the House of Lords. Walpole had never married, and he bequeathed Strawberry Hill to Mrs Anne Damer, the daughter of his friend and cousin, General Conroy.

Henry PELHAM
Prime Minister

22 Arlington Street **Map Ref 25**

Henry Pelham's house was in Arlington Street, but with offices being built in front of the original property, his plaque is located on the west side of the building, overlooking The Green Park. He was born in London, the eighth of nine children to Thomas Pelham (1st Baron Pelham of Laughton) and his second wife, Lady Grace Holles. He was educated at Westminster School and university at Hart Hall, Oxford.

At the age of 21 he commanded a troop of dragoons in the battle of Preston to overcome the Jacobite rising. His elder brother Thomas inherited their family estate in the north east of England, becoming the Duke of Newcastle, and 'arranged' his brother's election as a Whig MP for Seaford in east Sussex.

In 1721 he was appointed as a member of Prime Minister Robert Walpole's Treasury Board, then a year later as Secretary of War. Interestingly, Walpole lived opposite Pelham at 5 Arlington Street. Pelham was elected as MP for the County of Sussex in 1722, which he held throughout the rest of his life. In 1730, he was appointed Paymaster-General, and over the ensuing years he rose through the ranks and was appointed as 1st Lord of the Treasury, and in 1743, Chancellor.

During Henry Pelham's career, his brother Newcastle also held ministerial posts, but they were often at loggerheads. Pelham became Prime Minister in 1743, but King George II was not a fan, and in 1746 made an attempt to replace him with the Earl of Granville. However, Granville could not command the support of Parliament, and Pelham was reinstated hree days later.

Pelham had mixed success during his premiership. Not all his efforts at social and financial reform were realized, but he was successful in ending the War of American Succession in 1748, and achieved peace with France and trade with Spain. He helped to sort out the nation's finances, reorganized the navy and adopted the Gregorian Calendar – which moved the beginning of the year from 25th March to 1st January. He attempted to strengthen the rights of Jews, allowing them to become naturalized by applying to Parliament.

He had married Lady Catherine Mannors, the daughter of the 2nd Duke of Rutland in 1726, with whom he had four daughters. He had had a succession of illnesses during his life, and upon his death in 1754, his brother the Duke of Newcastle succeeded him as Prime Minister.

Rosa LEWIS
Hotelier
Cavendish Hotel, Jermyn Street — Map Ref 26

Rosa Lewis was born Rosa Ovenden in Leyton, Essex, the fifth of nine children. Her father became an undertaker after a career as a watchmaker. Her story is one of rags to riches, as she moved from domestic service to become the "Duchess of Jermyn Street". She left school at 12 to become a general servant for one shilling a week and her keep. It was rare that a general servant would become a cook, but Rosa displayed a flair, and at 16 a lucky recommendation took her to Sheen House in Mortlake, west of London, as a scullery maid at the home of the exiled Compte de Paris. Hardly a step-up, but it was a move that secured her future as "Queen of Cooks".

She rose through the ranks to Head Kitchen Maid, but in 1887 she was poached by Phillipe Duc d'Orleans in Sandhurst, a claimant to the French throne. He allowed his young cook to practice her skills in other grand houses, and society hostesses were keen to employ an English cook who could produce a lighter style of cooking. She was loaned to Lady Randolph Churchill for a night's entertaining, when Edward, Prince of Wales was at the head of the table and praised her cooking. Word travelled fast, and houses entertaining the future Edward VII were desperate to employ her. She became so popular amongst the rich and famous, that she had to employ teams of cooks to meet the demand.

"Not an 'otel, but an 'ome away from 'ome for my friends"

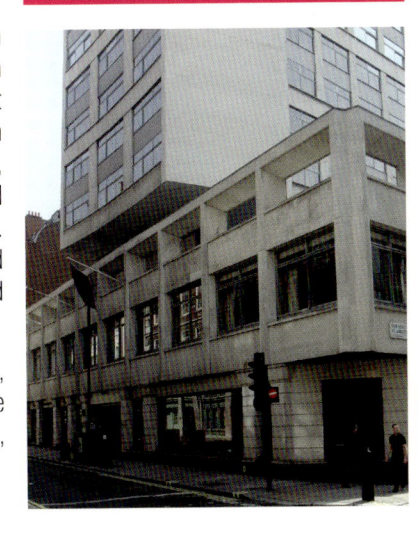

By 1902 she could afford to buy her own hotel, and perhaps with help from her Royal friend, she bought the Cavendish Hotel, which she ran as a kind of exclusive club. Distinguished families kept permanent rooms there, and her companion for over 30 years, Edith Jeffrey, arrived after the 1st World War to work as a seamstress, and became her personal and business assistant. The war affected the business, and it saw a 'majestic' decline from 1918 to 1952. The 1920's provided her with something she desperately needed – an audience, and she toured New York cooking in fine hotels and teaching her skills to eager young apprentices

She married a butler named Excelsior (Chiney) Lewis in 1893, and set-up home in Eaton Terrace. Her life was used as an outline for the popular late 1970's TV series, *The Duchess of Duke Street*, which starred Gemma Jones, who unveiled the plaque.

Sir Isaac NEWTON
Scientist and Mathematician

87 Jermyn Street **Map Ref 27**

Isaac Newton was born in Woolsthorpe, in Lincolnshire to Isaac, a yeoman farmer, who died before his son was born, and his wife Hannah. His mother remarried and when she went to live with her new husband, Newton was brought up by his maternal grandmother, Margery Ayscough. He was sent to boarding school in Grantham, and at 14 returned home, where the intention was that he would carry on with the family farm. He actually spent most of his time solving problems, making experiments or devising models.

Newton's uncle, who had been to Cambridge University, suggested that he should be sent there, to exploit his enquiring mind. At the age of 19 he entered Trinity College, Cambridge, and although he had not read any mathematics before going up to university, he quickly took-up the subject to study. As a mathematician, Newton invented integral calculus and differential calculus, and he made a huge impact on theoretical astronomy.

It has been claimed that he was the most influential scientist ever, and his accomplishments in mathematics, optics and physics laid the foundation for modern science, and revolutionized the world. He defined the laws of motion and universal gravitation, which he used to predict precisely the motions of stars, and the planets around the sun.

Using the lessons he learned from his discoveries, Newton constructed the first reflecting telescope. He had found science a jumbled mixture of isolated facts and laws, capable of describing some phenomena but predicting only a few. He left it with a unified system of laws that could be applied to an enormous range of physical phenomena, and that can be used to make exact predictions.

He lived in Cambridge for thirty five years, but when he was appointed Master of the Royal Mint, he moved to London in 1696, where he lived until his death. He was the first scientist to be honoured by being buried in Westminster Abbey. He had been engaged in his late teens to a Miss Storey, but it seems that his total commitment to his studies and his work was more important than contemplating marriage.

"If I have been able to see further, it was because I stood on the shoulders of giants".

A MESSAGE FROM THE AUTHOR

And so we reach the end of the last of 5 fascinating walks and the first London Plaques book from the Commemorative Plaques Explorer Series - I hope you enjoyed the journey.

Elgar Estates Publishing plans to move the series on with further books covering other exciting areas of London - and we are working on towns and cities around Britain where commemorative plaques are also in existence. We shall also be developing other products and services on the subject.

Why not subscribe to our mailing list to keep up to date with developments in the World of Commemorative Plaques? We promise not to bombard you with regular newsletters that fill up your Inbox, but will keep you updated on key news regarding plaques and new products and services from Elgar Estates Publishing.

To sign up visit the website shown on the logo below.

Thank you again for taking the time to read this book.

Doug Eaton

COMMEMORATIVE PLAQUES
www.commemorativeplaques.co.uk

INDEX

A
- ADAMS, John 70
- AMBROSE, Bert 14
- ARNOLD, Benedict 110
- ASHFIELD, Lord 77
- ASQUITH, Herbert 171
- ASTOR, Nancy 192
- AYER, Sir Alfred 103

B
- BABBAGE, Charles 119
- BALFE, Michael William 96
- BARING, Evelyn 153
- BASEVI, George 46
- BEAUFORT, Sir Francis 122
- BEDFORD-FENWICK, Ethel 150
- BEE GEES 68
- BENEDICT, Sir Julius 126
- BENTHAM, Jeremy 187
- BERLIOZ, Hector 143
- BEVIN, Ernest 58
- BLAKE, William 59
- BODLEY, George Frederick 158
- BOLIVAR, Simon 124
- BONN, Leo 86
- BRIGHT, Richard 49
- BROUGHAM, Lord Henry 44
- BROWNING, Elizabeth Barrett 108, 152
- BRUMMELL, Beau 32
- BUCHANAN, Jack 76
- BURGOYNE, General John 22
- BURNETT, Frances Hodgson 161
- BURNEY, Fanny 15

C
- CAMPBELL, Colen 69
- CANNING, George 39
- CAYLEY, Sir George 23
- CHARLES X of France 29
- CHICHESTER, Sir Francis 202
- CHOPIN, Frederic 201
- CHURCHILL, Sir Winston 180
- CLARENCE, Duke of 31
- CLIFFORD HALL, Keith 90
- CLIVE of India 40
- CLOVER, Dr Joseph T 174
- COLLINS, William Wilkie 109
- CONS, Emma 104
- CURZON, George 190

D
- De GAULLE, Charles 189
- DICK-READ, Dr Grantly 168
- DISRAELI, Benjamin 25, 84
- DONOVAN, Terence 42
- DOYLE, Sir Arthur Conan 151
- du PRÉ, Jacqueline 102
- DUKE-ELDER, Sir Stewart 156

E
- EDEN, Anthony 33
- EISENHOWER, Dwight D 72

F
- FARADAY, Michael, 121
- FISHER, Jackie 183
- FOX, Charles James 16

G
- GAGE, Thomas 163
- GAINSBOROUGH, Thomas 199
- GARRETT ANDERSON, Elizabeth 98

G	GIBBON, Edward	140
	GLADSTONE, William	157, 191, 195
	GODLEY, John	111
	GREEN, John	148
	GREY, Sir Edward	181
	GROSSMITH, George	127
	GROTE, George	48
	GWYNNE, Nell	200
H	HALDANE, Lord	186
	HALLAM, Henry	154
	HANDEL, George Frideric	62
	HANDLEY PAGE, Sir Frederick	73
	HARRISON, George	114
	HARTNELL, Sir Norman	43
	HENDRIX, Jimi	61
	HILL, Octavia	118
	HOGG, Quintin	172
	HUSKISSON, William	203
	HUTCHISON, Sir Jonathan	169
I	IRVING, Sir Henry	45
	ISAACS, Rufus	24
	IVES, Charles	19
J	JACKSON, John Hughlings	125
	JERMYN, Henry	193
K	KELLY, Sir Gerald	105
	KEMPE, Charles	116
	KITCHENER, Earl Horatio	188
	KORDA, Sir Alexander	67
L	LANE, Allen	50
	LEAR, Edward	97
	LENNON, John	100, 114
	LEWIS, Rosa	207
	LOGUE, Lionel	160
	LOVELACE, Ada	196
	LUTYENS, Sir Edwin	166
	LYELL, Sir Charles	157
M	MACAULAY, Rose	129
	MACKENZIE, Sir James	139
	MAHOMED, Sake	113
	MANSON, Sir Patrick	142
	MARRYAT, Captain Frederick	128
	MAUGHAM, William Somerset	34
	MAYER, Sir Robert	167
	MERYON, Edward	17
	MILNER, Lord Alfred	123
	MILSOM REES, Sir John	149
	MITFORD, Nancy	20
	MONTEFIORE, Sir Moses	85
	MOORE, Tom	112
N	NAPOLEON III	197
	NEAGLE, Dame Anna	82
	NELSON, Lord Horatio	65
	NEVILL, Lady Dorothy	36
	NEWTON, Sir Isaac	208
	NIGHTINGALE, Florence	81
O	OLDFIELD, Ann	66

P	PAGE, Walter Hines	71
	PALMERSTON, Lord	18, 185, 189
	PAOLI, General Pasquale	27
	PEARCE, Stephen	144
	PEARSON, John L	165
	PECZENIK, Charles	74
	PEEL, Sir Robert	83
	PELHAM, Henry	206
	PETTY, William	38
	PINERO, Sir Arthur	159
	PITT, William the Elder	194
	PITT, William the Younger	115
	PURDEY, James	75
R	RAGLAN, Lord	26
	RANK, J Arthur	78
	RAY-JONES, Tony	107
	RESCHID, Mustapha Pasha	99
	RICHARD, Wendy	21
	RICHMOND, George	106
	ROBERTS, Earl	162
	ROLLS, Charles	64
	ROSEBERY, 5th Earl of	35
	ROSS, Sir Ronald	170
S	SEFERIS, George	87
	SEGRAVE, Sir Henry	120
	SELFRIDGE, Harry Gordon	37
	SHERIDAN, Richard	22, 47
	SMITH, William	184
	SMITHSON, James	138
	SOPWITH, Sir Thomas	88
	SPRY, Constance	30
	STANHOPE, Charles	164
S	STANLEY, Earl Edward	195
	STARDUST, Ziggy	51
	STILL, Sir George Frederic	155
	STOKOWKSI, Leonard	117
	STREET, George Edmund	173
	SUNLEY, Bernard	41
T	TALLEYRAND, Prince	63
	TOSTI, Sir Paolo	130
	TOWNLEY, Charles	182
	TREVES, Sir Frederick	137
	TROLLOPE, Anthony	101
V	VAN BUREN, Martin	136
W	WALPOLE, Horace	205
	WALPOLE, Sir Robert	204
	WALTERS, Catherine	80
	WEISZ, Victor	146
	WESLEY, Charles	147
	WESTMACOTT, Sir Richard	28
	WINANT, John Gilbert	79
	WINSOR, Frederick	198
	WODEHOUSE, P.G.	89
	WOOLNER, Thomas	145
	WYATVILLE, Sir Jeffry	60
Y	YEARSLEY, James	52
	YOUNG, Thomas	141

WHERE THE PEOPLE WERE BORN

One third of the People commemorated with a Plaque were born outside England

Name	Role	Walk	Page
AUSTRALIA			
LOGUE, Lionel	Speech Therapist	Marylebone East	160
BELGIUM			
PEARSON, John [*]	Architect	Marylebone East	165
CORSICA			
PAOLI, General Pasquale	Statesman	Mayfair South	27
FRANCE			
BERLIOZ, Hector	Composer	Marylebone East	143
CHARLES X of France	Royalty	Mayfair South	29
DE GAULLE, Charles	Statesman	St James's	189
MAUGHAM, Somerset [*]	Novelist	Mayfair South	34
NAPOLEON III	Royalty	St James's	197
PECZENIK, Charles	Architect	Mayfair North	74
SMITHSON, James [*]	Sailor	Marylebone East	138
TALLEYRAND, Prince	Diplomat	Mayfair North	63
GERMANY			
BENEDICT, Sir Julius	Composer	Marylebone West	126
HANDEL, George Frideric	Composer	Mayfair North	62
MAYER, Sir Robert	Philanthropist	Marylebone East	167
MILNER, Alfred [*]	Statesman	Marylebone West	123
WEISZ, Victor	Cartoonist	Marylebone East	146
WINSOR, Frederick	Inventor	St James's	198
HUNGARY			
KORDA, Sir Alexander	Film Director	Mayfair North	67
IRELAND			
BALFE, Michael William	Composer	Marylebone West	96
BEAUFORT, Sir Francis	Inventor	Marylebone West	122
GODLEY, John	Statesman	Marylebone West	111
KITCHENER, Earl Horatio [*]	Soldier	St James's	188
MOORE, Tom	Poet	Marylebone West	112
PETTY, William	Prime Minister	Mayfair South	38
SHERIDAN, Richard	Playwright	Mayfair South	22
INDIA			
MAHOMED, Sake	Restaurateur	Marylebone West	113
ROBERTS, Earl [*]	Soldier	Marylebone East	162
ROSS, Sir Ronald [*]	Scientist	Marylebone East	170